THE FANTASY FOOT~~BALL~~
BLACK BOOK
2023 Edition

By: Joe Pisapia
@JoePisapia17

Featuring

Andrew Erickson @AndrewErickson
Derek Brown @DBro_FFB
Thor Nystrom @thorku
Scott Bogman @BogmanSports
Nate Hamilton @DomiNateFF
Chris Meaney @chrismeaney
Chris McConnell @WizardOfRoto
Andrew Seifter @andrew_seifter
Billy Wasosky @BillyWaz88
Travis Sumpter @tjsumpter55
Edited by Mike Maher @mikeMaher

RPV CHEAT SHEETS NOW AVAILABLE!

Want all the RPV for every format on one easy-to-reference cheat sheet PDF file?
Plus, <u>FREE</u> updates sent in July & Aug!?

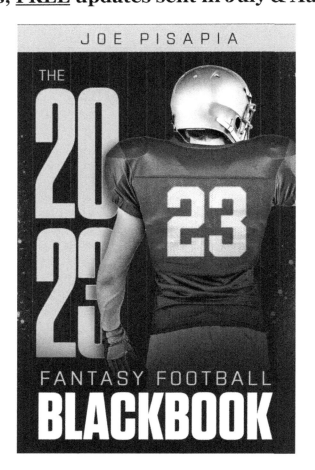

Send $5 to:
PayPal: <u>fantasyblackbook@gmail.com</u>
or
Venmo: @FantasyBlackBook
Be sure to write:
"Cheat Sheets" & add your <u>email address</u> in the comments!

About the Authors:

Joe Pisapia (@JoePisapia17 Twitter, @fantasyblackbook IG)
Joe is the author of the #1 best-selling Fantasy Black Book Series on Amazon and creator of the revolutionary player evaluation tool Relative Position Value (RPV). He's the host of the FantasyPros Fantasy Football Podcast, Leading OffMLB Podcast, and BettingPros Podcast. Joe is also currently the host of "Fantasy Sports Today (MLB/NFL)" on SportsGridTV.

Derek Brown *is a senior fantasy football analyst at Fantasypros. He's written previously for FTN, Playerprofiler, & FantasyData. Derek is a perennial contributor to the Fantasy Football Black Book. His DFS, redraft, and dynasty takes have been previously projected to the masses with recurring guest roles on Sirius XM and DK Sweat. Born in Louisiana, he is a diehard Saints fan (Whodat).*

Andrew Erickson *has been in the fantasy football space since 2017, but he finally got his break in the full-time business with PFF in 2020. He's since taken his talents to nerds over FantasyPros joining forced with Joe Pisapia and Derek Brown. He rests his laurels on living life by the 6 Fs: Family, Friends, Food, Fitness and Fantasy Football.*

Thor Nystrom *is a College Football & NFL Draft Analyst for FantasyPros and BettingPros. He previously spent 12 years at NBC Sports, where he held the same position. Thor also does Minnesota Vikings-centric shows on SkorNorth. He has won multiple national awards for his work, including from Rolling Stone magazine and FSWA, which named him the industry's top college football writer in 2019.*

Scott Bogman *has been in the Fantasy Sports industry since 2014, co-hosting Fantasy Football, Fantasy College Football and Fantasy Baseball shows for In This League as well as hosting the FantasyPros Dynasty Fantasy Football Podcast. Bogman also contributes to SportsGrid and CFB Winning Edge. This will be his 4th year contributing rookie profiles and 3rd covering IDPs for the Black Book. You can find his work by following him on Twitter @BogmanSports or check out the In This League Patreon at Patreon.com/ITLArmy!*

Nate Hamilton *is a senior football betting analyst & Editor for Gambling.com He spends his time immersed in analytics, stats, and betting lines. Nate has been a notable voice in the world of the NFL and fantasy football for over a decade producing valuable content for several leading sports media outlets around the country.*

Chris McConnell *Chris McConnell is an 18-year fantasy sports veteran. He currently runs the RotoBros Fantasy Lounge on Discord, and is the self-proclaimed chairman of the "RBDM" (Running Backs Don't Matter) community. Chris has also been a frequent guest on Sirius XM Fantasy Sports Radio and numerous other fantasy sports shows. Residing in Georgia, Chris is a diehard Atlanta sports fan and believes you're probably undervaluing Jordan Love in 2023.*

Billy Wasosky *is an accomplished high-stakes fantasy football player who has been playing for 33 years. He was inducted into the NFFC Hall of Fame in 2014 and is well known for his successes in standard, auction, and draft champion formats. In 2019, he co-owned championships in both the NFFC Playoff Contest and the NFFC Diamond league, was 2nd overall in the 2013 Fantasy Football Players Championship, and was the overall champion in the 1995 Sporting News Fantasy Football Championship. His career high stakes winnings exceed $425,000. 2022 Rotowire Online Championship winner ($200K).*

Andrew Seifter is a Featured Writer for FantasyPros, co-host of The Rest of Season Rankings Podcast, founder of ROSrankings.com, and a member of the Fantasy Sports Writers Association. He was previously a Featured Columnist for Bleacher Report and regular guest on ESPN Radio's Between the Lines with Scott Galeti and Chris Williams. According to FantasyPros' accuracy rankings, Andrew was the #1 most accurate ranker of kickers and #8 most accurate ranker of running backs during the 2021 fantasy football season.

Travis Sumpter *Lead Fantasy Analyst (@TruthSerumFF) Always a helping hand among the industry and am always willing to offer advice. Father of three beautiful boys Evan, Adler, and Kaleb. When the pandemic hit I really took more to fantasy and got more involved in the FFC(Fantasy Football Community). Writer, Podcaster, Contributor, Co-Social Media Manager for Truth Serum Football. I started my journey with the help of Chris Pinto from Fantasy First Rounders Live (@FantasyFRLive) and Ben, Jay, and Steve (@TotalForesight). I would to thank Joey Fickle and Jordan Thomas from Truth Serum Football. I would like to dedicate my portion of this to my beautiful wife Lindsay, who is my rock and my biggest supporter.*

Mike Maher *is the Senior Manager, Content at FantasyPros & BettingPros. In a previous life, he worked in book publishing for more than a decade, including several years as the Digital Operations Manager at one of the largest book publishers in the world, HarperCollins Publishers. But the allure of FantasyPros was too strong, and he made the jump from long-time freelancer to full-timer in March of 2022. He is also currently pursuing a Master of Professional Studies degree at George Washington University. When not talking about fantasy sports, sports betting, books, Chaim Bloom, AI, or the Eagles, he works on being a good dad to Nolan and Juliet, a good husband to Courtney, and adapting to life in Georgia.*

TABLE OF CONTENTS

INTRODUCTION

Working on this year's Black Book got me thinking of just how impactful the sport of football has been in my life. My earliest memories of the NFL were Ronnie Lott and Joe Montana Sunday afternoons at my grandmother's house. I would often be watching those games alone since I grew up in a baseball family. The '85 Bears captured my attention next. Their dominance and personality were unlike anything I had experienced. It would years before I landed on a team of my own to root for and that story probably is indicative of how I would end up where I have. Living in New York, to me the Jets and Giants were "Jersey Teams" and that left only one logical conclusion, the Buffalo Bills. That was the era of Jim Kelly, Thurman Thomas, Bruce Smith and arguably one the most talented football rosters the league had ever seen. It seemed like great timing. It was anything but.

We moved to New Jersey in the late '80's and by the early '90's the Bills would find themselves on a historic run of going to four straight Super Bowls and subsequently losing four straight Super Bowls. Every Monday following those crushing defeats I would wear my Bills Starter ® jacket, as was the fashion of the time, and take my harassment from the Giants fans and then the Cowboys fans (who apparently also inhabited NJ). I realized something after that final loss, the best team doesn't win. The team that plays the best wins. Talent was a big part of success, but without preparation, game plan, system and coaching it ultimately would fall short. This was my 14-year-old revelation. So, when the Bills didn't move on from Marv Levy I took my fandom to New England to followed the consensus best mind in the game. At the time Bill Parcells was touted as THE coach in the league. And guess what, they lost a Super Bowl a few years later too once I jumped on board. I was convinced it was me. But I stuck with the Pats process, through Pete Carroll and Bill Belichick. Eventually I enjoyed a dynasty of absurd modern-day proportions. But that's only part of the story.

As a kid, the biggest argument I ever had with my parents was wanting to desperately play freshman high school football and not being allowed. It went on for roughly two weeks. Basically, they didn't want me to get hurt and blow a potential baseball scholarship. Joke was on them, since I got offered a bigger scholarship to go to acting school over baseball. While at UArts in Philadelphia, I found an odd crew of dudes. Uncommon at an arts school. They had also been athletes like me and we played weekly park tackle football games every Fall Saturday. Sometimes we'd get challenged by some random UPenn or Temple frat boy types and the arts school kids frankly whooped their ass on a regular basis. Those Saturday afternoons were some of my favorite college memories.

Fast forward to adulthood, and I somehow over time combined my joys of sports and entertainment into a career, covering the NFL. The opportunity to write these books and broadcast over multiple platforms over the years saved me during some dark times and sustained me being a single parent of two incredible daughters. Not a day goes by I don't recognize how lucky I am to do what I do. However, it was a grind for over a decade filled with more disappointments that you can imagine. More losing of Super Bowls than winning them.

Speaking of daughters, here's the most unexpected wrinkle of the story. Two years ago, my youngest decided she wanted to try NFL Flag Football and joined. Of course, I got roped into coaching. Over two years and eight teams later I can easily say it has been an incredible bonding experience for us. She went from barely being able to throw a ball to being the only female quarterback in the co-ed league. We won three championships, two of which were undefeated seasons. We also had a few rough seasons too. Regardless, she loves to play and now watches games with me. Looking back at those afternoons watching games by myself in my grandmother's living room, I'm very grateful for the company I have now.

The one thing I always drive home to the squads I coach; the best team doesn't win, the team that plays the best does. Football has afforded me so many amazing friends and colleagues over the years and now I have the chance to pass down to the kids I coach that knowledge and love of the game. Weather you have a son or daughter, I recommend getting them involved with NFL Flag or just throw the ball around with them and see where it goes. My daughter comes home every day off the bus looking to throw and daily it's the best pause in my day.

It's pretty cool I finally got to see that name on the back of a football jersey.

Joe

Chapter 1

Relative Position Value (RPV)

Joe Pisapia

"The format and style of your league dictates the value of a player more than the talent of that player."

Rankings are good. Tiered Rankings are better. QUANTIFIED Rankings specific to your scoring system are best!

This is the creed of The Fantasy Black Book over the years and why **Relative Position Value (RPV)** is a difference maker for so many fantasy players over the last decade. If it didn't work, we wouldn't sell this many books and cheat sheets every season. There are other value systems out there, but they fall woefully short because they either look at positions as a whole or work solely on projections. RPV works of a hybrid of projections, previous season stats and three-year averages when applicable. With rookies, college stats get factored into projections along with previous seasons stats of the role they're assuming with their new NFL offense to make sure the picture is as clear as possible for their outlook. However, the biggest key to why RPV is superior is the fact it understands RB isn't a position, but RB1 is. Most teams in your league will have an RB1, a WR1, WR2 etc. So, how do you draft to create core roster strength and create an edge over your opponents? By using the RPV system to evaluate talent and build your roster. RPV goes beyond well informed analysis and creates a tangible strategy. When you combine both, as we do in the Black Book, you will be unstoppable.

Chances are you're playing in multiple leagues, with a myriad of different rules and scoring. That's why I created Relative Position Value (RPV), the one tool to rule them all. Even if you play in the oddest scoring on the planet, you can use the formula yourself and get a basic working model of how to approach your draft and evaluate in season trades using RPV. The RPV key will unlock your ability to maximize the available active roster spots you have on your team on a weekly basis.

RPV will automatically create player tiers -- and *define* them. It will also tell you how strong or weak a position player pool is entering the season. RPV is completely adaptable and adjustable to all league styles, depths and scoring systems. It's the single most useful player evaluation system available to fantasy owners and perhaps one of the easiest to grasp. I like simple and effective. RPV is both.

So, remember when I said "RB isn't a position, but RB1 is"? Well, let's dive into that and explain in more detail how RPV work and how to apply it.

STRIKING A BALANCE

It doesn't matter that Player A is ranked two slots above Player B on some "experts' board." What REALLY matters is how much more productive Player A is than Player B -- and how much better they are than the other options at their position. Projections can be helpful, but not relied upon solely. When's the last time projectionists were held accountable (or held themselves accountable) for their many failures? The answer is hardly ever. Projections can have their place when you couple them with reality.

RPV compiles projections, previous season stats and three-year averages (when applicable) before weighing them to create a Black Book Point Total. That number is ALWAYS format-specific and is historically more reliable than projections alone, hence the success of the Black Book series. When it comes to rookies or young players, clearly, we must rely more heavily on projections but use a cross-section to do so.

Now, what happens next to that Black Book Point Totals?

RPV IN THEORY

"RB isn't a position, BUT RB1 is!"

Considering a base of a 12-team league with two active RBs each week, a group of 24 running backs is a good starting point to grasp the RPV concept. However, it's NOT how we're going to truly utilize the tool.

Over 17 games in 2022, Austin Ekeler led all PPR running backs with 372 pts in PPR scoring. Derrick henry ranked fourth with 302 pts. The 12th-best running back was Leonard Fournette at 227, and the 24th was David Montgomery with 177.

So, how much more valuable is each one of these guys compared to the other? Before we get ahead of ourselves, let's first see the formula in action.

The Fantasy Black Book formula is more complicated than the "basic" version I will present to you here. At the core, the way to determine the RPV -- or the percentage in which a player is better than the fantasy league average -- is:

(Individual Player Point Value – Fantasy League Average of the Position) ÷ Fantasy League Average of the Position = RPV

So, what is "Fantasy League Average?" Well, every league has a different number of teams and a varying number of active players at a given position. Some have 1RB/3WR/1FLEX, others play 2QB/2RB/3WR, and the list goes on and on.

The Fantasy League Average is a position's average production, based on the depth of your league. For example, if your league has 12 owners and starts 2RB every week, the RB pool is 24. If the top player scored 250 points and the 24th scored around 120, the fantasy league's scoring average is likely somewhere around 185 points. All players who score above this mark are "Positive RPV" players. The ones below are "Negative RPV."

Fantasy sports is a simple game of outscoring your opponents as frequently as possible from as many active positions as you can. The more your team lives in the "Positive," the greater your chances are week-to-week. It's like playing the odds in Texas hold'em. If you have a strong starting hand, the odds are in your favor. Sure, you may take some bad beats, but often, the percentages will play in your favor.

Here's the trick! Even though there are 24 running backs, almost every team will likely have **one true RB1**, which means RB1 is its own unique scoring position. Rather than create a Fantasy League Average for 24 overall backs, it's more applicable to separate RB1s and RB2s into their own private groups and create an individual fantasy league average for each.

Now that we understand Fantasy League Average, let's get more specific. Last year, Austin Ekeler scored **372** (full point PPR) pts. The Fantasy League Average (or FLA) at RB1 last year (top 12) in that scoring was **281** pts.

Subtract that FLA (281 pts) from Austin Ekeler's 372 pts, then divide by that same FLA (281 pts) using the simple formula:

Relative Position Value of +32% RPV: [372-281] ÷ 281 = 32%.

Austin Ekeler was a +32% RPV better than the Fantasy League Average RB1 in 2020. #Quantified!!!

That means Taylor was 32% more productive than the average RB1 in fantasy leagues in PPR scoring.

That's substantial! That's not theoretical, it's definitive. That means something!

If we took the RPV of running back as a whole over the top 24, Ekeler's RPV would jump to a whopping +53% RPV, because the Fantasy League Average would be just 241 pts, creating a larger divide.

BUT we don't do that, because he'll be stacking up, head-to-head, against other RB1s most weeks in theoretical terms against other RB1 slots on other rosters. Calculating RB1s and RB2s as their individual positions gives a much more accurate depiction of a player's value, hence what makes RPV better than other value-based systems.

Are you in a 14-team league? Then use the top 14 to establish RB1 RPV. In a 10- team league? Adjust that way. The deeper the league, the more difficult it is to create an RPV advantage. The shallower the league, the less disparity you'll find (especially at WR). Therefore, you have more options to construct your roster in different ways. Have a wacky scoring system? Doesn't matter. RPV formula covers everything.

Below is the **Final RPV** for RB1s and RB2s from the end of 2022. You'll see not only the positive but also the negative side of RPV. The avoidance of over drafting/overspending on players that can't really supply you with "positive" production or as I like to say, 'move the needle". This clears the path to success. You will also see as we go on how to create an RPV advantage.

2022 FINAL RB RPV for RB1 and RB2 (Full PPR scoring)

RB 1 PPR				RB2 PPR			
	Player	FPTS	RPV		Player	FPTS	RPV
1	Austin Ekeler (LAC)	372.7	32%	13	Jamaal Williams (DET)	225.9	12%
2	Christian McCaffrey (SF)	356.4	27%	14	Najee Harris (PIT)	223.5	11%
3	Josh Jacobs (LV)	328.3	17%	15	Miles Sanders (PHI)	216.7	8%
4	Derrick Henry (TEN)	302.8	8%	16	Alvin Kamara (NO)	211.7	5%
5	Saquon Barkley (NYG)	284	1%	17	Travis Etienne Jr. (JAC)	205.1	2%
6	Nick Chubb (CLE)	281.4	0%	18	Kenneth Walker III (SEA)	202.5	1%
7	Rhamondre Stevenson (NE)	249.1	-12%	19	James Conner (ARI)	200.2	-1%
8	Tony Pollard (DAL)	248.8	-12%	20	Jerick McKinnon (KC)	196.3	-2%
9	Aaron Jones (GB)	248.6	-12%	21	D'Andre Swift (DET)	191.1	-5%
10	Joe Mixon (CIN)	240.7	-14%	22	Ezekiel Elliott (DAL)	185.8	-8%
11	Dalvin Cook (MIN)	237.8	-16%	23	Devin Singletary (BUF)	178.2	-11%
12	Leonard Fournette (TB)	227.1	-19%	24	David Montgomery (CHI)	177.7	-12%

You can see from last year's RPV not only the distinct advantage Austin Ekeler provided and why the "hero" RB strategy (drafting one elite RB early then waiting on RB2) has become more viable over the last few years. When you get to Nick Chubb, he's basically your benchmark, then even solid fantasy RB's are still negative in RPV RB1's. That lower tier are also only divided by 12 points between RB7 and RB 11, therefore why reach?. Any of those low end RB1's would be positive RB2 guys, so hitting elite RPV WR early in drafts is also viable if you can grab (2) low end RB1/high end RB2 candidates and maintain a decent RPV output. RPV shows you quite clearly the true value of a player compared to his peers.

So, how can the fantasy player exploit RPV?

By having a high-end RB1 and then drafting ANOTHER RB1 as your RB2, you have "frontloaded" the position and created an area of strength. That is one way to create an RPV advantage, but I prefer to use that same concept at WR in today's fantasy football world.

The BIGGEST mistake fantasy owners make in any sports in "filling their roster for positions," instead of filling their roster with talent and strength.

When you fill your roster for positions, you get a mediocre .500 team. When you fill your roster with strength, you have an advantage over the rest of the field. As long as you can responsibly fill the other positions and avoid Negative RPV as often as possible, that roster strength can carry your season.

With more NFL teams adapting backfield committees, the true starting running backs are worth more than ever in standard formats. That especially goes for the RB1s who get goal-line carries and the bulk of touches. In PPR, you can build the same strength of front-loading WR1s as you can with RB1s, then make up ground later by buying running backs in bulk with upside. The tough sell there is the difference between definitive running back touches as opposed to expected wide receiver catches. One is frankly more reliable on a weekly basis.

The same could be said for Superflex/2QB leagues. By "frontloading" elite QB play, you simultaneously create a team RPV strength and weaken the pool for the other owners. RPV shows you how stark the value can be position-to-position. Some will bottom out at -10% while others will be -20%. With middle-tier receivers, you'll see little advantage to be gained.

RPV is the ultimate tool to truly define talent and, even more importantly, where the drop-off in talent lies. Rankings are biased. RPV is honest.

Obviously, every league will be different. Flex players and OP (offensive player) slots will change values a bit, but the RPV theory holds in **EVERY LEAGUE and EVERY FORMAT!** It just needs to be adjusted according to each league's specifications. In the Black Book, I've done much of the work for you, but you must be sure to adjust the RPV for your league(s) quirky scoring wrinkles if you are going to truly achieve ultimate success.

Now that we've outlined RPV, let's dive deeper.

RPV IN PRACTICE (Draft and Trades)

Last year, so many folks asked, "How does the Black Book determine its RPV?"

The Black Book takes a combination of 3-year averages (when applicable/available), previous season stats, and the upcoming season projections, creating a hybrid point total for each player that then gets utilized within the RPV equation.

For rookies, clearly there is no track record from which to work to create that number. Therefore, I use a composite of projected stats from a few choice entities, their college statistical profile, and their potential use in their new team system in order to create each rookie's point total for the RPV formula.

With so many new styles of fantasy football, it's crucial to understand the value of each position in your league.

For example, I prefer PPR (point per reception) setups that play a lineup consisting of QB, RB, RB/WR, WR1, WR2, WR3, TE, K, 5 IDP and an OP slot (which can be a QB) or a second mandatory QB spot.

If a quarterback is the most important skills entity in *real* football, I want my fantasy experience to mirror that truth. The RPV for this kind of league is different than a standard league. Teams play 2 QBs every week, therefore QBs become the equivalent of the RB1/RB2 RPV I just laid out in the last section.

Another big adjustment: Since I technically only have to start 1 RB, the talent pool is adjusted back into a "one large group of running backs" theory. Possession WRs and big playmakers garner attention. This is a perfect example of why a tool like RPV is so necessary. If I were to use the standard old rankings from a website or a magazine in this format, I would get crushed.

Now more than ever, there is no "one ranking system" that will be useful to you in any format. Ignore these Top 100 lists and nonsense like that -- and instead focus on the true value and weight of the player in *your* league. That's why RPV works.

The last best thing about RPV is the fact it strips away a lot of the hype and noise surrounding the athletes, as well as the fictional computer projections that can be misleading and downright destructive.

RPV is about understanding a player's value -- his ACTUAL value. Not what his value may be projected to be while you sit in last place wondering where you went wrong. The best way to evaluate a player is through a mixture of career averages, previous statistics and projections that are then weighed against the other players of the same position. NOT PROJECTIONS ALONE!

Using only last year's numbers will give you a great team … for last season. Using just projections will give you a great team … in theory. RPV will give you a great team in REALITY!

You can choose to be great at one spot or two, but if you are below-average at other places, your overall RPV will even out. You may find yourself managing a middle-of-the-road team. Being above-average in as many places as you can, even without a top-flight star, you will find yourself consistently out-producing your opponents. If you use RPV correctly, you may even find yourself above average in most places and great in others, which makes you the one to beat. It's the ability to adapt, adjust and understand that separates us. RPV is the difference-maker.

RPV can tell you not only how much better a player is than the average for his position, but also how much better he is than the next guy available at his position on the draft board. Understanding these RPV relationships is key in maximizing your positional advantage.

To illustrate this point and its application, let's take a draft-day example. It's your turn to pick, and you have openings to fill at WR and TE. The top available players on the board at each position look like this:

WR

- Player A: +15% RPV
- Player B: +10% RPV
- Player C: +8% RPV
- Player D: +7% RPV
- Player E: +5% RPV

TE

- Player F: +8% RPV
- Player G: -2% RPV
- Player H: -2% RPV
- Player I: -4% RPV
- Player J: -6% RPV

At first glance, you might be inclined to take Player A, who is a +15% better than the average at his position. All other things being equal, however, Player F is probably the better choice.

Even though he is only +8% better than the average, the drop-off between him and the next-best player at his position is 10 percentage points. That's a significant dip. If you take Player A now, Player F almost definitely won't be on the board when your next pick rolls around, and at best you'll be stuck with an average or below-average tight end.

If you take Player F now, however, you'll be on the right side of that 10% RPV advantage over the teams who haven't drafted a TE yet. You'll also probably lose out on Player A at WR, but you will still most likely get someone from the above list (Player C, D or E) -- all of whom are trading in the same RPV range and, more importantly, still in the positive. It may not sound like a big deal with mere percentage points, but it adds up the more you rise above or fall below the average RPV threshold.

By picking this way, you end up with a strong advantage at one position while remaining above average at the other. The alternative is to be above-average at one position and decidedly average or worse at the other. That's the reason so many fantasy owners fail. Usually, they base these decisions on the *name* of the player instead of his Relative Position Value. The same can be said when evaluating trades. You must look at what advantage you're gaining and potentially losing in each deal.

The fantasy manager who does that effectively has a distinct advantage.

Remember, don't marginalize your strength!

Everyone has access to opinions, but now you have access to RPV.

Chapter 2

Draft Strategies

Joe Pisapia

PPR LEAGUE 4-ROUND MOCK

	Round 1	Round 2	Round 3	Round 4
Team 1	Justin Jefferson	Najee Harris	Patrick Mahomes II	Jerry Jeudy
Team 2	Ja'Marr Chase	Rhamondre Stevenson	Breece Hall	Drake London
Team 3	Bijan Robinson	DK Metcalf	Josh Allen	DJ Moore
Team 4	Christian McCaffrey	Garrett Wilson	Jalen Hurts	Keenan Allen
Team 5	Austin Ekeler	Tee Higgins	DeVonta Smith	Tyler Lockett
Team 6	Tyreek Hill	Derrick Henry	Dalvin Cook	T.J. Hockenson
Team 7	Cooper Kupp	Tony Pollard	Chris Olave	Cam Akers
Team 8	Travis Kelce	Nick Chubb	Josh Jacobs	Amari Cooper
Team 9	Saquon Barkley	Jaylen Waddle	Travis Etienne Jr.	Miles Sanders
Team 10	A.J. Brown	Amon-Ra St. Brown	Aaron Jones	George Kittle
Team 11	CeeDee Lamb	Jonathan Taylor	Dameon Pierce	Justin Fields
Team 12	Stefon Diggs	Davante Adams	Joe Burrow	Mark Andrews

2023 PLAYER POOL OVERVIEW

In recent seasons, I've been at the forefront of leading the early and often wide receiver strategy. One can take numerous approaches to this format, including "Hero RB," where you invest in a top-tier RB early and then pound the WR picks. One could also go heavy WR the first few rounds, take RB values as they present themselves, and even speculate on committee backfield situations. I prefer the latter, but both strategies have their merit. The fact is, the NFL has evolved into a wide receiver-dominated space. NFL teams show you in the draft how they value the running back position and, with the cap, their unwillingness to overpay running backs or even give them second contracts.

The trick to succeeding at RB in fantasy is looking for touches, health, and, typically, youth nowadays. You can even target those RBs that aren't necessarily "3 down backs" but are heavily involved in their offense's passing game. The high injury quotient in the position also lends itself more to waiver wire streaming throughout the season at a higher clip than the wide receiver position.

The other major change in philosophy is QB strategy. For many years in single QB leagues, you could wait on QB and still land on a strong option late in the draft. With so many rushing QBs and certain elite-level offenses, there's a definitive advantage to having an elite-level QB on your roster. You could roll the dice with taking an upside play like Anthony Richardson this season and then a "safe" Kirk Cousins or Aaron Rodgers veteran as insurance. If you hit on this strategy, you could see a similar situation as in 2022 with those who had Justin Fields, who became a huge fantasy impact player, despite the low passing totals. Again, both have merit, but I prefer locking in a good value elite QB because you know you're paying a premium and receiving premium productivity in return.

10 TEAM V 14+ TEAM LEAGUE DRAFT SLOT APPROACHES

Varying league depths should always adjust your draft strategy. In shallower 10-team formats, I'm more at peace with "Hero RB" because there is an even greater abundance of wide receiver talent based on simple supply and demand. I'm also more apt to let top talent at TE slide because the streaming pool at the position will be much stronger. When it comes to quarterback in 10-team leagues, it's all about value and where they fall. Drafting the last of the "top tier" makes the most sense if you can pull it off in the draft.

When you add in more than 12 teams, the strategy should become very simplified: draft talent when it presents itself. That sounds simplistic and obvious, but you'd be surprised how often above-average fantasy players make bad decisions. I'd hyper-target players throughout the draft in above-average offensive ecosystems with strong QB play. You can love a player's talent or upside, but the fact remains if the QB/OC/HC can't execute a strong offense, then unlocking that potential from that player is going to be next to impossible. Another common mistake is fantasy managers trying to fill roster spots too soon rather than drafting the talent on the board at value.

You can have a theoretic strategy all you like, every draft is a unique snowflake, and you're best served always to take the best talent available as early as often as you can to build core roster strength. Then, a well-informed fantasy player like you can take calculated risks later to fill out their roster later in the draft. In a 14 or more-team league, the drop-off from TE is more drastic, so it's more sensible to take a top talent in the earlier rounds, but ONLY if that value makes sense when compared to what else is available. For instance, I wouldn't take Mark Andrews over Amon-Ra St. Brown in round two simply because TE is a shallow talent pool.

IF YOU COULD PICK YOUR DRAFT SLOT

This year I'm more apt to be at the top of drafts if I had my say in picking my draft slot. There are a ton of young and relatively young quarterbacks starting this year, and there will be a clear division of "haves" and "have nots" when it comes to NFL offenses. A top pick gives me three top 25 players, one of which is elite, and that's how I prefer to start. This is a change from the last few years when I almost preferred a bottom pick near the turn. In superflex, I don't mind that spot as much, but in single QB leagues, the top 3 is where I want to be. The middle of the draft is where you are at the whim of runs on both sides, which can be very frustrating.

SUPERFLEX LEAGUE 4-ROUND MOCK

	Round 1	Round 2	Round 3	Round 4
Team 1	Justin Jefferson	Deshaun Watson	Kirk Cousins	Aaron Jones
Team 2	Ja'Marr Chase	Dak Prescott	Amon-Ra St. Brown	Dameon Pierce
Team 3	Patrick Mahomes II	Davante Adams	Jaylen Waddle	Josh Jacobs
Team 4	Josh Allen	Jonathan Taylor	Nick Chubb	Derek Carr
Team 5	Jalen Hurts	Stefon Diggs	Tony Pollard	Anthony Richardson
Team 6	Bijan Robinson	Trevor Lawrence	Daniel Jones	DK Metcalf
Team 7	Christian McCaffrey	Justin Herbert	Breece Hall	DeVonta Smith
Team 8	Austin Ekeler	CeeDee Lamb	Tua Tagovailoa	Najee Harris
Team 9	Tyreek Hill	A.J. Brown	Geno Smith	Derrick Henry
Team 10	Cooper Kupp	Saquon Barkley	Aaron Rodgers	Russell Wilson
Team 11	Travis Kelce	Justin Fields	Tee Higgins	Jared Goff
Team 12	Joe Burrow	Lamar Jackson	Rhamondre Stevenson	Garrett Wilson

The superflex format is my favorite by far since we live in an unprecedented era of open-air offenses. There are numerous ways to approach this format, depending on the year's talent pool. Last season, I still wanted Justin Jefferson or Ja'Marr Chase in Round 1 and take care of QB in Rounds 2-4. That strategy led me to a second Flex Expert superflex League Championship. This year, the pool is different, and I want to be slightly more aggressive and get an elite QB if I'm picking outside of the top 3 picks. JJ, Chase, and Bijan Robinson are the only guys I would take over Mahomes, Allen, or Hurts.

Typically, wide receiver ADP gets pushed in superflex drafts with the rush for running backs and quarterbacks. That's usually where a smart fantasy manager can make up ground in Rounds 4-6. The QB drop-off is even worse than last season. There are so many rookie and second-year QBs that are going to be very dicey investments, as well as some aging veterans that could be on the downside of their careers.

I've seen the "fade QB" strategy work in this format, but only when you lock in two stable fringe QB1/QB2 types (ex. Jared Goff and Aaron Rodgers). Regardless of when you pull the trigger on QBs, I would be hesitant to leave the 4th round without 2 QBs, 5th round, if your draft is very conservative and the QB run doesn't happen early.

STANDARD LEAGUE 4-ROUND MOCK

	Round 1	Round 2	Round 3	Round 4
Team 1	Justin Jefferson	Jalen Hurts	Garrett Wilson	Drake London
Team 2	Ja'Marr Chase	Josh Allen	Dalvin Cook	T.J. Hockenson
Team 3	Bijan Robinson	Tony Pollard	Justin Fields	Tyler Lockett
Team 4	Christian McCaffrey	Patrick Mahomes II	Tee Higgins	Cam Akers
Team 5	Austin Ekeler	Amon-Ra St. Brown	Aaron Jones	Keenan Allen
Team 6	Tyreek Hill	Najee Harris	Josh Jacobs	DJ Moore
Team 7	Cooper Kupp	Breece Hall	DK Metcalf	George Kittle
Team 8	Travis Kelce	Davante Adams	Dameon Pierce	Miles Sanders
Team 9	Saquon Barkley	Stefon Diggs	Travis Etienne Jr.	Mark Andrews
Team 10	A.J. Brown	Rhamondre Stevenson	Joe Burrow	Chris Olave
Team 11	CeeDee Lamb	Derrick Henry	Jaylen Waddle	DeVonta Smith
Team 12	Jonathan Taylor	Nick Chubb	Lamar Jackson	Amari Cooper

In standard league scoring formats (non-PPR), touchdown equity matters greatly. It's why three-down backs with goal-line touches are more valuable than in PPR formats. Rushing QBs like Jalen Hurts, Lamar Jackson, and Justin Fields are also key pieces in these leagues because they basically control all the scoring for their teams. They're either throwing a TD or rushing for one for the most part. Controlling that offensive scoring is key in standard. Make no mistake, yards are yards, and TDs are TDs, so great wide receivers still deserve early investment. It's just that you'll see a slight shift in bell cow back value and elite QBs over the #1A/#2 WRs.

GUILLOTINE LEAGUES

Guillotine Leagues I just started playing two years ago, and I love them. Basically, you draft, and every week the lowest-scoring team gets cut from the league, and all their players become free agents. I've personally had a fair amount of success with being reasonably aggressive on free agents. That means if there's a game-changing round one talent, I will be ultra-aggressive with my FAAB budget to acquire them. I'd also highly recommend combing the wire post waiver wire run for other players left or dropped, picking good talent up on the cheap, and stashing them on your bench. This may be tedious, but it will serve you well in the long run. Remember, the longer you last in this format, the less competition for free agents you will have and the cheaper good talent becomes. But that's only if you are still alive in the league to claim it, so play every week like it's your last and hope that you can get through the bye weeks. By the way, looking ahead on bye weeks and utilizing your bench in preparation for them is a great way to get an advantage over your opponents.

CLICK AD BELOW TO PLAY!

DYNASTY LEAGUE START-UP 4-ROUND MOCK (SUPERFLEX)

	Round 1	Round 2	Round 3	Round 4
Team 1	Justin Jefferson	Travis Kelce	Rhamondre Stevenson	Quentin Johnston
Team 2	Ja'Marr Chase	Trevor Lawrence	Jahmyr Gibbs	T.J. Hockenson
Team 3	Bijan Robinson	Justin Herbert	Chris Olave	Christian Watson
Team 4	Patrick Mahomes II	Cooper Kupp	Tony Pollard	Jaxon Smith-Njigba
Team 5	Josh Allen	Tyreek Hill	Kyle Pitts	C.J. Stroud
Team 6	Jalen Hurts	Saquon Barkley	Stefon Diggs	Dameon Pierce
Team 7	Joe Burrow	Garrett Wilson	Tee Higgins	DJ Moore
Team 8	Lamar Jackson	Amon-Ra St. Brown	Mark Andrews	Davante Adams
Team 9	A.J. Brown	Jaylen Waddle	Deshaun Watson	Nick Chubb
Team 10	CeeDee Lamb	Anthony Richardson	Austin Ekeler	DK Metcalf
Team 11	Jonathan Taylor	Breece Hall	Dak Prescott	Drake London
Team 12	Christian McCaffrey	Justin Fields	DeVonta Smith	Najee Harris

The majority of dynasty startups are superflex formats, as they should be. The key with dynasty is to create a roster that will be good for a two-year window. Most leagues have deeper rosters, therefore, constantly acquiring talent and quality depth is important. The biggest mistake people make is constantly trying to load up on picks and not proven NFL talent. Now in TE premium formats (which are the bane of my existence and I strongly recommend against), the calculus changes, as it should with any unique scoring wrinkle. However, above all, you should be acquiring talent first and foremost, regardless of position first and foremost.

A mix of proven guys and young up-and-coming talent is how you stay relevant year after year. Personally, I always value players over non-first-round rookie draft picks. If your roster is a failure, turn it over and keep your best assets. There's nothing wrong with admitting your team isn't a contender. Don't be afraid to use future rookie draft picks to move up in a current rookie draft if you feel there's talent on the board that can help you this coming season. You can always make deals in-season to acquire draft picks for the following year's draft and make up that deficit. One final note: typically, building around elite young wide receivers is a better short and long-term investment over running backs. Also, and especially in superflex leagues, elite QBs are worth the premium investment.

HIGH STAKES/NFFC SALAY CAP STRATEGY

Billy Wasosky

Close your eyes, and picture yourself sitting at a table with 11 other people. You have all your projections and auction values in front of you and are "ready"! One person starts and says, "Justin Jefferson.....$50." Then multiple people start shouting "52!, 55!, 56! Your budgeted value for Jefferson was $55. In a matter of seconds, you need to decide whether you would like to go $2 past your budget or miss out on the potential No. 1 overall player in fantasy football. You yell, "57!" and say to yourself, "I'm getting JJ!"

After the bidding ends, Justin Jefferson is now on your roster for a mere $64 (32% of your entire $200 budget). The strategy you came into the auction with can now be thrown out, as you have to now allocate $9 less at multiple positions, and the WR you wanted to get (CeeDee Lamb) just went for $3 less than you had him valued for. The auction has been rolling for about an hour and a half, and you have been drinking your favorite beverage and forgot to go to the bathroom before the draft.

You are anxious, have to use the bathroom (but you can't since this isn't a snake draft where you can make your pick and walk away), and now need to decide which of the remaining tight ends that no one really wants you are going to bid on. Welcome to the world of high-stakes auction drafting in the National Fantasy Football Championship (NFFC)! If you want to take your drafting to a different level, these are the leagues you want to be drafting in this year.

All the auction leagues I currently play in are at the NFFC (nfc.shgn.com/football). The NFFC offers online auctions and live auctions ranging from $150 - $5,000 entries. While an online auction is certainly more exciting than a snake draft, there is nothing that parallels a live auction in New York or Las Vegas. Getting that player, you wanted for a few dollars cheaper than you had allocated, losing out on a player at the last millisecond, watching everyone react when that final player in a tier keeps getting bid up, etc...it is without a doubt the absolute 2.5 - 3 hours you can spend putting together a fantasy team. At the time of this article, these are the current top 10 in ADP at the NFFC since the NFL Draft. This table shows each of the four skill positions, along with a combination of approximate auction values (based on last two year averages) and projected values for this year.

	QUARTERBACKS	$$	RUNNING BACKS	$$	WIDE RECEIVERS	$$	TIGHT ENDS	$$
1	Patrick Mahomes	$24	Christian McCaffrey	$58	Justin Jefferson	$62	Travis Kelce	$40
2	Josh Allen	$23	Austin Ekeler	$54	Ja'Marr Chase	$57	TJ Hockenson	$27
3	Jalen Hurts	$22	Bijan Robinson	$48	Tyreek Hill	$52	Mark Andrews	$26
4	Joe Burrow	$18	SaQuon Barkley	$46	Cooper Kupp	$50	George Kittle	$15
5	Lamar Jackson	$10	Jonathan Taylor	$44	Stefon Diggs	$48	Dallas Goedert	$12
6	Trevor Lawrence	$10	Josh Jacobs	$40	CeeDee Lamb	$47	Kyle Pitts	$10
7	Justin Herbert	$9	Derrick Henry	$38	AJ Brown	$43	Darren Waller	$9
8	Justin Fields	$9	Nick Chubb	$38	DaVante Adams	$43	Evan Engram	$8
9	Dak Prescott	$7	Breece Hall	$37	Amon-Ra St. Brown	$42	Pat Freiermuth	$6
10	DeShaun Watson	$6	Tony Pollard	$37	Garrett Wilson	$37	David Njoku	$5

"QB OR NOT QB?"

Since the NFFC rewards 6 points for all touchdowns, the QB position has more value than it does in a league that rewards 4 points per passing touchdown. That being said, in the past, the top 2 or 3 QBs would usually go for about $15-$17, but we are seeing a change in the position in the NFFC this year. The foursome of Mahomes, Allen, Hurts, and Burrow have crept their way into the late 1st and early 2nd round of snake drafts, and that means that people are valuing the top signal callers like they were back in the mid-2000s when Brees, Brady, and Rodgers were annual first-round selections.

Last year, Mahomes, Allen, Hurts and Burrow each averaged at least 5 points per game more than the next QB. While many have gotten away with spending $5-$10 of their $200 at this position, the predictability that these top QB's just might be well worth the money spent. It all comes down to whether you believe that these QBs will have a repeat performance this year, and if so, you probably have to allocate at least $20-$25 (maybe more) to obtain their services.

"RUNNING, CATCHING, AND GOAL LINE, OH MY"

Just like in your standard snake draft, the true three-down workhorse running backs that get the carries, catches, and goal line are "fantasy gold." In the past three years of the NFFC, the overall #1 RB has outscored the 5th overall RB by 91, 118, and 119 points, respectively. As you can see, there is very little room for error when drafting a RB. While it seems easy enough to just pay whatever it takes for Christian McCaffrey this year, and that he has been the overall consensus RB #1 (along with Jonathan Taylor last year) for the last three years going into drafts, he has not finished #1 overall since his remarkable 2019 campaign. There are a multitude of ways to attack the RB position, but you better believe that the top 4-5 RBs will command a hefty price tag on draft day.

"WIDE RECEIVERs: THE LIFEBLOOD OF NFFC AUCTIONS"

In the NFFC, you must start 3 WRs each week, and you can start a 4th at the flex position. Due to this, and the fact that WRs don't get hurt as often as RBs, and the top WRs almost always return their value (unless, of course, they get injured), this is arguably the most important position in the NFFC. So it shouldn't be a shock to anyone that owners will pay top dollar, and often go over their budget to get the top 10-15 WRs in an auction. As you can see from the table above, the RBs and WRs clearly go for the most money in an auction. What the table doesn't show is that the RB's fall off considerably, after the top 10-15, while the top WR's will still command a $20+ price tag up to about WR 25.

"TIGHT END: THE FORGOTTEN POSITION"

While a lot of people will try to skimp at QB, you will see many more people choosing to play "TE roulette" to save even more money at this position. What I have learned over the years is that if you have a top producing TE, it can be a significant advantage at that position. If you pay up for Travis Kelce, you just have to treat him like a top 5 WR (which he certainly was last year that you got for about $10-$15 less). Or maybe you just took a stab at a TJ Hockenson last year for $7-$8.....and stole yourself a championship? One thing is for sure about this position, there is always one (Kelce in 2022 and 2020) or two (Andrews and Kelce in 2021) who absolutely dominate the TE landscape each year. Having one of these difference makers at the position will have you scoring boatloads of points over your competition each and every week.

SO WHAT IS THE BEST WAY TO BUILD YOUR TEAM IN AN AUCTION?

This question has been debated for years and has been proven right and wrong equally over that same period. Below are three ways you could build an auction team (and there are hundreds of similar variations to these).

#1 "STARS AND SCRUBS"

This is exactly what it sounds like. You are going to buy 3-4 mega studs that will burn up 75-80% of your money, and the rest of your roster will be made up of players that go for $10 or less, and many $1 stabs in the dark. You are in business if your studs stay healthy and you hit on a few sleepers. If you get one stud hurt, you are in trouble, if you get two injured for an extended period......better luck next year!

#2 "DOMINATING THE "ONE-OFF" POSITIONS"

The "one-off" positions are QB and TE. So in this strategy, you would maybe stack Patrick Mahomes and Travis Kelce for $65 - $70, then have plenty of money to buy another top player, or maybe three $25 guys you can mix in. The problem is when another owner gets Joe Burrow and TJ Hockenson last year for about a total of $20, they obviously have a lot more money to spend elsewhere than you and may get close to the same production.

#3 "THE BALANCED APPROACH"

You guessed it, you are going to get (3) $30 players and another (3) $20 guys, go cheap at QB or TE, and have a team that won't have many holes after it is drafted. This strategy only seems to work when you hit one or two studs who vastly outplay their ADP, as those $50+ RBs and WRs can be equivalent to 2-3 players on most rosters on many given weeks.

If you have never done an auction draft, I highly recommend that you at least convince your home league to give it a try. Or, if you have been doing that, take your game to the next level and try an online auction or draft live at the NFFC in New York City or Las Vegas.

The camaraderie at these events is second to none. I have drafted at least one live auction with the NFFC each year since 2004, and have met some of my best friends to date, who I talk or text frequently about football and life on a regular basis. While every player has a perceived value in an auction, the lifelong friendships and competition in the NFFC auctions are something you simply cannot put a price on!

Chapter 3

Quarterbacks

	SINGLE QB LEAGUE	RPV		QB2 SUPERFLEX	RPV
1	Patrick Mahomes	13%	13	Jared Goff	10%
2	Josh Allen	11%	14	Aaron Rodgers	9%
3	Jalen Hurts	10%	15	Anthony Richardson	8%
4	Joe Burrow	7%	16	Russell Wilson	6%
5	Lamar Jackson	4%	17	Tua Tagovailoa	6%
6	Justin Fields	-2%	18	Daniel Jones	5%
7	Justin Herbert	-4%	19	Kenny Pickett	-3%
8	Trevor Lawrence	-5%	20	Derek Carr	-5%
9	Deshaun Watson	-5%	21	Matthew Stafford	-6%
10	Kirk Cousins	-8%	22	Jimmy Garoppolo	-8%
11	Dak Prescott	-10%	23	Mac Jones	-10%
12	Geno Smith	-11%	24	Jordan Love	-12%

Get updated RPV Cheat Sheets for one time $5 cost, updates included, 10 & 12 team league RPV PayPal: FantasyBlackBook@gmail.com or Venmo: @FantasyBlackBook with your email address

Player Profiles and Overview

Joe Pisapia

Like last season, there's a clear separation between the top of QB and the rest of the position. There are also a ton of rookie and second year QB's starting in 2023 which will drag down many NFL offenses and talented fantasy players alike. Understanding the QB is to understand the offense. When you understand the offense, evaluating a team for overall fantasy value becomes simpler. There will inevitably be some surprises like Geno Smith, but for the most part, you know what you're paying for here. In single QB leagues, I love getting Joe Burrow, Lamar Jackson or Justin Fields. This strategy doesn't require you to take the first QB off the board, but you can follow the trend and maybe get a value a round or two later without sacrificing RB/WR quality. The single QB league strategy of a "safe" Kirk Cousins and a "wild card" Anthony Richardson is also a viable way to give your roster floor and upside at the position. In superflex, you better have a plan. The back end of QB2 is littered with youth, inexperience, injury plagued players and giant question marks. Sure, you could buy in bulk and hope you hit on 2 of 3, but that's not an approach I would advise in 2023.

THE ELITE

1. **Patrick Mahomes, KC:** Last season, we underestimated Patrick Mahomes. There was cause, having lost Tyreek Hill to the salary cap via trade and left with a host of new and largely unproven receivers. He led the league in QB fantasy points (428.4) and finished second in fantasy points per game to Jalen Hurts (25.2). Mahomes might not be the rushing threat his elite fantasy QB peers are, but when you throw 40 TDs, it doesn't really matter. Let's not be fooled again in 2023. Skyy Moore, Kadarius Toney and Marques Valdes-Scantling are what he's working with, and the best tight end on the planet, Travis Kelce. He's been the best quarterback in the league since his second season and arguably the most consistent. He may not spike like Jalen Hurts and Josh Allen, but he did have (10) 300-yard games in '22. If throws for more than 5,000 yards and 40 TDs again in '23, he'll more than likely finish as the best QB in fantasy. Another unsung virtue of Mahomes is the fact he takes almost half as many sacks as his counterparts. That means he keeps drives going, makes plays, and gives himself more opportunities to produce fantasy points. I can keep going all day, but there are other QBs to discuss.

2. **Josh Allen, BUF:** There's been some off-season buzz that Josh Allen will "run less" in 2023. Frankly, I'll believe it when I see it. Allen is an instinctual player. That was his blessing and curse coming out of college. While many scouts dinged him for that, I had him in 2018's Black Book as the best QB in that class, despite the consensus in fantasy ranking Baker Mayfield, Sam Darnold, Josh Rosen, and Lamar Jackson all ahead of him. My argument was always he can do what no one else can, the rest he can learn and work at. To his credit, he has. It's hard to knock that raw athletic instinct out of a player like Allen. His 776 rushing yards and seven rushing TDs certainly did add to his fantasy appeal. If he shaves that number down to 600, he'll still be top 5 in that category at the position and an elite fantasy QB. Gabe Davis failed to make himself a valuable piece of the offense and James Cook only showed flashes. Stefon Diggs is still by far the #1 target. While Khalil Shakir could surprise in the slot, the fact the only offensive move the Bills made this season was signing Damien Harris. To be truthful, that's not exactly a game changer. While balancing this offense is important because Josh Allen can get "pass-happy" and start forcing balls into windows they don't belong, Allen remains my #2 QB based on the fact his passing stats regressed ever so slightly last year and the Bills really didn't acquire a true second receiving threat. Expect 35 passing TDs, half a dozen rushing TDs, over 4K parks passing and 600+ rushing yards when vying for his services.

3. **Jalen Hurts, PHI:** I'll be the first to admit I've been very reserved in years past when recommending Jalen Hurts. Last year assuaged all those fears. The acquisition of A.J. Brown was the perfect fit for Hurts, and the emergence of DeVonta Smith in his second full season gave the Eagles a 1-2 punch that helped guide Hurts to new heights. He was the number one QB last year in fantasy points per game (25.6) and was third overall (384.1), despite playing in only 15 games. His 13 rushing TDs led all QBs, and his 760 yards on the ground was 4th best. If he can approach 3.7K passing yards again (even over a full, healthy season) and duplicate that rushing total, Hurts will easily be a top 3 fantasy quarterback. Former OC Shane Steichen left for the Colts HC job, leaving Brian Johnson as the new play caller. While Johnson was the QB coach last year, sometimes these promotions do have some bumps in the road. But really, that's the only real concern about Hurts coming into this season, and a minimal one at that.

4. **Joe Burrow, CIN:** If Joe Burrow and Ja'Marr Chase can get a full, healthy season together, they could unlock a fantasy ceiling that could help Burrow challenge Patrick Mahomes for the top spot. Yeah, I said it. Last year, Joe B. threw for 4.5K yards, 36 TDs and 12 INTs. While rushing isn't his game, Burrow is mobile enough to add five rushing TDs and actually had a slightly higher CMP% than Mahomes (68.5%). To put it kindly, the offensive line is still a work in progress. Burrow is on the precipice of a mega contract extension and having Tee Higgins and Chase as his dynamic duo will help him close the deal. The run game is suspect right now with Joe Mixon's potential looming issues/potential of being cut. However, the Bengals kept things rolling with Samaje Perine last year so...MORE TO COME TE OR RB IN DRAFT.

TOP TALENT

1. **Lamar Jackson, BAL:** After a long and winding road, Lamar Jackson finally signed an extension to stay in Baltimore. Jackson has struggled with health the last two seasons, playing just 12 games in each. Just a few years ago, Lamar was MVP of the league just four years ago and he has multiple 1,000-yard rushing seasons under his belt. The Ravens have failed miserably to supply him with weapons over his career. Now, he has Odell Beckham to join Mark Andrews as well as drafting Zay Flowers. Flowers may be undersized, but he's explosive and fights for the football. I'm not holding my breath, but maybe even Rashod Batemen stays on the field for more than a few weeks. This offense could look completely different under new OC Todd Monken, and it's long overdue. Lamar got paid, got his toys and now it's time for him to put up numbers again. The recent injury issues are the only reason I have him not ranked in the "elite" range.

2. **Justin Fields, CHI:** In Week 6, something clicked for Justin Fields, and he basically took the ball in his own hands and proceeded to run all over opposing defenses. He had very few weapons and a poor offensive line, but Fields became a fantasy revelation for many last season. They drafted Tennessee OT Darnell Wright, who should help that line out, and acquired D.J. Moore from Carolina. Moore is by far the best receiver Fields has worked with year to date in Chicago. Fields was a QB1 in 9 of his last 10 games. His style of play does make him an injury risk, but in single QB leagues, he's absolutely worth that risk, as replacement value is easier to find. If you miss out on the top fantasy QBs waiting for Fields a round or two later is a great strategy. He still has plenty of development left to go as a passer, but the arm strength is certainly there. Even if the passing prowess doesn't improve by leaps and bounds, his 1K+ yards rushing and likely double-digit rushing TDs will make up for that deficit.

3. **Justin Herbert, LAC:** In 2022, Justin Herbert fell short of expectations, but still finished as QB12 overall. He did the best he could with Keenan Allen and Mike Williams each missing significant time. It was a rotating cast of characters for Herbert, but this season the Chargers drafted Quentin Johnston who is practically a Mike Williams clone. So, WHEN (not if) Mike Williams goes down again, Johnston can step in and provide some immediate upscale help to the offense. Despite falling short of lofty expectations, Herbert still crossed 4.7K passing yards. The TD total falling from 38 to 25 is where the fantasy value took a hit. There's still some risk here considering the age and health of Keenan Allen and the walking IR stint that is Mike Williams. However, Justin Herbert remains a relatively safe fantasy QB in 2023. The Chargers picked up his 5th year option and Herbert is about to get handed a huge extension.

4. **Trevor Lawrence, JAC:** What a difference a year makes, with a REAL coach and some weapons. Trevor Lawrence was rescued in 2022, and the future looks even brighter in 2023. He doubled his TDs year-over-year from 12 to 25 and cut his interceptions in half from 17 to 8. Oh, and he took the Jags to the playoffs! These are all excellent trends. There are still some offensive line questions in Jacksonville, but bringing in Calvin Ridley to join Christian Kirk, Zay Flowers and Evan Engram gives Lawrence the toys he needs to have a big season. He should reach 4K yards easily and possibly knock on the door of 4.5K. Lawrence is set up for success in 2023, which sometimes takes a toll on young QBs. Not Lawrence, though. He's a generation prospect for a reason and he's poised to break out in 2023.

SOLID OPTIONS

1. **Deshaun Watson, CLE:** After a year away from football, Deshaun Watson was noticeably rusty. He was one of the worst in the NFL in terms of getting the football out of his hands, so one would hope the processing and timing will return this off-season. Watson is a top 5 fantasy QB when he's at his best. Amari Cooper will be his main target and he has enough to work with on this Browns roster. I'd be lying if I said I wasn't slightly concerned about Watson. I was hoping as the season ended that he would look more like himself. The rush ability was still there, but he looked slow on the trigger and shaky on the

playbook. Nonetheless, I'm going to invest in the larger body of work here and have faith he gets back to his old self. He's still just 27 years old, so technically, he's entering his prime years. Let us not forget that in 2020 Watson threw for 4.8K passing yards, 33 TDs and ran for nearly 450 yards. This will be my mantra all summer as I reinvest in Watson. It's a failure I'm willing to risk in single QB leagues all day long, but less so in a shaky superflex QB pool.

2. **Kirk Cousins, MIN:** He was QB in 2022. Yes, Kirk Cousins. He's also been a QB1 for three straight seasons now, so although Monday nights are not his bag, and he falls short in big games, when it comes to fantasy, Kirk Cousins is a quality vanilla ice cream. It will get it done on a hot day, but never have the flavor profile of an elite mint chocolate chip or cookie dough. Kevin O'Connell's offensive scheme was as advertised and having the all-world Justin Jefferson goes a long way. They drafted wide receiver Jordan Addison to join K.J. Osborn and TE T.J. Hockenson was a baller down the stretch after being acquired from Detroit. Despite throwing for 4.5K passing yards (his best total since 2016), Cousins had only (3) 300-yard games. He did have at least one passing TD in 16 of 17 games, so Cousins was consistent. You will always get a few rough Cousins games every year, but he's a decent fantasy starter and ideal second QB if you can pull it off in a superflex format. I would expect another 4.5K year with 30 TDs and 15 INTs again, so bid accordingly.

3. **Geno Smith, SEA:** Well, look who decided to save his NFL career! Geno Smith on his fourth organization, Smith took down a QB6 finish with over 4K passing yards, 30 TDs and 11 INTs. He was a QB1 in 8 of his final 10 starts, so it wasn't like he got off to a great start and then faded away into oblivion down the stretch. Smith won many a superflex league last year off the scrap heap and it feels like he's in a position to repeat close to what we saw in '22. He still has D.K. Metcalf, another year of Tyler Lockett, drafted Jaxon Smith-Njigba for the slot role that's been vacant for some time and they have a two-headed running back monster with Ken Walker and Zach Charbonnet. I don't expect the 2022 Comeback Player of the Year to be a top 6 QB again, but I think he can be a QB1 and a strong fantasy value in 2023. Many won't buy last year. Take advantage of that fact when he inevitably falls in drafts.

4. **Daniel Jones, NYG:** I did a lot of defending of Daniel Jones when he was drafted. Now, everybody loves him after a QB7 finish in '22. Where were you in 2019!!?? Daniel Jones had Saquon Barkley and a cast of no-name WRs last year but managed to make the most of what he had, dropping his best passing yard total to date (3.2K). He threw just 15 TDs, but did run for seven along with a whopping 708 yards. That rushing total was 5th best for all QBs last year. His 18.4 FPPG were 11th best in fantasy. There will be some that now will expect too much of Daniel Jones this year. They brought in Darren Waller, who, in theory, should be a bug weapon, but he has not been healthy the last two seasons, so don't hold your breath. Parris Campbell was signed at WR and Sterling Shepard returned with Isaiah Hodgins, Darius Slayton and Wan'Dale Robinson to the WR corps. Not exactly a murderer's row here. Jones has to run for 600+ yards again to maintain QB1 status because his pass catchers have not improved year over year enough to make him a 25-TD guy. Some will take him over the vanilla Kirk Cousins, but I would still lean the boring pocket passer over the head of this still suspect Giants offense. Even Geno feels like a safer repeat based on his surroundings.

5. **Jared Goff, DET:** It's hard for most of us to accept that Jared Goff was the 10th best QB in fantasy last year. But alas, we must. I'll be holding my hands over my eyes in 2023, because I expect he could actually be even better. Swapping out the oft-injured D'Andre Swift for Jahmyr Biggs, the eventual return of Jameson Williams, and drafting of Sam LaPorta could all keep the trajectory of the Lions offense facing upwards. Even as I write this, I feel as though I'm living in The Upside Down. A lot of this cautious optimism has to do with Amon-Ra St. Brown's star power. Goff threw for 4.4K passing yards, 29 TDs and just 7 INTs. It's the limiting of turnovers that was the secret sauce here for Goff. It also helps to have playmakers who can pad your stats, and he has those as well. He will undoubtedly have some "shake your head moments," but Goff has established a floor and should be motivated with a potential contact extension looming.

6. **Aaron Rodgers, NYJ:** The overpay market for Aaron Rodgers could be fascinating, especially in local area fantasy drafts of the NY and Wisconsin areas. The facts are, Rodgers is coming off a middling season (QB14), he will turn 40 in December, and although he's familiar with the offense (his former OC and failed Head Coach of the Broncos Nathaniel Hackett will be calling plays for the Jets) he still must navigate a lot of NEW; new teammates, new surroundings and a New York media that is vastly different than what he was used to in the Green Bay bubble. His YPA was just 6.8. His 26 TDs were his lowest total in three years. He had ZERO 300-yard games and just one QB1 finish (Week 9 he finished as QB12). To me, Rodgers has big-time fools' gold vibes in 2023. Could the Jets offense and environment rekindle this Hall of Famer's spark? Perhaps, their offensive line is going to be a marked improvement over what he had with the Packers. I would much rather take a flier on Anthony Richardson's upside in single QB leagues and use Rodgers as an insurance plan than a starter. In superflex formats, He's just a QB2. That's fine, but to rank him as more than that at this stage is almost like buying into the idea that nothing could go wrong…like in Denver last year for Russell Wilson. Remember, all the hype that move came along with that scenario and we all know how that turned out.

SUPERFLEX QB2

1. **Dak Prescott, DAL:** 2022 was a frustrating season for Dak Prescott, his fantasy managers, the Cowboys, all of humanity. Ok, that last bit was maybe one too far. But, Dak Prescott finished as QB20 last year after turning in just 12 games. Those 12 were enough to lead the league in interceptions (15!). The picks are a huge problem because they steal away drives that could be equally fantasy points. One of Dak's early hallmarks was being careful with the football, but that was not the case last season. He did manage 17.8 FPPG, so he's not completely bereft of value, but the Cowboys offense is a bit of an enigma right now. They have an alpha dog WR in CeeDee Lamb, and brought in veteran Brandin Cooks, but their depth at WR and TE is "sus" as the kids would say. Prescott is at a fork in the road after the last two years, and if he doesn't improve, Dallas could be looking elsewhere for QB. Prescott is a low-cost investment, but with reason. There doesn't feel like a big return on the investment is coming.

2. **Derek Carr, NO:** We know who Derek Carr is at this stage and that's a QB2 who can offer some low-end QB1 finishes some weeks. Carr now seeks redemption with the Saints after being cast aside by the Las Vegas Raiders. His Raider tenure certainly had its challenges over multiple coaches and systems. We can all root for him to use it as motivation, but let's be honest, New Orleans is a work in progress at best. As much as I love Chris Olave, he's not Davante Adams, Michael Thomas never sees the field and Alvin Kamara is facing a looming suspension. At 32, he has a few decent seasons left in the tank, but Carr is better suited to bye week streaming in single QB formats or a mid-low QB2 in superflex. The fact he posted career-high INT rate and career-low CMP% isn't exactly making me feel excited about his 2023 trajectory.

3. **Mathew Stafford, LAR:** At 35 with a back issue, Matthew Stafford is one of the bigger superflex risks of 2023. We all know the Rams literally sold out for a championship and they got it, but like Avengers Infinity War, we can ask Sean McVay, "what did it cost?" and the answer is: everything. The Rams roster is a shambles, it's old and extremely top-heavy. Star weapon Cooper Kupp is also coming off an injury, so a lot of faith is needed to make fantasy investments in this Rams offense. To chase the 2021 peak of Stafford with his 41 TDs and 4.8K passing yards is folly. If he comes at an extreme discount on draft day in superflex, you can pull the trigger off a healthy training camp. However, you better be drafting a third QB on that roster for safety purposes.

4. **Kenny Pickett, PIT:** I stuck my neck out for Kenny Pickett last year and defended his honor, and I'm glad I did. The Steelers literally threw him to the wolves last year (well, the Jets and Bills to start to be exact, neither an easy situation), and he battled through bad offensive line play, injuries, and elements all year long. He showed some heart and the Steelers made some fixes to the O-Line, including drafting T Broderick Jones. Does he have big, flashy upside? No, he does not. Can he give you 13-15 points a week in 2023 in his second year with more time under center this off-season with first-team reps? I think he can. He has decent mobility and should be a low-end QB2 in superflex this year.

RED FLAGS

1. **Tua Tagovailoa, MIA:** I wish it wasn't so, but Tua is a risky pick in 2023 fantasy. He finally had a great system with talent around him, but the concussion issues are a very serious concern and that feeling of uneasiness rostering him will linger all year. It's far more of a superflex concern. You basically have to draft a third QB if you take a flier on him. From a performance standpoint, he had a higher FPPG than Daniel Jones and Trevor Lawrence. His 3.5K passing yards and 25 TDs were both career highs. When he returned to the field, Tua had four straight weeks of QB1 finishes. However, after the Week 11 bye, he had none (topping out at QB13 in Week 15). The big concern is that Tua was thinking about retirement after the multiple concussions. His health and wellbeing is far more important than football and fantasy. For the sake of this profile, not only is a tough sell for '23, but his dynasty value is even cloudier.

2. **Russell Wilson, DEN:** Well, that didn't go well, now did it? Russell Wilson got a new city, a new team, a new coach, a new playbook and a new cast, and it all culminated in a massive disappointment. Now, he gets another new coach and a new playbook. Now, Sean Payton is a huge theoretical upgrade from the previous regime, but there's no telling how quickly he can steer Wilson and the Broncos out of the skid. Wilson had arthroscopic knee surgery this off-season but should be a full go for training camp. More concerning was his low completion percentage compared to expectations. My fear is that folks will see Sean Payton and forgive and forget the disaster of '22. There's no guarantee everything reverses course and Wilson becomes a top 12 QB in fantasy again. For now, he's a superflex QB2 with risk. With just 16 TDs and 11 INTs in '22, I'd prefer to look elsewhere for my second QB.

3. **Kyler Murray, ARZ:** Kyler Murray's season ended with a torn ACL. Currently, the plan is a "mid-season" return. But, what does that mean? Do we think the Cardinals, one of the worst rosters in the NFL, will be relevant by that juncture in the season? Would tanking for the #1 overall pick be a desired result and would a Murray return put that plan in jeopardy? Murray makes his fantasy living with his legs, but his size was always going to be a long-term question and now he's played 25 games in the last two seasons. It appeared his rushing yardage totals were back on the upswing after a down 2021 prior to the injury. However, his passing stats were less impressive. In all fairness, DeAndre Hopkins did miss significant time, but even when they were on the field together, they seemed at odds. That's not a good thing. I would hard pass on Murray for '23. Perhaps in superflex he could make a late push, but depending on the draft capital he'll cost, returning to a poor team with a new offense doesn't sound like a good investment to me. In dynasty, I'd wait for him to be healthy and look to move him and attack the '24 rookie QB class instead.

4. **Jimmy Garoppolo, LV:** Jimmy Garoppolo outside of the 49ers offense is frankly an enigma. He's efficient with the football, but lacks deep play ability. How the Raiders offense functions with him as opposed to Derek Carr is basically an experiment. Davante Adams is still around, as are possession WRs Hunter Renfrow and newly acquired Jacobi Meyers and the drafted Notre Dame TE Michael Mayer. If Garoppolo finds himself in a new version of the old Patriots dink and doink offense, he could be useful in superflex formats. As long as he's healthy and not asked to do too much, Jimmy G's ceiling is serviceable. Don't look for more.

5. **Mac Jones, NE:** Rumors swirled that the Patriots were kicking the tires on other QB options not named Mac Jones this off-season. Sure, Jones regressed in year two, but can you blame him, considering he didn't have an offensive coordinator and what he did have was a former defensive coordinator in Matt Patricia pretending to call plays. It was a hot mess. Now that Bill O'Brien is back as OC, Jones should find more stability. However, he still doesn't have great weapons to work with and the Patriots will continue to be a run first offense with Rhamondre Stevenson leading the way. The potential Bailey Zappe controversy will resurface if Jones struggles and there's no guarantee Mac starts every game for the Pats in 2023. Jones absolutely deserves a pass, but that doesn't mean he deserves a fantasy investment either. This is a make-or-break season for Jones' future. The supporting cast doesn't leave me hopeful this story ends well.

6. **Desmond Ridder, ATL:** I'm in the minority here, but I think Desmond Ridder can be decent for the Falcons in 2023. He was a great leader in college at Cincinnati and really elevated that program. It's clear he doesn't have an elite skill set, but he's going to have an incredible run game led by Bijan Robinson (who will also catch plenty of dump offs and pad his stats). Ridder will also have Drake London and Kyle Pitts, two premium talents at their respective positions. Ridder is mobile too, which can help his fantasy value. As a third QB in superflex, I would rather invest in him at no cost than some other veterans like Ryan Tannehill.

7. **Jordan Love, GB:** The Jordan Love Era has begun. The trouble is, no one knows what that necessarily means. Outside of Christian Watson and Aaron Jones, it's hard to know who else he can confidently throw the football to in 2023. This is a young team, that's green as grass and could be headed for last place in this division. We can hope that all the reports of the "massive improvement" the team has seen in Love over the last year is true. He's a fascinating dart throw as a QB3 in superflex, because he may indeed outperform expectations and make some spot starts for you in a pinch. Outside of that, it's about waiting and seeing how Love handles the starting job. Love is an intriguing buy low in dynasty because if he does over-deliver, he'd be a make for a nice return on investment.

8. **Ryan Tannehill, TE:** Ryan Tannehill is on notice. The Titans drafted Will Levis, and Tannehill is coming off a terrible season. To be fair, the Tennessee offensive weapons not named Derrick Henry were basically non-existent. There's speculation he could be dealt this summer as well, but regardless, Tannehill's 2020 QB7 performance undoubtedly seems like the outlier of his career. Both of his QB1 season finishes came with 7 rushing TDs and at 35 those rushing days may be behind him.

9. **Sam Howell/Jacoby Brissett/ WAS:** All reports say the Commanders are ready and confident to roll with Sam Howell and that Sam Howell is the starter this season. Color me skeptical that the 5th round QB is ready to be a fantasy player, especially after his final season of college was a disappointment. He would have to have some serious rushing totals to make up for his subpar throwing skills to be an asset. On the other hand, Jacoby Brissett played admirably for the Browns last season and was well-regarded as a leader in that locker room (something the Commanders have lacked). I would be far from shocked if started more games for Washington than any other QB in '23. I'd hedge here on the Brissett side.

10. **Trey Lance/Brock Purdy/Sam Darnold SF:** When you have three quarterbacks, you likely have no quarterback. Trey Lance carries the draft capital and athleticism that's so highly valued in the NFL and fantasy alike. Unfortunately, injuries have derailed his development and he was already a player coming out of college that needed more reps. Irrelevant Brock Purdy came out of nowhere and was surprisingly solid, getting the 49ers to the playoffs and throwing in 3 QB1 performances over his final 5 starts. The bad news, Purdy tore his UCL in the NFC Championship Game and is still in that recovery process. We don't know if he'll be ready for the start of the regular season. Enter Sam Darnold. The man has had more OC's

than Nick Cannon has baby mommas (maybe an exaggeration). Now, Darnold is in camp and technically is the "safest" option to start the season. The truth is, nobody knows how this will all shake out which makes me want to run in the other direction when it comes to fantasy. Lance is the dynasty buy low (and I mean low). Purdy was a fun story, but health and pedigree is a real question. As far as Sam Darnold, I've seen enough of him to know what he is already. Sure, if one wins out in this offense it could work out in fantasy, but the signing of Darnold says to me, there's massive uncertainty under center for San Francisco.

THE WILD CARD

1. **Anthony Richardson, IND:** If there's a man who could break the NFL, and more specifically fantasy football, it's Anthony Richardson. He's bigger than George Kittle, heavier than Hassan Reddick, has bigger hands than DeAndre Hopkins, a higher vertical jump than Davante Adams and a longer jump than Odell Beckham. The man is a freak of nature athlete. But, as a passer, he has a lot of room to grow after just starting 13 games for Florida. Richardson's combine and pro day were utterly fascinating. At the pro day, you saw the struggles with touch and consistency, but those are all things he can improve upon with reps and work ethic. The same way I felt about Josh Allen a few years ago (when I called him the best QB prospect in his class, despite going 4th amongst his peers), is the same way I feel about Richardson. New HC Shane Steichen (former Philadelphia OC) worked with Jalen Hurts and his journey from project to MVP candidate was impressive. Richardson could end up being the best fantasy QB on the planet in 2-3 years. In single QB leagues, I would draft Richardson aggressively and then take a stable veteran like Kirk Cousins or Aaron Rodgers to back up the investment. If he fails or doesn't start right away, you're covered. But if he does start Week 1 or even has a run like Justin Fields did last year of being a fantasy stud for most of the second half, then you could have a league winner on your hands.

UP AND COMING

1. **Bryce Young, CAR:** Bryce Young made great strides year after year in Alabama. Two years ago, he struggled under pressure, despite posting career-high stat totals. Last season, he improved his pocket presence and mobility, which in my opinion, enamored him to NFL teams. Make no mistake, his size is an issue, no matter what anyone may tell you. He's the smallest quarterback in the NFL and playing with an offensive line in progress doesn't make me feel warm and fuzzy. Where Young shines is football intelligence and leadership qualities. It's those traits that anointed him as the 1.01 in this year's draft. He's always been surrounded by elite talent, so seeing how he responds with far less to work with in Carolina will be interesting. He's not bereft of weapons, though, as they signed veteran wide receivers Adam Thielen and D.J. Chark running back Miles Sanders this off-season. The redraft outlook for Young is probably 20 TDs and 3.5K yards passing. The long-term outlook for Young is tenuous based on his size. We've seen a far faster Kyler Murray struggle with health taking hits at the NFL level. Young will need to utilize 100% of that football IQ if he's going to be a productive dynasty asset. I'm rooting for him but leery of investing too heavily.

2. **C.J. Stroud, HOU:** I was adamant that C.J. Stroud would be the second quarterback taken in the draft and despite two weeks of utter nonsense leading up to the draft, he was indeed selected second overall by the Houston Texans. My favorite thing about Stroud was how he showed up in big games. His performance against Alabama showed me everything I needed to feel comfortable about him as an NFL quarterback. Houston has a long way to go to surround him with an offense, but I believe Stroud is a safer long-term investment than Bryce Young. He is elusive, athletic and can make every throw. His rookie year will be rough, but look how quickly the Jags turned over a bad team and launched Trevor Lawrence in just two years. Turnarounds can happen quickly, but 2023 will be a year of growing pains for the Texans and Stroud. The future, however, is bright.

3. **Will Levis, TEN:** Will Levis has a quick release and a strong arm. However, he struggles with reading defenses, and it wasn't that long ago he left Penn State for KU because he couldn't beat out Sean Clifford. Levis didn't elevate the talent around him in college and had plenty of bad days along with the good. Throughout the whole process, I was never drinking the Levis Kool-Aid. He may ultimately prove me wrong, but Levis fell to day two for a reason, and he's more of a thrower than a quarterback at this stage of his development. A less polished Carson Wentz would be my comp, so do with that as you will. Expect Levis to sit behind Ryan Tannehill for the season, unless injury strikes again.

4. **Hendon Hooker, DET:** Coming off an ACL, the 25-year-old Tennessee QB saw his draft stock fall a bit in 2023. Hooker was a solid QB prospect before the injury but not an elite one. Hooker has size and can run, which is positive. While he has a good arm and is accurate, but neither the arm or the athleticism is "elite." Regardless of lacking big flash, Hooker is a capable and competent QB who landed in a spot where he can continue to get healthy, learn and possibly take over the reins of a Detroit offense eventually that's pretty loaded with talent. Hooker is a sneaky low-cost dynasty investment, but likely not relevant in 2023.

Chapter 4

Running Backs

RB 1 PPR		RPV
1	Bijan Robinson	19%
2	Christian McCaffrey	16%
3	Austin Ekeler	13%
4	Saquon Barkley	9%
5	Jonathan Taylor	6%
6	Nick Chubb	-1%
7	Derrick Henry	-3%
8	Tony Pollard	-4%
9	Breece Hall	-10%
10	Najee Harris	-15%
11	Rhamondre Stevenson	-15%
12	Josh Jacobs	-16%

RB2 PPR		RPV
13	Dalvin Cook	11%
14	Aaron Jones	9%
15	Joe Mixon	7%
16	Jahmyr Gibbs	7%
17	Travis Etienne Jr.	4%
18	J.K. Dobbins	0%
19	Dameon Pierce	-3%
20	Kenneth Walker III	-5%
21	Miles Sanders	-7%
22	Cam Akers	-7%
23	James Conner	-7%
24	Alvin Kamara	-9%

RB3 PPR		RPV
25	David Montgomery	17%
26	D'Andre Swift	17%
27	Isiah Pacheco	14%
28	Javonte Williams	8%
29	Rachaad White	1%
30	Rashaad Penny	1%
31	Khalil Herbert	-5%
32	AJ Dillon	-7%
33	Antonio Gibson	-8%
34	Alexander Mattison	-11%
35	Samaje Perine	-11%
36	Zach Charbonnet	-15%

RB1 STND		RPV
1	Bijan Robinson	31%
2	Christian McCaffrey	19%
3	Derrick Henry	8%
4	Austin Ekeler	4%
5	Saquon Barkley	0%
6	Jonathan Taylor	-4%
7	Nick Chubb	-6%
8	Breece Hall	-6%
9	Josh Jacobs	-8%
10	Tony Pollard	-11%
11	Dalvin Cook	-13%
12	Najee Harris	-13%

RB2 STND		RPV
13	Aaron Jones	9%
14	Rhamondre Stevenson	9%
15	Joe Mixon	8%
16	J.K. Dobbins	7%
17	Dameon Pierce	3%
18	Travis Etienne Jr.	1%
19	Kenneth Walker III	1%
20	Isiah Pacheco	1%
21	James Conner	-5%
22	Alvin Kamara	-10%
23	Miles Sanders	-10%
24	Cam Akers	-13%

RB3 STND		RPV
25	Javonte Williams	16%
26	David Montgomery	16%
27	Jahmyr Gibbs	12%
28	Rashaad Penny	8%
29	AJ Dillon	1%
30	D'Andre Swift	-2%
31	Brian Robinson Jr.	-2%
32	Ezekiel Elliott	-6%
33	Rachaad White	-6%
34	Damien Harris	-10%
35	Antonio Gibson	-13%
36	Alexander Mattison	-13%

Get updated RPV Cheat Sheets for one time $5 cost, updates included, 10 & 12 team league RPV PayPal: FantasyBlackBook@gmail.com or Venmo: @FantasyBlackBook with your email address

Player Profiles and Overview

Andrew Erickson

Whether it's best ball or redraft fantasy football, the golden standard approach of selecting a running back with your first-round pick or second-round pick has not changed. Although, of course, the landscape at the very top has changed slightly to favor the league's top-tier WRs such as Justin Jefferson and Ja'Marr Chase. But this isn't the first time we have seen elite WRs favored against their running back counterparts.

Not long ago, the elite tier of WRs like Davante Adams, Julio Jones, Odell Beckham Jr., DeAndre Hopkins and Antonio Brown were drafted in the top half of Round 1. So, WRs being drafted ahead of many RBs is just part of the natural fantasy football cycle. There's a strong argument that today's top WRs are just better than the top RBs. However, with a strong crop of diverse running backs entering the player pool, I'd bet we return to the glory days where RBs reign supreme in Round 1 – as they did just one season ago between Jonathan Taylor, Christian McCaffrey, Austin Ekeler, Joe Mixon, Saquon Barkley, Alvin Kamara and Dalvin Cook.

Because one thing's for certain — running backs are the drivers behind fantasy-winning teams. So, get your talented studs early in Rounds 1-2.

The cleverly coined and my personal favorite "Hero RB" approach sets you up nicely with a locked-and-loaded stud in your RB1 slot. You've got one spot dialed in, and the other spot can be filled by the rotating carousel of remaining RBs on your roster.

Solidifying a top dog in Rounds 1/2 also helps you avoid reaching for running backs in the upcoming RB Dead Zone, where your primary focus should be drafting WRs poised for significant leaps in 2023.

You take shots on RBs with potential red-zone roles and pass-catching chops until the later rounds. You'll also want to hone in on impending free agents, proven running backs and RBs in ambiguous backfields. That's where we'll find the next breakout at the position.

It's the exact balancing act of drafting up-and-coming running back breakouts with the elites/top talents – while also playing matchups and avoiding red flags – that will help you DOMINATE your fantasy football league in 2023.

Let's go.

THE ELITE

1. **Christian McCaffrey, SF:** Christian McCaffrey joined the 49ers midway through the 2022 season and quickly became a key player, recording over 40 fantasy points in just his second game with the team. From Weeks 8-17, McCaffrey led all running backs in fantasy points scored, averaging 20.5 fantasy half-points per game - a feat that would have also ranked him first among all RBs in 2022. He maintained an average of 19.5 points per game and 17.3 expected fantasy points per game during the 13 games (including postseason play) from Week 8 onward. Despite being part of a crowded offense, McCaffrey should have the highest production among the talented group of weapons in the Bay Area, thanks to his combination of high-value usage, rushing ability, pass-catching skills, and touchdown-scoring potential. According to PFF, he averaged nearly 20 touches per game and a 76% average snap share in non-blowout games for San Francisco while also catching nearly five balls per game, earning him the third-highest grade among running backs. Fantasy football managers can count on McCaffrey to be a reliable and high-performing player as long as he stays healthy.

2. **Bijan Robinson, ATL:** Bijan Robinson, the highly touted rookie running back from Texas, was selected 8th overall in the 2023 NFL Draft by the Atlanta Falcons, and his fantasy football ceiling is sky-high. In his final college football season, Robinson was the second highest-graded rusher in the FBS per PFF and posted a staggering 37% dominator rating with 18 rushing TDs and 1,575 rushing yards. His impressive 40% broken

tackle rate and 104 missed tackles forced demonstrate his ability to thrive at the NFL level. Robinson's versatility is also noteworthy, as he finished third among RBs in yards per catch (16.5) with zero drops. In Arthur Smith's run-heavy offense last season, Tyler Allgeier, a former 5th-round pick, finished as PFF's highest-graded rookie RB and ranked 6th in rushing EPA. Allgeier averaged nearly 18 carries and 96 rushing yards per game from Week 13 onward in 2022. Given Robinson's superior talent and size compared to Allgeier, the first-year rusher is primed to be a three-down back for the Falcons. Considering the offense ranked first in early down run rate and +13% in run rate above expectation in 20202, Robinson has the potential to eclipse 300 carries and 1,500 rushing yards in 2023 and beyond, making him a top-3-ranked running back in season-long formats. Atlanta also boasts the second-easiest schedule based on Vegas' forecasted win totals. The schedule from Weeks 1-5 is extremely favorable toward the Falcons' ground game with matchups versus the Panthers, Packers, Lions, Jaguars and Texans. Although it won't be just a strong start, considering they also own the easiest schedule from Week 9 onward. Robinson sure fits the profile of a late-season hammer to drive home fantasy titles with the Panthers, Colts and Bears teed up in the fantasy playoffs.

3. **Nick Chubb, CLE:** As one of the league's premier pure rushers, Nick Chubb quietly amassed an impressive 1,525 rushing yards (5.0 yards per carry again) and 13 touchdowns in 2022, finishing as the RB6 overall with a top 10 backfield opportunity share (64%). From Weeks 1-12, he was the RB4 overall and in points per game. However, his production tailed off towards the end of the season with the return of Deshaun Watson to the lineup, dropping him to RB23 overall in Weeks 13-17. However, with Watson expected to raise the ceiling of the Browns' offense with a full offseason back to football, Chubb's fantasy production should remain more consistent throughout the 2023 season, making him a near-bust-proof draft pick. Additionally, Chubb could see increased opportunities in the receiving game with the departure of running backs Kareem Hunt and D'Ernest Johnson. He demonstrated his ability in this area with a strong Week 18 performance, playing a season-high 75% snap share, running a route on 71% of dropbacks and catching 5-of-6 targets (22% target share) for 45 yards. 2022 5th-rounder Jerome Ford is currently pegged as the No. 2 RB.

4. **Jonathan Taylor, IND:** Jonathan Taylor is expected to bounce back after a disappointing 2022 campaign where he finished as the RB30 in 11 games played. Despite being 8th in expected points per game and 4th in touches per game, Taylor's lack of touchdowns hurt his fantasy value in the Colts' struggling offense. After scoring a combined 33 TDs through his 1st two seasons, Taylor scored just four rushing TDs in 2022. The Colts RB scored only thrice from inside the 5-yard line on 16 goal-line carries. Woof. However, with Taylor being healthier – he was the RB3 when healthy from Weeks 10-13 last season – and rookie QB Anthony Richardson's mobility expected to boost Taylor's per-carry efficiency, JT should experience positive TD regression in the final year of his rookie deal. Even with Richardson potentially taking some goal-line carries, Taylor's proven production and talent make him a strong bet to reach double-digit scores in 2023. Remember, a mobile quarterback didn't stop Shane Steichen's running back, Miles Sanders, from scoring 13 TDs in Philadelphia last season. Considering the wide talent gap and proven production from Taylor compared to Sanders, I'd bet Steichen's new RB1 will reach double-digit scores even if his rookie QB runs in a few himself. Taylor should also hit right from the get-go, opening the year versus the Jaguars and Texans. JT also has the No. 1-easiest schedule for fantasy RBs per FantasyPros' strength of schedule tool and a juicy Week 17 playoff matchup versus the Raiders. Wheels Up.

5. **Austin Ekeler, LAC:** Austin Ekeler has been a touchdown-scoring machine for the past two seasons, scoring a combined 38 touchdowns. He's been a reliable fantasy RB1, and his dual-threat ability has made him a staple in PPR leagues. In 2022, Ekeler led all running backs in receptions and targets, resulting in an RB3 finish in half-point scoring. His role as a receiver is particularly valuable in the Chargers' pass-heavy offense, especially with the team's WRs struggling to stay healthy. Ekeler is the focal point of the offense and should continue to see a high volume of touches in the final year of his deal. And better yet, the lack of RB depth behind him ensures

his stranglehold on high-value touches. If the Chargers don't add any significant competition to their backfield, Ekeler should remain a top fantasy option in a Kellen Moore-led 2023 Chargers offense.

6. **Saquon Barkley, NYG:** Saquon Barkley proved his worth as a top-tier running back in 2022 after returning to full health and playing in an improved offensive system. In 16 games, he finished as the RB5 overall and in points per game, showcasing his explosive upside as both a rusher and receiver. With the Giants using the franchise tag on him for 2023, Barkley will be highly motivated to prove his value. One area where Barkley shines is as a receiver out of the backfield, and he finished with 57 catches for 338 yards in 2022. With the Giants lacking depth at the running back position, Barkley is poised to see a heavy workload and should be a focal point of the offense on another one-year deal. He scored 10 rushing touchdowns in 2022 and had 23 carries inside the 10-yard line, showcasing his potential for goal-line carries. Big Blue's RB1 also finished second in overall touches (352) and backfield opportunity share (80%) behind only Josh Jacobs through 17 weeks. With Barkley's proven track record of production and lack of competition for touches in the Giants' backfield, he should be considered a top-tier fantasy option in 2023. Fantasy managers can rely on him to produce consistent points week in and week out, especially as he looks to prove his worth on the franchise tag. Expect Barkley to be a workhorse for the Giants and a major asset for fantasy teams.

7. **Josh Jacobs, LV:** Josh Jacobs was a league winner for many fantasy managers in 2022, as he outperformed his draft day ADP to finish as the RB2 overall. Despite concerns of a committee backfield, Jacobs proved to be a bellcow for the Raiders, leading the league in touches throughout the regular season. Now returning to Las Vegas on the franchise tag, Jacobs is poised to be the focal point of the Raiders' offense once again. While the lack of depth behind him on the depth chart may be a concern for the real-life Raiders, it foreshadows that Jacobs will likely see heavy volume as the clear lead back. As long as he stays healthy, the 24-year-old should be a reliable RB1 option for fantasy managers in 2023.

8. **Derrick Henry, TEN:** Derrick Henry proved all his doubters wrong in 2022, finishing as the RB4 overall and in points per game (18.3). He dominated the league, finishing second in carries and third in rushing yards with 23.4 touches per game. Henry also posted career highs in targets, receptions, and yards per route run, showing he's more than just a traditional workhorse running back. Despite a poor offensive line, Henry continued to excel in 2022, with the Titans' poor offensive situation not impacting his fantasy production. 2023 is a contract year for Henry, and the Titans may look to ride him even harder as they look to secure their star running back long-term. However, there are concerns that this could be the year Henry hits the wall. With the Titans facing major questions on offense, including the potential change at QB, there are valid concerns about drafting Henry early in 2023. While his impressive 2022 season shows he's still an elite back, the risk of injury and burnout is always a concern with such a heavy workload. It will be interesting to see how the Titans utilize Henry in 2023 and whether he can continue to perform at an elite level despite the questions surrounding the offense.

TOP TALENT

1. **Breece Hall, NYJ:** Breece Hall burst onto the scene in 2022, showcasing his talent and proving that he has the potential to be one of the NFL's best running backs. Unfortunately, his season was cut short due to a torn ACL, but Hall is expected to make a full recovery and be ready for training camp. In just seven games played, Hall was the RB6 in half-PPR points per game, averaging an impressive 5.8 yards per carry as a rusher and ranking fourth in yards after contact per attempt (4.13). He also made an impact as a receiver, ranking fourth in RB receiving yards with an elite 34.4% target rate per route run. While Hall's talent is undeniable, his ACL injury raises concerns about his durability and ability to bounce back. However, recent reports suggest that Hall is making significant progress in his recovery and could be back fully in 2023. Fantasy managers should consider Hall a high-upside target with top-tier rushing and receiving potential. However, his injury history should be a factor

in the decision to draft him. Keep an eye on his recovery progress throughout the offseason and preseason to make an informed decision on drafting him for the 2023 fantasy football season.

2. **Tony Pollard, DAL:** Looking ahead to the 2023 fantasy football season, Tony Pollard will be playing for the Cowboys on the franchise tag after an impressive 2022 campaign. With Ezekiel Elliott no longer on the roster, Pollard can take over as the team's lead back. Last season, he finished as the RB7 in fantasy despite ranking outside the top 25 in touches per game. Pollard's efficiency was on full display as he averaged 5.3 yards per carry and was the third-highest-graded running back by PFF. From Weeks 7-16, Pollard was the highest-scoring running back in fantasy with 19.3 points per game while playing as the team's featured back. Although the Cowboys added Ronald Jones in free agency and drafted Deuce Vaughn late in the 2023 draft, neither player poses a significant threat to Pollard's touch volume, as a healthy Pollard should continue to be a formidable asset in fantasy football. Even if Dallas eventually does bring in another body, Pollard's efficient play style will mitigate any workload limitations.

3. **Rhamondre Stevenson, NE:** Rhamondre Stevenson is poised to have an even bigger role in the New England Patriots backfield with Damien Harris now in Buffalo. Although Stevenson shared touches with Harris in 2022, he still managed to finish as a fantasy RB1 with a solid RB10 finish. In fact, during Weeks 5-16, when Harris was either inactive or not at 100%, Stevenson was the RB13 in points per game. Despite struggling to convert goal-line carries into touchdowns in 2022, Stevenson still made an impact in the passing game, which should continue as he improved his route running as the season progressed. Stevenson finished third in route participation (58%) and targets (82) among all running backs. Expect his receiving numbers to stay high, with the Patriots facing probable negative scripts in 2023 based on the league's most difficult schedule. With Harris now gone, Stevenson's touchdown potential is set to increase, and his lack of competition for touches in the Patriots' backfield only adds to his upside. Moreover, the arrival of James Robinson in Buffalo means that Stevenson's path to touches and production is clearer than ever. Robinson, who was benched in favor of an undrafted free agent in 2022, is unlikely to challenge Stevenson for touches, and Stevenson's strong performance last season indicates that he is more than capable of handling an expanded role. With positive touchdown regression likely to come his way, Stevenson is a strong bet to build on his impressive sophomore campaign and provide consistent RB1 value for fantasy managers in 2023.

4. **Travis Etienne Jr., JAC:** Travis Etienne Jr. proved himself to be a solid fantasy asset during the 2022 season, averaging 15 fantasy points per game from Weeks 7-17 (RB8 in points per game) and finishing tied for 5th in carries inside the 10-yard line (23) despite only scoring four touchdowns on those carries. In 2023, with the backfield his to lose and the Jaguars' offense on the rise, Etienne is poised for a breakout year with increased touchdown production. Additionally, Etienne's potential as a receiver is tantalizing. While he had a limited role in the passing game in 2022, he was the primary route runner among the Jaguars' running backs, and his 22% target rate per route in 3 of his last four games played is a strong indication of his receiving upside. The possibility of injury to one of the team's top receivers, such as Calvin Ridley, Christian Kirk, Zay Jones, or Evan Engram, could result in an even greater receiving role for Etienne in 2023. Though JaMycal Hasty, D'Ernest Johnson, Snoop Conner and Tank Bigsby are all behind him on the depth chart, it remains to be seen how much of a threat any will pose to Etienne's workload. Regardless, Etienne's potential as a dual-threat running back and his status as the clear lead back on an improving offense make him an enticing option for fantasy managers in 2023. He has the upside to finish as a top-10 RB and is worth targeting in the early rounds of fantasy drafts.

5. **J.K. Dobbins, BAL:** J.K. Dobbins' 2022 campaign got off to a sluggish start as he was recovering from major knee surgery and missed the first two weeks of the season. Even when he returned, his performances were middling, failing to surpass 50 rushing yards or 13 carries in any game with little involvement in the passing game. Unfortunately, he required another knee surgery after Week 6 and was placed on IR until Week 14. However, when Dobbins finally returned later in the year, he showed why he's such a highly regarded talent. In his last

five games, including the playoffs, he averaged an impressive 6.6 yards per carry, 92 rushing yards, and 14 carries per game. This strong finish is a promising sign for his 2023 prospects in an offense that should light the league ablaze under the QB/OC combination of Lamar Jackson/Todd Monken. And although he continued to split carries with Gus Edwards in 2022, Dobbins' explosive running style and effectiveness in the Ravens' offense make him a highly desirable fantasy asset. Additionally, with little receiving usage during his limited playing time in 2022, it's possible that he could see an increased role in the passing game this season in Monken's offensive attack. Despite the presence of Edwards and Justice Hill in the backfield, Dobbins is the clear lead back for the Ravens and should be viewed as a top-tier fantasy option in 2023. Helps his case further than Baltimore could ride him into the ground as an impending free agent.

SOLID OPTIONS

1. **Najee Harris, PIT:** Najee Harris had a disappointing sophomore campaign for the Pittsburgh Steelers, finishing as RB14 in points per game, down from his top-5 finish in his rookie year. However, his workload metrics were still impressive, as he ranked 6th in opportunity share (70%) and 8th in total touches through the first 17 weeks of the season. Harris also showed significant improvement down the stretch, finishing as the RB7 in points per game over the last nine weeks of the season. He had five games with 20-plus carries during the second half of 2022, compared to zero in the first eight weeks. What's even more exciting for Harris' fantasy outlook in 2023 is Pittsburgh's vastly improved offensive line. The Steelers used their first-round pick in the 2023 NFL Draft on offensive tackle Broderick Jones and signed guards Nate Herbig and Isaac Seumalo in free agency. These additions should help open running lanes for Harris and give him more opportunities to break big runs. With the potential for an improved offense led by second-year quarterback Kenny Pickett, Harris is in line for a bounce-back effort in 2023. Fantasy managers can confidently draft Harris as a workhorse back with RB1 upside.

2. **Miles Sanders, CAR:** Miles Sanders has found a new home in Carolina, reuniting him with familiar faces from his Eagles days in Duce Staley, Frank Reich, and Josh McCown. His previous success with these coaches was surely a factor in his signing, as he replaces D'Onta Foreman as the Panthers' RB1. Sanders will likely be the primary back on early downs, while Chuba Hubbard and Raheem Blackshear split work on third downs. However, Sanders can be a full-blown three-down workhorse, as Hubbard and Blackshear have yet to prove themselves to the new coaching staff. Sanders had a great 2022 campaign, finishing as the RB10 in half-point scoring overall and RB13 in points per game from Weeks 1-17. The former Eagle averaged nearly five yards per carry and scored 13 rushing TDs, a significant improvement from his zero rushing TDs in 2021. He was also loaded with carries inside the 10-yard line, ranking in the top five among all RBs. Sanders' best receiving usage to date came under Staley's tenure, when he had 50 receptions for 509 yards as a rookie in 2019. And the Colts running backs under Reich's coaching the past three seasons have averaged a 21% target share or higher – a top-12 mark among all teams. With the Panthers, Sanders can expand his receiving role, as evidenced by the team's four-year, $25 million ($13 million guaranteed) commitment to him. He will be running behind an offensive line that finished 9th in adjusted line yards in 2022, making Carolina an excellent landing spot for him. Looking at Foreman's production after the team traded away Christian McCaffrey, he finished as the RB21 in total points, RB22 in points per game and fourth in the NFL in total rushing yards (852) from Week 7 onward. Foreman's inconsistency was due to a lack of pass-game work, which caused him to be phased out of games where the Panthers were outmatched. However, Sanders is expected to have an expanded receiving role, which should prevent him from being phased out of games. Therefore, Sanders can potentially be a back-end RB1, and fantasy managers should target him as such in their drafts.

3. **Aaron Jones, GB:** Although Aaron Jones didn't quite live up to his lofty expectations in 2022, the Packers running back still managed to finish as the RB9 in fantasy points and the RB12 in points per game. His 59 catches ranked second on the team, behind only Allen Lazard, and his 72 targets were a career-high. However, Jones caught fewer passes than the previous year and was inconsistent, often becoming a boom-or-bust

option for his fantasy managers. Better in best ball, am I right? One of the biggest concerns for Jones heading into 2023 is the competition for touches in the Green Bay backfield. A.J. Dillon emerged as a red zone threat last season, out-carrying Jones inside the 10-yard line 14 to 5 from Week 9 onward. This resulted in Dillon scoring six rushing touchdowns during the season's final seven weeks. If Dillon continues to receive a significant amount of goal-line work, it could cut into Jones' fantasy upside and limit his touchdown potential. Despite the competition for touches, Jones remains tantalizing due to his ability as a receiver. He has consistently been one of the better receiving backs in the league and has a good chance to lead the Packers in receptions in 2023. However, the uncertainty surrounding the quarterback position with Jordan Love taking over for Aaron Rodgers adds another layer of risk to Jones' fantasy outlook. Overall, Jones' fantasy value largely depends on his usage in the Packers' offense and the extent of A.J. Dillon's role. While he has shown the ability to produce at a high level in the past, fantasy managers should be aware of the potential downside in an offense that is in transition and has a new quarterback under center. A lack of established pass-catchers in Green Bay's offense could end up as the deciding factor to what makes or breaks Jones' fantasy upside in 2023.

4. **Cam Akers, LAR:** Cam Akers had a rocky start to the 2022 season, getting benched in Week 1 and facing doubts about his role in the Rams' backfield. However, Akers eventually emerged as the team's RB1 and finished the season as the RB4 in the final six weeks leading the NFL in rushing yards (85 yards/game). As the Rams enter a new season, Akers' potential for high volume makes him an appealing option in fantasy football. One reason for optimism is that Sean McVay is staying in Los Angeles, which bodes well for Akers to remain the primary option in the backfield. Akers played every snap in the Rams' season finale, and the team did not select any running backs until the sixth round of this year's draft. This means that Akers will face little competition for touches, with only Day 3 picks Kyren Williams, Ronnie Rivers, and Zach Evans as potential "threats." What's more, Akers is still only 24 years old, and with free agency looming after this season, the Rams have every reason to ride him hard in 2023. His 2022 finish and potential for heavy volume make him an excellent fantasy football value.

5. **Joe Mixon, CIN:** Joe Mixon had an up-and-down 2022 season but finished the year as a top-10 fantasy running back in points per game. Mixon struggled to find his footing in the first eight games, averaging just 3.3 yards per carry and ranking as the RB19 in points per game. However, as the season progressed and the offensive line started to gel, Mixon's production soared, culminating in an incredible 5-touchdown performance against the Panthers in Week 9. In his final eight healthy games, Mixon was the RB5 in points per game, averaging 16.7 fantasy points per game. Despite the emergence of Samaje Perine during Mixon's midseason injury absence, Mixon remained the workhorse back for the Bengals, finishing sixth in touches per game and second in carries inside the 10-yard line. However, Mixon only scored five touchdowns at the goal line despite the high volume, likely due to early-season negative touchdown regression. His career-high receiving usage helped salvage his fantasy season, as he finished as the RB8 in points per game. Looking ahead to 2023, Mixon should be in line for another heavy workload, as the Bengals did not add any notable competition for touches in the backfield. Chris Evans may take on a larger role on third downs after the departure of Perine to the Broncos, but Mixon's role as the primary back on early downs is secure. The Bengals did draft Chase Brown in the fifth round, but he is unlikely to have a major impact in his rookie season. With his ability to contribute as both a runner and a receiver, Mixon should once again flirt with RB1 status in 2023, especially if he can continue to find the end zone with more consistency. And, of course, if he doesn't have any off-the-field issues that influence his playing time and starter status in Cincinnati.

6. **James Conner, ARI:** When healthy in 2022, James Conner was an elite fantasy producer and a key part of the Arizona Cardinals' offense, finishing as the RB4 overall in his last eight games with an average of 17 fantasy points per game (RB6). He also ranked highly in overall usage, with at least a 90% snap share in five contests. With no significant investments made in the No. 2 running back position this offseason for the Cardinals, it's

likely that Conner will maintain his high workload, making him a solid asset for fantasy managers. However, durability issues and his age are factors to keep in mind. Conner missed four games entirely and left three others early due to injuries in 2022, and he is entering his age-28 season. Nonetheless, with a potential out in his contract at the end of the season, the Cardinals have every reason to ride him hard in 2023.

7. **Dameon Pierce, HOU:** Dameon Pierce was a bright spot for the Texans during his rookie campaign in 2022, quickly becoming the team's bell cow and finishing the year as the fantasy RB12 overall and in points per game. Pierce ranked fifth in the NFL in rushing yards from Weeks 2 to 10, averaging over 19 carries and 92 rushing yards per game. He displayed his ability to break tackles, finishing fourth in missed tackles forced and first in missed tackles forced per attempt (28%) among RBs with at least 100 carries. However, Pierce hit a wall mid-season and suffered a season-ending ankle injury just 61 yards shy of hitting the century mark on the year. Assuming he recovers fully from his injury, Pierce is expected to lead the Texans' backfield in 2023. However, the team's new coaching staff and Pierce's 4th-round draft capital suggest that his role could change. The addition of veteran Devin Singletary on a one-year deal worth $3.75 million could cut into Pierce's workload. While Singletary is unlikely to unseat Pierce as the team's No. 1 rusher, he presents a much bigger threat than other Texans RBs who combined for just 11 carries during Pierce's hot start in 2022. Singletary's PFF pass-blocking grade (73.2, 8th) could also earn him usage on passing downs, where Pierce struggled in his rookie season. However, Singletary's addition should not cause fantasy managers to fully fade Pierce. Singletary is not the worst running back the Texans could have added, but he is not a reason to completely lose faith in Pierce's fantasy value. The team also did not draft any running backs in the 2023 NFL Draft. If Pierce can improve his pass protection in his second year, he still has a chance to earn a full three-down workload, as Singletary has never been a standout receiver. Overall, while Pierce's role may not be as undisputed as it was in 2022, he still has the potential to be a valuable fantasy asset in 2023.

8. **David Montgomery, DET:** David Montgomery signed a lucrative contract with the Detroit Lions, making him the potential goal-line and red-zone back for the team in 2023. Despite his overall inefficiency last season, Monty's upside lies in his ability to score touchdowns. In his 15 healthy games, he averaged 10.9 fantasy points per game, finishing as the RB26. However, his production decreased in the 11 games he played alongside Khalil Herbert, averaging just 9.2 fantasy points (RB35) and 48 rushing yards per game (13 carries per game, 32nd in rushing EPA/attempt. But with the departure of Jamaal Williams, Montgomery has an opportunity to claim a similar red-zone role that led to Williams carrying the ball a league-high 45 times inside the 10-yard line and scoring 17 rushing touchdowns. The Lions also drafted Jahmyr Gibbs 12th overall, creating competition for touches in the backfield. This may limit Montgomery's overall production, but his contract and projected role suggest that he will be involved enough (likely as a rusher on early downs) to maintain his fantasy viability alongside Gibbs. Therefore, while Montgomery may not be the flashiest pick, he presents a solid value at a relatively cheap price tag as a potential RB2/RB3 with touchdown upside in an above-average offense.

RED FLAGS

1. **Kenneth Walker III, SEA:** Kenneth Walker III emerged as a fantasy-relevant player in 2022, finishing as the RB9 in points per game and the RB8 from Weeks 6-17 after Rashaad Penny went down with an injury. Walker got absolutely FED after returning from a late-season ankle injury playing 70 percent-plus snaps or carrying the ball 23-plus times. He proved to be a steal for those who drafted him late, but his overall outlook for 2023 is less certain. While Walker took over RB1 duties and received a heavy workload after Penny's injury, he underwhelmed as a receiver and had a low rushing success rate, ranking second-to-last among rushers with at least 100 carries. Injuries were also a concern for him. The Seahawks added Zach Charbonnet in the second round of the 2023 draft, a back who excels as a receiver and is highly efficient as a rusher. Charbonnet's skill set will likely earn him playing time, and he could cut into Walker's touches. While Walker has shown the ability to deliver explosive rushes, Charbonnet's reliability as a rusher and receiver could make him the more

appealing option for the Seahawks on a down-to-down basis. Fantasy managers hoping for Walker to be the workhorse in Seattle this season may need to temper their expectations.

2. **Javonte Williams, DEN:** Javonte Williams had a rough go in his sophomore season, seeing just four games of action before being sidelined for the remainder of the year due to a devastating knee injury. However, the silver lining to his abbreviated campaign is that he may have been spared from further struggles in the Broncos' dismal offense. Before his injury, Williams had a middling RB35 ranking in points per game, but don't be fooled by the numbers. His underlying metrics were elite, with a PFF elusive rating of 116.3 that was tops among all RBs with at least 45 carries. While Williams's expected to be back at the start of the 2023 season, concerns loom about how he'll bounce back from such a severe and complex injury, much like J.K. Dobbins from the previous year. In addition, the Broncos' offseason moves suggest that they may not be fully confident in Williams' ability to return right away and for him to handle a full workload with the addition of Samaje Perine to the backfield under new head coach Sean Payton. Fantasy managers should temper their expectations for Williams heading into 2023, but if he can overcome his injury concerns, he has the potential to make a major impact on the Broncos' offense in the second half of the year.

3. **Dalvin Cook, MIN:** Dalvin Cook had a somewhat underwhelming 2022 season, which might make fantasy managers question his elite status going into 2023. Despite finishing as the RB8 overall and RB10 in points per game, he ranked last in rushing EPA and percentage of rushes for zero or negative yardage among all ball carriers. Cook still managed to earn a hefty opportunity share, placing fourth in the league at 78%. However, Cook's future with the Vikings is a bit murky, with the latest reports as of this writing suggesting "all signs point" to the team moving on from the veteran with claims reporting he will indeed be a post-June 1st cut. The team has invested in the running back position by bringing back Alexander Mattison, which could lead to a reduced role for Cook in the offense. Additionally, there are reports that the Vikings could potentially look to trade Cook or even cut him due to his high salary. This uncertainty creates a lot of ambiguity around Cook's fantasy value heading into 2023. Cook has stated that his preferred landing spot is with the Miami Dolphins. While Cook has been a dominant fantasy force when healthy, the possibility of a reduced role or a move to another team should give managers pause when considering him in drafts. It will be important to monitor Cook's situation closely throughout the offseason and preseason to get a better sense of his expected usage in 2023.

4. **Alvin Kamara, NO:** Alvin Kamara had a tough 2022 season with the Saints, and he has multiple red flags for fantasy managers heading into 2023. Kamara saw his touchdown upside capped due to the presence of Taysom Hill, who took on an increased role as a backfield rusher at the goal line and limited Kamara to just two rushing touchdowns. With Jamaal Williams joining the backfield this offseason, Kamara's touchdown production could face further challenges. His overall touches could also be limited, with the Saints drafting TCU's Kendre Miller in the 3rd round of the 2023 NFL Draft. Kamara's receiving usage also took a hit towards the end of the year, with his target share dropping from 22% to 11%. He never caught more than two passes in any game from Weeks 13-18, and his days as a game-breaking receiver seem to be long gone. His rushing production was also subpar, finishing second worst in the rushing EPA (-41) and managing only two games with over 65 rushing yards before the schedule eased up in the final four games. Kamara's 2023 fantasy outlook is further complicated by potential suspension due to events from the previous year's Pro Bowl. With so many question marks, he is a risky pick in the early rounds of drafts. Kamara's days as a fantasy superstar are likely over.

5. **D'Andre Swift, PHI:** D'Andre Swift is in a new situation after being traded from the Lions to the Philadelphia Eagles. While his efficiency in 2022 was impressive, his injury history and lack of projected usage in the passing game may temper expectations for his fantasy output in 2023. Despite missing time due to injury in his final year with Detroit, Swift still showed promise, ranking fourth in fantasy points per touch and third in yards per

carry among all RBs. He created yards after contact and remained efficient on a per-touch basis despite his reduced workload in the Lions' offense. However, he struggled to find the end zone and didn't receive the featured role in Detroit's backfield. Now in Philadelphia, Swift should benefit from a change in scenery and the opportunity for more involvement in the offense. However, he will have to compete with Rashaad Penny for touches, who has shown himself to be a solid rusher in his own right. Additionally, the Eagles ranked last in RB target share in 2022 (12%), which could limit Swift's value as a receiver. Despite the uncertainties, Swift's talent is undeniable, and he should be productive on a per-touch basis in 2023. However, fantasy managers should be aware of his injury history and the potential for limited receiving work in the Eagles' offense. While Swift has the potential to be a league-winner, there is also some risk involved if his ADP rises too high.

6. **Ezekiel Elliott, FA:** Ezekiel Elliott had a down year in 2022, and I was among those who advised against drafting him in fantasy leagues. His yards per carry dropped to a career-low of 3.7, and he saw decreased usage in the passing game. However, he was still a touchdown machine, finishing second in expected touchdowns with 12 real rushing scores. Only Joe Mixon and Jamaal Williams had more carries inside the 10-yard line than Elliott. His scoring prowess made him a viable fantasy option, especially after he returned from injury, scoring eight touchdowns from Weeks 11-17. Despite his up-and-down 2022 season, Elliott's potential value in fantasy for 2023 and beyond could be a factor if he lands on a new team. He was released by the Dallas Cowboys in the offseason, leaving him free to sign with any team that wants him. He will need to carve out a role as a team's primary red-zone back to have sustained fantasy value. Depending on where he signs, he could be a valuable addition to fantasy rosters, especially if he becomes the primary option goal-line option in a high-powered offense. Keep an eye on his landing spot, as it could be the difference between him being a top-tier fantasy running back or a major bust.

7. **Leonard Fournette, FA:** After being released from the Tampa Bay Buccaneers due to salary cap restrictions, Leonard Fournette finds himself searching for a new team and a fresh start in 2023. Fournette's 2022 season was a letdown after his impressive 2021 campaign with the Bucs. His efficiency as a runner took a significant hit, finishing as the 4th-worst in NFL next-gen stats rushing yards over expectation per attempt (-0.36) and 6th-worst in PFF rushing grade (67.6.) In Tampa, Fournette faced competition from rookie Rachaad White and saw his role diminish as the season progressed. White split time with Fournette and emerged as the 1A in the backfield, averaging 11 fantasy points per game (RB26) from Weeks 10-17 compared to Fournette's 11.3 (RB23). Despite Fournette's struggles in 2022, his potential fantasy value remains intriguing. He's only one year removed from a strong season where he led Tampa Bay's backfield with over 1,300 scrimmage yards and 12 touchdowns. With a new team, Fournette could carve out a primary goal-line and short-yardage back role with his three-down skillset and large frame. Additionally, Fournette could continue to see a receiving role, especially if he signs with a team that utilizes running backs in the passing game. He's caught 74-plus passes in three of the last four seasons and finished last year 6th in PFF receiving grade. If Fournette can find the right landing spot and return to his 2021 form, he could be a valuable asset for fantasy managers looking for a low-cost, high-upside running back option in 2023. But there's no doubt that his disappointing 2022 campaign, which featured a surplus of dump-off catch production, has hurt his interest in the free agency market.

8. **Kareem Hunt, FA:** Kareem Hunt had a rough 2022 season with the Cleveland Browns, where he played second fiddle to Nick Chubb in a struggling offense. Despite Hunt's proven ability as a dual-threat RB and his past fantasy success, he saw limited usage and averaged only 9.4 touches per game. Hunt played over 50% of the snaps just once all season, which severely limited his fantasy value. He also struggled to generate yardage with a career-low 3.8 yards per carry, making it hard for fantasy managers to trust him even when he did see the field. Despite his struggles, Hunt remains a talented back and could see a resurgence in fantasy value if he signs with a new team in 2023. However, Hunt's free agency has been relatively quiet thus far, indicating that teams may not see him as a bellcow back or the player he once was. If Hunt does sign with a team and earns a larger workload, he has the potential to return to RB1 status in fantasy. He has proven to be an effective pass-

catcher and red-zone weapon in the past, making him worth a late-round flier for fantasy managers. Keep an eye on Hunt's situation throughout the offseason, as he could be a sneaky value pick in the later rounds of fantasy drafts.

UP AND COMING

1. **Jahmyr Gibbs, DET:** Jahmyr Gibbs, the highly-touted rookie running back, is set to take the field for the Detroit Lions in the upcoming 2023 fantasy football season. Gibbs displayed his impressive skills in college, with a 24% dominator rating during his time at Georgia Tech, where he played alongside future NFL running back Jordan Mason. In his first year with the Crimson Tide, Gibbs demonstrated his receiving prowess, ranking third in the FBS in receiving yards and leading all RBs in the nation in receiving yards in the previous year. Gibbs' breakaway run rate was fifth in the class, indicating his explosiveness as a rusher. At 5-foot-9 and 199 pounds, Gibbs is smaller than some other backs, but his speed and receiving ability more than make up for it. The Detroit Lions invested heavily in Gibbs, selecting him 12th overall in the NFL Draft, indicating that he is likely to take on a significant workload. Gibbs is expected to fill the role previously held by D'Andre Swift, who was highly efficient last season. Despite splitting touches with Jamaal Williams, Swift managed to rank highly in fantasy points per touch, yards per carry, and yards after contact per attempt. With Swift now with the Eagles, Gibbs is expected to inherit a workload of at least 224 touches (based on the usual workload for a first-round rookie RB), with the potential for even more if he takes the lion's share of the carries. With his size and receiving ability, Gibbs could be a back-end RB1, making him an attractive prospect for fantasy football enthusiasts in the upcoming season.

2. **Rachaad White, TB:** Rachaad White's rookie season saw him flash his legitimate 3-down back skill set in the Buccaneers' offense. Despite working in a timeshare with Leonard Fournette, White was able to average 11 fantasy points per game (RB26) and operate as the 1A back in the second half of the season despite averaging just four yards per carry. While he wasn't particularly efficient on the ground, White was still a better rusher than Fournette. And more importantly, he showed proficiency as a receiver with 50 receptions (11th among all RBs), which helped him solidify his role as the team's RB1 for the upcoming 2023 season. However, there is a downside to White's projection for the upcoming season, given the potential struggles of the Tampa Bay offense without Tom Brady. But with White's work as a receiver, he could still be valuable in games where the Buccaneers are chasing points. Additionally, the release of Fournette and the addition of cast-off Chase Edmonds and UDFA Sean Tucker gives White less competition for touches in the backfield. White's versatility and solidified role as the RB1 make him a solid pick in fantasy drafts for the 2023 season, especially in PPR formats. While there may be some concern about the overall state of the Tampa Bay offense, White's receiving skills and potential for an increased workload make him a player to target in fantasy drafts.

3. **Isiah Pacheco, KC:** Isiah Pacheco's emergence as a late-round rookie for the Chiefs in 2022 was nothing short of remarkable. After taking over as the team's starting running back in Week 10, Pacheco quickly established himself as a reliable and explosive option in the Chiefs' high-powered offense. He finished the season as the RB21 in points per game and sixth in total rushing yards from Weeks 10-17. In the postseason, Pacheco continued to shine, averaging 13 touches for 65 rushing yards per game, while Jerick McKinnon saw his role decrease. Pacheco's strong Super Bowl performance (15-76-1) helped the Chiefs secure their championship victory. As he enters his second season, Pacheco is expected to be the lead back in Kansas City's backfield, with zero noteworthy additions made to the roster. His physical running style and ability to break tackles make him a perfect fit for the Chiefs' scheme. Moreover, Pacheco showcased his receiving ability with a six-catch game against the Bengals in the conference championship, suggesting he could see an increased role as a receiver in 2023. Fantasy managers should target Pacheco as a high-upside RB2 with the potential to exceed expectations in both the rushing and receiving games.

4. **Devon Achane, MIA:** Devon Achane is one of the most exciting rookie running backs entering the league this season. In his final year at Texas A&M, Achane exploded for 1,100 rushing yards and eight touchdowns while also catching 36 passes (3.6/game) for 196 yards. He finished the season with a 33% dominator rating, proving that he can handle a large workload as the clear-cut No. 1 back for the Aggies. Despite concerns about his size, Achane proved his toughness by carrying the ball 38 times for 215 yards and two touchdowns in his final game against LSU. The Miami Dolphins made a smart move by selecting Achane in the third round of the 2023 NFL Draft. He is a perfect fit for their outside zone running offense, and his elite track speed will make him a terror for opposing defenses. The current depth chart in Miami consists of an injury-prone Raheem Mostert and journeyman Jeff Wilson Jr., so Achane has a real chance to earn opportunities, if not the starting job altogether. Not only is Achane a dynamic runner, but he is also an elite kickoff returner. He finished last season as PFF's third-highest graded kick returner among 2023 draft-eligible players. This ensures he will be an active player on game days, giving him additional opportunities to make an impact. Achane's potential in Miami's offense and lack of competition behind him make him a high-upside pick in fantasy drafts.

5. **Zach Charbonnet, SEA:** Zach Charbonnet had an impressive college career, starting ahead of future NFL draft selection Hassan Haskins at Michigan in 2019. However, his numbers regressed in 2020 due to COVID-19, splitting time with Haskins and losing work to other NFL-drafted players. In 2021, Charbonnet transferred to UCLA and saw his production skyrocket, posting a 25% dominator rating as a junior and finishing third among all RBs in PFF rushing grade. His 2022 senior production was also elite, finishing fourth in PFF rushing grade among all RBs, while improving his receiving game, catching 37 balls for 320 yards on 44 targets. Charbonnet's collegiate accolades made him an attractive option for the Seattle Seahawks, who selected him in the second round of the 2023 NFL Draft (52nd overall). Paired with last year's second-round pick, Kenneth Walker III, Charbonnet's skills complement Walker's home run rushing ability. While Charbonnet can't match Walker's explosive plays, he can be counted on to deliver consistent production as a rusher and receiver. His 3-down skill set and draft capital suggest that he will be heavily involved in the Seahawks' offense as a rookie, and he may even be the better fantasy asset compared to Walker when you consider the difference in ADP. It's worth noting that Seahawks head coach Pete Carroll has a history of shaking up his backfield. Despite drafting Rashaad Penny in the first round of the 2018 NFL Draft, former seventh-round pick Chris Carson led the team in rushing from 2018 to 2020. Charbonnet's closest comparison based on his size and weight is Carson, so he could be in line for a similar role in the Seahawks' offense. Charbonnet's talent and situation make him a great late-round running back option for fantasy managers in the 2023 season.

6. **James Cook, BUF:** James Cook had a limited role during his rookie season, but he showed flashes of explosiveness and received praise for his receiving abilities out of the backfield. Cook forced a 60-40 snap split with Devin Singletary from Week 13 onward, and he matched Singletary in points per game (RB25) over the final seven games. Additionally, Cook was the superior rusher, averaging 5.3 yards per carry (5th) and earning PFF's top ranking in breakaway run rate (44%). With the signing of Damien Harris, Cook is expected to take on the pass-catching role in the backfield. Singletary finished third among running backs in route participation (57%) in 2022, but Cook's 27% target rate per route run was equal to or better than Christian McCaffrey and Alvin Kamara and 5th among all RBs with at least 30 targets. The Bills also made significant offensive line improvements during the offseason, which bodes well for Cook's outlook. The team added left guard Connor McGovern during the free agency period and drafted O'Cyrus Torrence in Round 2 to upgrade the offensive line. With Harris as his main competition, Cook has a chance to emerge as the Bills' starting running back in 2023. Cook's receiving ability and explosive runs will drive his fantasy value.

7. **Kendre Miller, NO:** Kendre Miller was a highly productive running back during his college career at TCU, often splitting carries with Zach Evans before becoming the bell cow in 2022. Standing at 5-foot-11 and 215 pounds (identical to Bijan Robinson), Miller possesses the ideal size for an NFL running back. He showcased his efficiency and explosiveness on a per-play basis, leading the FBS in yards after contact per attempt in 2021 and

finishing fourth in career yards per play among his RB draft class. Miller's 23 percent dominator rating in 2022 shows that he can handle a heavy workload, rushing for nearly 1,400 yards and demonstrating a nose for the endzone with 13 rushing touchdowns. He's also elusive, as indicated by his 18 broken tackles per 100 touches, which was the highest among his draft class. Despite not testing due to recovering from a knee injury, the New Orleans Saints selected Miller in the third round of the 2023 NFL Draft. He may not have an immediate opportunity to start, given the presence of Alvin Kamara and Jamaal Williams on the depth chart, but Miller's explosive running style and big-play ability make him an exciting stash across deeper formats. Miller is an ideal complement to Williams, who is more of a grinder, and he could see increased opportunities should Kamara miss any time due to injury or suspension. Miller's low bust run rate and ability to break tackles bode well for his fantasy prospects, and he should be on the radar of all fantasy football managers looking for a high-upside running back with big-play potential in the later rounds. The Saints also benefit from the league's easiest schedule, putting Miller in a spot to face soft matchups when he finally earns opportunities.

8. **Brian Robinson Jr., WAS:** Brian Robinson Jr. proved himself to be a capable bellcow in his rookie season, despite missing the first four games after suffering gunshot wounds in August. From Week 6 onward, he averaged 9.4 fantasy points per game (RB34), but don't let the point totals fool you - Robinson's rookie campaign was all about volume. He was fourth in the league in carries, averaging 17.8 per game and over 70 rushing yards per game. PFF even ranked him as the ninth-highest-graded running back with a grade of 82.1. However, fantasy managers were left wanting more due to Robinson's lack of receiving usage (just 9 catches for 60 yards on a 6% target share) and the absence of touchdowns. Although his usage in the receiving game is unlikely to change significantly with Antonio Gibson returning in 2023, Robinson should experience positive touchdown regression if he sees a similar volume workload. In 2022, he finished 13th in carries but only scored two rushing touchdowns despite having 14 carries from inside the 10-yard line, which was the most of any player with fewer than three rushing TDs. It's worth noting that Robinson's lack of explosiveness and stylistic limitations as a "plodder" runner may keep him from reaching true fantasy stardom, but with the Washington Commanders' upgraded offensive line in 2023, Robinson should be a solid RB2/RB3 option who can provide steady production on the ground. Just be wary of overpaying for a two-down grinder on a team with one of the most-difficult projected schedules based on forecasted betting win totals.

9. **Roschon Johnson, CHI:** Meet Roschon Johnson, the Bears' fourth-round pick in the 2023 NFL Draft. Despite sitting behind Bijan Robinson at Texas, the 8th overall pick in the 2023 NFL Draft, Johnson managed to post an impressive 49% missed tackle rate and finished fourth in yards after contact per attempt among the 2023 draft class. With bell-cow size at 6 feet and 219 pounds and tenacity to match, Johnson has the potential to become a major player in the Bears' backfield. Johnson only started five games in his 47 total games played as a Longhorn, but his size and athleticism caught the attention of the Bears, who drafted him with the hope that he could compete with veterans D'Onta Foreman and Khalil Herbert for snaps. Despite being a mid-round pick, Johnson has a good chance to rise the depth chart and make an impact early on, especially since he won't have to compete with the likes of an elite stud like Robinson for playing time. In fact, don't be surprised if Johnson beats out Foreman by the time training camp concludes. His reliable work on special teams and pass protection should earn him early playing time, and if he can continue to display his impressive ability to make defenders miss, he could end up being a steal for fantasy football managers. Keep an eye on Johnson as a potential sleeper pick who could pay big dividends down the road. Chicago has the fifth-easiest schedule overall, and they also boast a juicy playoff schedule (CLE, ARI, ATL) that could benefit whichever Bears RB emerges late into the season.

MATCHUP PLAYS

1. **Samaje Perine, DEN:** RB Samaje Perine could be a valuable pickup for fantasy managers in the 2023 season. Perine signed a 2-year, $7.5 million contract with the Denver Broncos with $3 million guaranteed after the team released Chase Edmonds and Mike Boone. With Javonte Williams potentially delayed in his return from a 2022 multi-ligament knee injury, Perine has a chance to make an impact early in the season. Perine played a role in the Bengals' offense last year, serving as the primary third-down back and earning the starting nod from Weeks 11-13. During that stretch, he averaged an impressive 23.6 fantasy points per game. He also showed his versatility as a pass blocker and receiver, finishing 6th in PFF pass-blocking and 14th in RB targets. If Williams' injury lingers, Perine could become a major factor in the Broncos' backfield, potentially taking over passing-down duties and even challenging Williams for early-down work. Perine is undervalued in ADP and could provide significant value for those who take a chance on him.

2. **Rashaad Penny, PHI:** Rashaad Penny is in a new situation in Philadelphia, signing a one-year deal with the Eagles in the offseason. He's expected to compete for the early-down lead-back role, following in the footsteps of Miles Sanders. In 2022, Penny's on-field production was impressive, averaging over six yards per carry and ranking second among all RBs in rushing percentage, resulting in 10-plus yards. However, he missed a significant amount of time due to injuries. Quarterback Jalen Hurts' presence at the goal line will obviously hinder Penny's TD potential to some extent but make no mistake that the former first-round pick can score beyond just the 5-yard line. Of his 14 career touchdowns, 11 have come on 10-yard-plus plays, with seven of those being 30-plus plays from scrimmage. However, the addition of D'Andre Swift and the re-signing of Boston Scott could hinder Penny's chances of a significant role in the Eagles' offense. While Swift and incumbent Kenneth Gainwell are expected to be the superior pass-catchers, Penny's efficiency as a pure rusher should not be overlooked. However, his injury track record could impact his availability and overall production. With his low-risk contract, fantasy managers should consider Penny as a high-upside late-round selection, but it's important to monitor his role in the Eagles' backfield throughout the offseason.

3. **Damien Harris, BUF:** Damien Harris had a lackluster 2022 campaign with the New England Patriots, playing in just 11 games due to injuries and averaging only 8.8 fantasy points and 49 rushing yards per game when he was on the field. However, he has found a new home with the Buffalo Bills, who signed him to a one-year contract to add more size to their backfield. With the Bills prioritizing a more balanced run-pass offense this offseason and improvements made to their offensive line, Harris could be in for a bounce-back season. While Rhamondre Stevenson was the primary RB for the Patriots last season, Harris could carve out a role as the Bills' featured red-zone back. In 2022, former Bills RB Devin Singletary totaled just four rushing TDs inside the 10-yard on 16 carries. Harris scored just as many times from inside the ten-yard line as Stevenson (three times) despite being out-carried in that area of the field 19 to six. However, it's worth noting that QB Josh Allen is often used as a goal-line rusher, which could limit Harris' touchdown upside. But we have seen quarterbacks run less at the goal line as they get older, so there's still a chance that Harris flirts with double-digit scores should his arrival mean the team leans on him more as their preferred rusher near the pylon to protect their franchise quarterback in the long term. Harris has landed in a situation that could provide him with plenty of scoring opportunities in 2023. If he can stay healthy, Harris has a chance to be a valuable contributor to fantasy rosters, especially in touchdown-heavy leagues. He has the size, talent, and opportunity to make a significant impact in the Bills' backfield and is a solid late-round draft target for fantasy managers looking for RB depth.

4. **Antonio Gibson, WAS:** Antonio Gibson had a polarizing 2022 season, splitting work in the Commanders' backfield with rookie Brian Robinson. However, Gibson's proven track record of production, ideal size, and pass-catching chops make him an enticing buy-low running back target for the 2023 season. Despite operating as an RB3 for much of the second half of 2022, Gibson remained much more involved in the passing game

than Robinson, with an impressive 14% target share and an 80.5 PFF receiving grade. The release of J.D. McKissic further solidifies Gibson's role as the primary receiving back for Washington. As a free agent at the end of 2023, the team could ride Gibson till the wheels fall off. Additionally, new offensive coordinator Eric Bieniemy's arrival may lead to more opportunities for Gibson, as he has no prior commitments to the backfield hierarchy from the 2022 season. We could easily see him in a Jerick McKinnon-esque role in Washington. While Gibson may be overshadowed by Robinson's rushing volume in the short term, his proven receiving ability and potential future opportunities make him an intriguing fantasy option. If you're willing to overlook the presence of Robinson, Gibson's three-down skillset and track record of production make him an ideal buy-low target for the 2023 fantasy football season. The Commanders' tough schedule foreshadows negative scripts favoring Robinson's pass-catching abilities.

5. **Khalil Herbert, CHI:** Khalil Herbert proved to be an efficient player in 2022, outshining David Montgomery in nearly every rushing metric. He averaged an impressive 5.7 yards per carry to Montgomery's 4.0 and finished with a rushing EPA ranked 12th compared to Montgomery's 32nd. However, with Monty leaving in free agency, the Bears brought in D'Onta Foreman, who has also shown flashes of high-end early-down potential the last two seasons. While Herbert has demonstrated his abilities on limited opportunities, the team will likely use a similar RB usage split as they did between Herbert and Montgomery in 2022. Fantasy managers should consider taking the cheapest option in drafts, as there may not be a clear No.1 rusher in Chicago unless there is an injury. The 4th-round rookie draft selection, Roschon Johnson, adds another wrinkle to the Bears backfield, potentially making it a three-headed monster. While Herbert has a high upside as an efficient player on a per-touch basis, his downside is the increased competition in the Bears backfield, which could limit his fantasy value and make him extremely tough to predict what weeks he can be confidently started.

6. **A.J. Dillon, GB:** Despite a sluggish start to the 2022 season, A.J. Dillon eventually found his footing as a red-zone threat for the Packers. He out-carried Aaron Jones inside the 10-yard line 14 to 5 from Week 9 onwards while splitting snaps equally with his backfield teammate. Dillon scored six rushing TDs during that stretch, demonstrating his value as a potential goal-line back. However, there are some concerns heading into the 2023 season. With Aaron Rodgers no longer leading the Packers' offense, the team will turn to Jordan Love to lead the way. It remains to be seen how effective the offense will be under his leadership, and that uncertainty could impact Dillon's fantasy value. Additionally, Dillon will have to compete with Jones for touches and snaps in the backfield. Jones is an established receiving stud and has proven to be a reliable weapon in the Packers' offense. On the plus side, Dillon finished the 2022 season with the fifth-highest PFF rushing grade, demonstrating his impressive skills on the field. He also showed his potential as a top-tier handcuff when Jones got injured in Week 13, putting up a strong performance with 18 carries for 93 yards, a touchdown, and three catches for 26 yards. Dillon's contract will expire at the end of the 2023 season, so he will be looking to make a big impact this year to secure his future in the league. Overall, Dillon has the potential to be usable for fantasy managers as a potential goal-line back, but his upside may be limited by the uncertainty surrounding the Packers' offense and the competition with Jones for touches.

7. **Jeff Wilson Jr., MIA:** Jeff Wilson Jr. had a polarizing 2022 season, joining the Miami Dolphins in Week 9 and immediately taking on a sizable role. He averaged 10 carries for 49 yards and almost 0.4 TDs per game from Weeks 9 through 18. Although Raheem Mostert averaged a similar workload with ten carries for 55 yards and 0.25 TDs per game, Wilson had the slight edge in expected points based on usage, out-targeting Mostert 23 to 20. Wilson also posted an almost identical fantasy point-per-game output of 10 points per game (RB32/33). However, Mostert was the superior back on a per-touch basis, excelling in yards after contact per attempt and catching 18 of his 20 targets, while Wilson only converted 12 of his 23 targets into receptions. The Dolphins opted to bring back both Mostert and Wilson for the 2023 season, but Wilson's contract is worth more and has more guaranteed money. Plus, at just 27 years old, Wilson has a longer runway for his career. He will be competing with rookie Devon Achane for snaps in the backfield but given his experience and demonstrated

ability to produce in the Dolphins offense, Wilson should be considered the better option than Mostert among the two veterans. His ability to contribute to the passing game and his larger role in the offense make him a strong late-round flier option for fantasy managers looking for running back depth.

8. **Jerick McKinnon, KC:** Jerick McKinnon proved to be a valuable fantasy asset in the second half of the 2022 season, finishing as the RB7 in points per game from Weeks 10-17. He was especially effective as a receiver, finishing third among running backs with 35 receptions and seven receiving touchdowns during that span. McKinnon's increased usage in the passing game was largely due to the absence of Mecole Hardman, who missed several games with an injury. In the eight games with Hardman in the lineup, McKinnon was targeted less than three times per game on average. However, when Hardman was out, McKinnon saw five targets per game and his receptions and yardage totals increased significantly. His yardage spiked from just under 20 yards to nearly 40 receiving yards per game. At 30 years old, McKinnon's best role is likely as a pass-catching back in a rotation with another running back. His return to the Kansas City Chiefs is ideal for anyone invested in Isiah Pacheco, as McKinnon's return makes it less likely that the team will invest significantly in another veteran running back option. While McKinnon's fantasy value may not be as high as it was in the second half of 2022, he could still be a valuable depth piece for fantasy managers in PPR formats. Keep in mind that the team did not re-sign Hardman this offseason.

9. **Kenneth Gainwell, PHI:** In 2022, Kenneth Gainwell's role on the Philadelphia Eagles was limited due to the team's dominant performances, which resulted in him rarely being needed as a pass-catcher out of the backfield. However, his usage increased towards the end of the season, and he out-targeted Miles Sanders 18-5 from Week 15 onward. Sanders played fewer than 40% of snaps in his last five games, after never playing fewer than 50% of snaps from Weeks 1-16, and Gainwell/Sanders split touches nearly 50/50 in the team's last four games, with Gainwell seeing preferred usage on passing downs. With Sanders gone and the Eagles backfield almost completely overturned, Gainwell could see an expanded role on the ground, in addition to his confirmed receiving role on offense. The key question for Gainwell's fantasy prospects will be the health of newcomers Rashaad Penny and D'Andre Swift. If they can stay healthy for a full season, Gainwell's workload could be limited, but if they cannot, Gainwell will benefit. Currently, Gainwell is the cheapest ADP option in the Eagles' backfield.

HANDCUFFS

1. **Alexander Mattison, MIN:** Alexander Mattison has been a reliable handcuff for Dalvin Cook managers the past few seasons, but his true potential as an RB1 has yet to be seen. Mattison showed flashes of his capabilities in 2020 and 2021 when Cook was sidelined, averaging 23.7 PPR points and 90 rushing yards per game in games where he saw at least 23 touches. However, in 2022, Mattison remained relegated to a backup role as Cook stayed healthy for the entire season. But Mattison's efficiency with the ball was still on display, finishing with a career-high 84.2 PFF rushing grade, ranking 15th among running backs with at least 70 carries in 2022. Mattison's future with the Vikings looks bright, especially if Cook is traded or released. The team can save nearly $8 million if they release Cook, leaving a potential opening for Mattison to step up as the team's RB1. And if given the opportunity, Mattison's history of success when Cook has been sidelined suggests that he could thrive in a larger role. While his contract extension with the Vikings was not an endorsement of his projected starting role, it does show that the team values his contributions and trusts him to fill in should Cook miss time. Mattison should be on every fantasy manager's radar as a high-upside sleeper pick in 2023.

2. **Jamaal Williams, NO:** Jamaal Williams may have been an unexpected fantasy star in 2022, but his role with the New Orleans Saints is even more uncertain. Despite catching only 12 passes last season, Williams managed to finish as the RB12 thanks to his league-leading 41 carries inside the 10-yard line, which led to 13 touchdowns goal-line scores (17 total rushing TDs). While TD regression may be on the horizon, Williams' situation in New Orleans is cloudier due to the potential absence of Alvin Kamara. With Kamara potentially

facing a suspension, Williams could see a significant uptick in touches and become the Saints' primary red-zone back. Williams' past usage projects limited involvement in the passing game, but his potential for goal-line work is undeniable. While his overall production may not match his 2022 output, with Hill/Kamara also seeing some work in the red zone, Williams has a clear path to fantasy relevance if Kamara misses time. The Saints coaching staff has never shied away from featuring the likes of backup grinders such as Latavius Murray or Mark Ingram when AK41 has missed time in the past.

3. **Elijah Mitchell, SF:** Elijah Mitchell had an up-and-down second season in 2022, mainly due to injuries. Mitchell got injured in Week 1 and couldn't return to the field until Week 10 after the team traded for Christian McCaffrey. However, in his first game back, he showed flashes of his potential by rushing for 89 yards on 18 carries. Unfortunately, Mitchell got hurt again after seeing middling usage over the next two weeks. Despite his injury downside, Mitchell's efficient play last season solidified him as the primary handcuff to McCaffrey in 2023. He could see occasional spikes in production even while CMC is healthy, as he did at times in 2022. However, it's unlikely he'll have a consistent role as the No. 2 running back on the depth chart. It's worth noting that Jordan Mason, the 49ers' No. 3 running back in 2022, graded out as PFF's second-highest graded rusher last season. Mason's larger stature could help him hold up over an 18-week season, and he could potentially push Mitchell for the backup job. Overall, Mitchell's injury history is a downside factor, but his potential and role as the primary handcuff to McCaffrey make him a valuable late-round pick in fantasy drafts.

4. **Tyler Allgeier, ATL:** Tyler Allgeier was a standout rookie in the 2022 season, earning the highest PFF grade among all rookie running backs (86.7), even beating out highly-touted prospects such as Kenneth Walker and Breece Hall. His strong finish saw him ranked sixth among all RBs in rushing EPA, and his impressive play earned him an elite rookie status alongside the likes of Nick Chubb, Jonathan Taylor, Alvin Kamara, and Rhamondre Stevenson. While adding Bijan Robinson in the 2023 NFL Draft may have relegated Allgeier to backup duties, he remains a valuable handcuff for Robinson managers due to his proven production and potential upside if given the opportunity. His solid performance last season suggests that he can be a reliable contributor if called upon, making him an excellent option for Robinson managers and zero-RB truthers looking to secure their fantasy backfield.

5. **Jaylen Warren, PIT:** Jaylen Warren, a 2022 undrafted free agent, made the most of his opportunities in the Steelers' backfield last season, showcasing his potential as a solid fantasy football asset. Despite being the No. 2 back behind Najee Harris, Warren ranked third in rushing success rate at 45.5% and second among all 2022 rookie RBs in yards per route run, second only to Breece Hall. His impressive efficiency suggests he will continue earning snaps alongside Harris in the Pittsburgh backfield. However, what really boosts Warren's fantasy upside is his potential role as the bell-cow back if Harris were to miss any time. Standing at 215 pounds, Warren would be the clear beneficiary of a potential injury to Harris, with no other Steelers running back behind him to compete for touches. He could see a significant workload and become a potential league-winner for fantasy managers who are wise enough to stash him on their benches. Keep an eye on Warren's usage and snaps in training camp and the preseason, as his role in the Steelers' offense could expand beyond just being a handcuff to Harris.

6. **Devin Singletary, HOU:** Devin Singletary joins the Houston Texans on a one-year deal worth $3.75 million, where he is expected to back up the team's lead rusher, Dameon Pierce. Singletary's 2022 season with the Buffalo Bills was productive as he operated as the 1A in the team's backfield, finishing as the RB23 overall and RB27 in points per game. However, he shared touches with rookie James Cook, leading to a full-blown committee situation. Cook matched Singletary point-for-point and averaged a 40% snap share over the final seven games. Singletary totaled just nine more carries than Cook from Weeks 13-20 but ended the year 10th in PFF rushing grade (two spots ahead of Pierce). While Singletary's strong finish over the last two seasons won't help his case to become Houston's lead rusher, he is a credible threat to Pierce's workload compared to

the other available options on the team. Singletary's PFF pass-blocking grade (73.2, 8th) could also secure his usage on passing downs, where Pierce struggled as a rookie (32.3, 52nd) in that capacity. Still, Pierce's potential to be a three-down back is higher as Singletary hasn't thrived as a receiver. Singletary's role in Houston's backfield is ambiguous, but he brings quality depth and veteran experience to the team. With a history of being productive in committee situations, he could become a valuable fantasy asset if Pierce suffers an injury or if the team decides to rely more heavily on its running game.

7. **Tyjae Spears, TEN:** Tyjae Spears was a standout rusher at Tulane, and his draft stock skyrocketed after impressive showings at the Senior Bowl and the 2023 NFL Scouting Combine. Standing at 5-foot-10 and weighing in at 201 pounds, Spears impressed with his explosiveness, ranking in the 92nd percentile for vertical jump (39") and in the 89th percentile for broad jump (125"). Although he didn't run the 40-yard dash, his performance in the explosion drills was enough to put him high on the radar of NFL teams. In college, Spears posted impressive numbers, including a 31 percent dominator rating in 2022, finishing fifth in the FBS in rushing yards (1,586), second in rushing touchdowns (19), and fourth in yards after contact per attempt (4.55). His career average of 3.00 yards per play ranks seventh in his class, highlighting his potential to succeed at the NFL level. The Tennessee Titans selected Spears in the third round of the 2023 NFL Draft, making him a solid backup option for Derrick Henry. However, concerns about his knee injuries led to his draft stock falling. Spears was projected to go higher than the 83rd overall pick, but his health concerns scared teams away. For 2023, he offers excellent value as a handcuff to Henry, making him a valuable addition to fantasy football rosters. In the long-term, Spears' prospects are uncertain due to his knee issues, which include a missing ACL and knee arthritis. However, with Henry hitting free agency in 2024, Spears could become the Titans' RB1 as soon as next season.

8. **Chuba Hubbard, CAR:** Chuba Hubbard's 2022 season showed glimpses of his potential as a dual-threat running back in the NFL. He finished as PFF's 21st-highest graded rusher, averaging a solid 4.9 yards per carry, and also proved efficient in the receiving game, tying for 6th in yards per route run with Austin Ekeler. After the Panthers traded Christian McCaffrey to the 49ers, Hubbard's role increased from Week 7 onwards as he split the backfield duties with D'Onta Foreman. With a three-down skillset, Hubbard has the potential to become a valuable handcuff to Miles Sanders in 2023. Furthermore, if he can continue to impress as a receiver, he may even have a chance to take over as the primary pass-catching back in the Panthers' backfield. While Hubbard's role may be limited to a backup role behind Sanders, his potential upside makes him an intriguing late-round target in fantasy football drafts. Given his dual-threat skillset, he could be a usable piece in PPR formats, particularly if Sanders misses time due to injury.

9. **D'Onta Foreman, CHI:** D'Onta Foreman's performance in 2022 with the Panthers was enough to convince the Bears to sign him to a one-year contract worth $3 million. He joins a crowded backfield with Khalil Herbert, Travis Homer, and 2023 fourth-round pick Roschon Johnson. While Foreman's late-season breakout was impressive, his inconsistency raises questions about his potential usage in 2023. From Week 7 on, Foreman was the RB21 in fantasy scoring and RB22 in fantasy points per game. He ranked fourth in the NFL in rushing yards (852) over that span. But his production wasn't consistent week-to-week, as he rushed for more than 110 yards in half of his last 10 games while finishing with fewer than 40 rushing yards in four of the others. His weekly half-point PPR fantasy finishes over those last 10 games were RB13, RB5, RB42, RB9, RB48, RB27, RB27, RB70, RB3, and RB53. Additionally, Foreman was not involved in the passing game, recording only five receptions as the team's starter. Despite his potential, Foreman will have to compete with Herbert, Homer, and Johnson for snaps in the Bears' backfield. While Herbert has shown the most promise on limited opportunities to the current staff, it's hard to predict how the workload will be divided among the trio of veteran backs, especially with a fourth option added in the form of Johnson. Fantasy managers should monitor Foreman's usage during training camp and preseason to gauge his potential value for the upcoming season.

He could easily be cut or emerge as the Bears RB1, given the wide range of outcomes regarding Chicago's backfield.

10. **Tank Bigsby, JAC:** Tank Bigsby was a standout performer for the Auburn Tigers throughout his college career, earning a dominant rating of 20% as a freshman in 2020. The 6-foot, 210-pound running back continued to impress in his sophomore and junior years, recording a 25% and 27% dominator rating, respectively. Bigsby also proved to be a force on the field, finishing 6th in yards after contact per attempt (4.16), 11th in forced missed tackles, 11th in PFF rushing grade and 7th in breakaway run rate among his 2023 draft-eligible RB peers. Despite Bigsby's lackluster combine performance, which included a 26th percentile vertical jump, 54th percentile broad jump and a 4.56 40-yard dash (47th percentile), he showed improvement at Auburn's pro day, running a 4.45. This improvement caught the eye of the Jacksonville Jaguars, who selected him in the third round of the 2023 NFL Draft. Bigsby will compete for the backup job behind fellow established Jaguars RB1 Travis Etienne. Head coach Doug Pederson has made it clear that he wants to build a deep RB room, giving Bigsby a chance to earn significant touches in his rookie year. JaMycal Hasty, D'Ernest Johnson, and Snoop Conner will also be fighting for backup duties, but Bigsby's impressive college career and draft capital make him a strong contender for the No. 2 role, especially as a rusher on early downs or in the red zone. Fantasy managers should keep an eye on Bigsby's progress throughout the offseason, as he has the potential to make a significant impact in 2023 if given the opportunity in an up-and-coming offense.

11. **Zach Evans, LAR:** Introducing Zach Evans, the new rookie running back for the Los Angeles Rams. Evans may not have had a breakout college career, but his efficient play on the field suggests he has the potential to deliver when called upon. Despite sharing the backfield with Kendre Miller at TCU and losing touches to freshman Quinshon Judkins at Ole Miss, Evans still managed to post a career average of 3.47 yards per play, which ranks second-best among incoming rookie RBs. Yards per play is a great indicator of future success, with recent late-round standouts in that category the past two years including Elijah Mitchell, Rhamondre Stevenson, Rachaad White, and Tyler Allgeier. Although he has no significant role as a receiver, Evans' college counting stats and class-leading 15% boom percentage (per Sports Info Solutions) indicate that he can contribute to the Rams' offense. At 5-foot-11 and 202 pounds, Evans boasts decent size, and his pro day results show he has the speed and agility to make an impact in the NFL. The Rams traded up in the 2023 NFL Draft to select Evans with the 215th pick, which could signal the team's confidence in his potential. With nobody threatening behind the No. 1 running back Cam Akers on the depth chart, Evans can carve out a role in the Rams' backfield as the primary handcuff. In fantasy football terms, Evans is a high-upside late-round pick or a player to stash on your bench. He may not be an immediate starter, but if given the chance, he has the potential to surprise and post solid numbers. Consider drafting Evans as a sleeper pick, especially in deeper formats where he could have a long-term impact.

12. James Robinson, NE: James Robinson was unwanted by two teams in 2022 and was benched in favor of an undrafted free agent Zonovan Knight after landing with the New York Jets. It's still Rhamondre Stevenson's backfield in New England, with the former undrafted free agent unlikely to push him for legitimate touches. All J-Rob does is likely prevent the Patriots from adding anybody else better. In the best case, from the Robinson perspective, the former Jet operates in a Damien Harris role as a red-zone/goal-line running back. But Robinson's contract is also very incentive-based, meaning he must really earn his playing time. It's not guaranteed he sniffs the field, even as Stevenson's primary backup, if he can't recapture his pre-torn Achilles form. Robinson was a complete shell of his former self in 2022, finishing the season as PFF's 59th-graded rusher among 62 qualifiers. He also ranked fourth worst in yards after contact per attempt (2.44) with an abysmal 11% forced missed tackle rate. Simply put, if Stevenson fails in 2023, it probably won't because of James Robinson.

13. **Chase Brown, CIN:** Looking ahead to the 2023 fantasy football season, rookie Bengals RB Chase Brown is a name to watch. With the potential of No. 1 RB Joe Mixon missing some time due to injury, salary cap concerns or off-the-field issues, Brown could see increased usage in the Bengals backfield. However, it's important to note that Brown's college profile doesn't necessarily suggest that he's poised to seize the starting job and excel in an NFL offense. Despite his lack of efficiency, Brown put up impressive counting stats in college, rushing for over 1,600 yards and 10 touchdowns in his final season at Illinois. His 329 carries ranked second in the nation, and his 83 forced missed tackles were the third-most among all college RBs. However, his career average of 2.4 yards per play is concerning. On a positive note, Brown performed well at the NFL scouting combine, finishing first in both the vertical jump (94th percentile) and broad jump (93rd percentile) while running a 4.43 40-yard dash. His athleticism should translate well to the NFL level.Even though Brown has experience leading a backfield, it's more likely that he will provide empty volume rather than improve the overall efficiency of an NFL offense. It's possible that his ADP could rise in fantasy drafts if negative reports come out regarding Mixon, but managers should be cautious not to overvalue him based solely on his potential increased workload. Brown is a name to monitor in the Bengals backfield, but he may not be a reliable option for fantasy managers in 2023.

14. **DeWayne McBride, MIN:** The Vikings' 7th-round pick DeWayne McBride headlines the RB class this season with a 4.18 average yards per snap. It's the highest mark I've tracked over the past three draft classes. It's a testament to just how elite McBride was as a rusher in three years at UAB, considering he was a complete non-factor in the passing game with just five receptions during his entire collegiate career. Even so, McBride totaled a top-five dominator rating (27%) for his excellent efforts. If the Vikings move on from Dalvin Cook, it's just McBride competing with Alexander Mattison for starting reps in the Minnesota backfield.

Chapter 5

Wide Receivers

	WR1 PPR	RPV
1	Justin Jefferson	18%
2	Ja'Marr Chase	16%
3	Tyreek Hill	11%
4	Cooper Kupp	6%
5	A.J. Brown	3%
6	CeeDee Lamb	-2%
7	Stefon Diggs	-2%
8	Davante Adams	-6%
9	Amon-Ra St. Brown	-7%
10	Garrett Wilson	-10%
11	Jaylen Waddle	-12%
12	Chris Olave	-14%

	WR2 PPR	RPV
13	DK Metcalf	9%
14	Amari Cooper	6%
15	Keenan Allen	6%
16	DeVonta Smith	3%
17	Tee Higgins	2%
18	Drake London	-2%
19	DJ Moore	-2%
20	Tyler Lockett	-2%
21	Deebo Samuel	-4%
22	DeAndre Hopkins	-5%
23	Jerry Jeudy	-6%
24	Christian Watson	-6%

	WR3 PPR	RPV
25	Chris Godwin	4%
26	Terry McLaurin	4%
27	Mike Williams	3%
28	Michael Pittman Jr.	2%
29	Calvin Ridley	2%
30	Christian Kirk	0%
31	Diontae Johnson	-1%
32	Brandon Aiyuk	-1%
33	Elijah Moore	-2%
34	Marquise Brown	-3%
35	Mike Evans	-4%
36	Courtland Sutton	-5%

	WR4 PPR	RPV
37	JuJu Smith-Schuster	7%
38	Treylon Burks	6%
39	George Pickens	6%
40	Brandin Cooks	4%
41	Skyy Moore	4%
42	Kadarius Toney	3%
43	Darnell Mooney	-1%
44	Elijah Moore	-3%
45	Jakobi Meyers	-6%
46	Allen Lazard	-6%
47	Jahan Dotson	-6%
48	Adam Thielen	-9%

	WR5 PPR	RPV
49	Rashod Bateman	12%
50	Quentin Johnston	12%
51	D.J. Chark	10%
52	Jaxson Smith-Njigba	7%
53	Romeo Doubs	4%
54	Zay Flowes	0%
55	Marquez Valdes-Scantling	-3%
56	DeVante Parker	-6%
57	Gabriel Davis	-7%
58	Hunter Renfrow	-7%
59	Michael Thomas	-9%
60	Jameson Williams	-13%

WR1 STND		
	Player	RPV
1	Justin Jefferson	23%
2	Ja'Marr Chase	18%
3	Tyreek Hill	12%
4	Cooper Kupp	6%
5	A.J. Brown	0%
6	CeeDee Lamb	-2%
7	Stefon Diggs	-3%
8	Davante Adams	-8%
9	Amon-Ra St. Brown	-9%
10	Garrett Wilson	-12%
11	Jaylen Waddle	-12%
12	DK Metcalf	-14%

WR2 STND		
	Player	RPV
13	Chris Olave	7%
14	Amari Cooper	5%
15	DeVonta Smith	5%
16	Tee Higgins	3%
17	Christian Watson	3%
18	Keenan Allen	1%
19	Tyler Lockett	-1%
20	DJ Moore	-2%
21	Jerry Jeudy	-2%
22	Drake London	-4%
23	Deebo Samuel	-8%
24	Terry McLaurin	-8%

WR3 STND		
	Player	RPV
25	Calvin Ridley	9%
26	DeAndre Hopkins	9%
27	George Pickens	7%
28	Christian Kirk	5%
29	Mike Evans	5%
30	Brandin Cooks	0%
31	Jakobi Meyers	-4%
32	Marquise Brown	-4%
33	Michael Pittman Jr.	-7%
34	Jahan Dotson	-7%
35	Brandon Aiyuk	-7%
36	Mike Williams	-7%

WR4 STND		
	Player	RPV
37	Elijah Moore	4%
38	Kadarius Toney	4%
39	JuJu Smith-Schuster	2%
40	Diontae Johnson	2%
41	Courtland Sutton	2%
42	Chris Godwin	2%
43	D.J. Chark	2%
44	Odell Beckham Jr.	0%
45	Michael Thomas	0%
46	Allen Lazard	-3%
47	Jaxon Smith-Njigba	-3%
48	Gabriel Davis	-8%

WR5 STND		
	Player	RPV
49	Quentin Johnston	12%
50	Treylon Burks	6%
51	Jordan Addison	6%
52	Rashod Bateman	2%
53	Skyy Moore	2%
54	Marquez Valdes-Scantling	0%
55	Darnell Mooney	0%
56	Adam Thielen	0%
57	Nico Collins	-3%
58	Zay Jones	-6%
59	Zay Flowers	-6%
60	Jameson Williams	-12%

Get updated RPV Cheat Sheets for one time $5 cost, updates included, 10 & 12 team league RPV PayPal: FantasyBlackBook@gmail.com or Venmo: @FantasyBlackBook with your email address

Player Profiles and Overview

Derek Brown

The age of the bell cow running back is dead outside of a few outlier situations and players. More and more NFL teams are utilizing committee backfields with the unfortunate reality that running backs get banged up and routinely miss time. This has all led to heavier wide receiver drafting in recent years. It's rare if I'm not walking away from the top three rounds of a typical (one quarterback) redraft league with at least two (at bare minimum one) wide receivers. As you progress through drafts, projecting 100 or more targets to wide receivers becomes more difficult. Even in the final rounds of fantasy drafts, I can pick out a few running backs that could be one injury away from substantial workloads. That argument doesn't cross over to wide receivers.

Target volume is not only a by-product of the offensive system but also a reflection of talent. Targets are earned, and it makes sense that the farther you go down the board, the upper-tier target-earning talent disappears. Over the last three seasons, 54-56% of the top 50 players in fantasy points per game have been wide receivers.

Draft wide receivers early and often. I'll attack most of my drafts by building rosters utilizing a Zero RB or a "wide receiver heavy" approach. This is the way.

ELITE

1. **Justin Jefferson, MIN:** Justin Jefferson should be the 1.01 in every non-Superflex draft this year. Last season he was second in total fantasy points among skill players, behind only Austin Ekeler. Jefferson is in the prime of his career and isn't slowing down anytime soon. He was a top-five wide receiver in weekly fantasy scoring in a whopping 52.9% of his games. He ranked first in target and fifth in yards per route run. The arrival of Jordan Adidson should free up Jefferson to see more single coverage in 2023.

2. **Ja'Marr Chase, CIN:** After returning from injury in Week 13, Chase went on a tear, proving that he should be a top 3-5 selection in every single quarterback league this year. Across his final five games of the season, he led all wide receivers with 11.8 targets per game, ranked fourth in target share (30.9%), and was the WR3 in fantasy points per game. Over that same span, he also led all wideouts with 1.2 end-zone targets per game. If Chase had kept up that type of blistering pace for 17 games, he would have walked away with 204 targets, 136 receptions, 1,499 receiving yards, and ten receiving scores. No one should be surprised if Chase puts up 2022 Justin Jefferson-type numbers this year. The duo of Burrow and Chase could post video game numbers in 2023.

3. **Tyreek Hill, MIA:** Hill showed no signs of slowing down or dropping off moving from Kansas City to South Beach. He finished as the WR3 in fantasy points per game with career highs in targets (170), receptions (119), and receiving yards (1,710). If Hill gets a full season with a healthy Tua Tagovailoa, he could post even better numbers in 2023. Last year in the 13 games he played with Tagovailoa, he averaged 21.4 fantasy points per game which would have still been WR3 in fantasy points per game, but it was within spitting distance of Jefferson's 21.7 points per game. Hill ranked first in yards and fantasy points per route run last year. He could challenge for WR1 overall this season.

4. **Stefon Diggs, BUF:** Diggs' excellence has almost become boring at this point. He's finished as the WR9 or better in fantasy points per game in each of the last three seasons (WR6, WR9, WR3). In that stretch, he's caught at least 103 balls each season while never finishing with less than 1,225 receiving yards. On the surface, last year's numbers look par for the course, but Diggs did deal with a dropoff in the second half of last year. In the first nine games, Diggs rolled up six games with at least 100 receiving yards, a 29.4% target share (10.9 targets per game), a 47.6% end zone target share, and 2.88 yards per route run. His numbers over his final seven games weren't nearly as glamorous. Diggs only managed one game with at

least 100 receiving yards while seeing his target share drop to 25.3% (7.9 targets per game), his enzone target share fall to 27.3%, and his yards per route run dwindle to 1.95. This could be a blip on the radar or a sign of things to come for 2023. Diggs' floor remains high, but if those stretch run numbers persist into 2023, his ceiling will be lowered considerably.

5. **Cooper Kupp, LAR:** The Los Angeles Rams disintegrated before our eyes in 2022. The roster was left in shambles due to injuries. This didn't stop Cooper Kupp from posting another amazing season before the injury bug turned to bite him too. Kupp ranked third in target share, 12th in air-yard share, and was the WR1 overall in fantasy points per game. At his floor, he's still a top-five fantasy wide receiver. A WR1 overall ceiling remains if Matthew Stafford can stay healthy and upright. The Rams should be throwing early and often weekly with a putrid defense backing them. Los Angeles could be down multiple scores early in every game. Assuming health, Kupp should have no problem challenging for the league lead in targets.

TOP TALENT

1. **Amon-Ra St. Brown, DET:** After proving that his rookie season wasn't just smoke in mirrors in 2022, St. Brown could step into the top-shelf elite tier of wide receivers this year. Last season St. Brown continued to draw targets at a ridiculous rate ranking third in target per route run rate and eighth in raw target volume. He was ninth in yards per route run and eighth in red zone targets. He could post double-digit receiving touchdowns this season if his late 2022 usage continues. St. Brown rolled up 15 red zone targets across his final nine games. Add in that Jameson Williams is out for the first six games of the year, and St. Brown looks destined for a career year.

2. **CeeDee Lamb, DAL:** CeeDee Lamb emerged as the "dude" we've been waiting to see since his arrival in Dallas. He finished last year top-six in receptions, receiving yards, and touchdowns among wide receivers. Lamb was an elite target earner ranking ninth in target share (28.7%) and seventh in target per route run rate (30.1%). The Cowboys used him in various ways, as evidenced by his 26 deep targets (ninth-most) and 15 red zone targets (18th). I won't tell you that I don't have some squirmy feelings about Mike McCarthy taking over as the offensive play caller, but Lamb is a true alpha wide receiver that still stands out among the rest of Dallas's receiving weapons. If Dak Prescott can shake last year's roller-coaster play at times, Lamb could post even better numbers in 2023.

3. **Davante Adams, LVR:** Davante Adams should have at least one more monster season left in him. Adams still emphatically checked the efficiency boxes ranking eighth in yards per route run and fifth in total route wins. If you look at his volume numbers last season, you'd never know he left Green Bay. He was first in target share (32.6%), fifth in air yard share (39.4%), and second in deep targets. Jimmy Garoppolo might not be amazing, but he can deliver an accurate ball, and with talent like Adams, that's all he'll need. Last year Garoppolo was eighth in catchable pass rate and 16th in quarterback rating. Just get the ball to Adams and let him do his thing, Garoppolo.

4. **A.J. Brown, PHI:** A.J. Brown wasted no time making the Titans wish they had never traded him away. He was the WR8 in fantasy as he crushed every statistical category with career marks. Brown finished top-12 in receptions (88, 11th), receiving yards (1,496, fourth), and total touchdowns (11, second). Brown and Hurts didn't need brunch or mid-afternoon snack time to develop a rapport like some other duos around the league. Brown and Hurts were simpatico from Day 1. Brown walks away from the 2022 season ranking second in yards per route run and top 15 in route win rate. Brown remains an upper-echelon wide receiver tied to one of the league's best young passers.

5. **Jaylen Waddle, MIA:** Waddle and Hill formed the South Beach bash brothers. They were the unstoppable receiving duo that fueled the Dolphins' offensive engine. While Hill took the top off defenses, Waddle cut them to pieces with YAC. Waddle ranked tenth in YAC and fourth in yards per route run as he cruised to a WR1 season (WR12 in fantasy points per game). Waddle can put you over the top weekly as your WR2, but if you lean into other positions early, he is a viable WR1 for your team. If Hill slows down at all, don't be surprised if Waddle takes over the throne for Miami's wide receiver room.

6. **Keenan Allen, LAC:** Recency bias can be a helluva drug. Don't let this cocktail of lies and deceit turn you off, Allen, for 2023. Is he a young pup anymore? No. Is he injury prone after being held to ten games last year? No. Allen has started at least 13 games in each of his previous five seasons. Allen didn't look like he declined at all last year when he was finally healthy. If anything, he looked rejuvenated. In Weeks 12-18 last year, he was the WR3 in fantasy points per game, ranking 15th in target share and target per route run rate. In Kellen Moore's fast-paced pass-heavy approach, Allen should eat this year.

7. **Calvin Ridley, JAC:** I'm rooting for a beautifully savage comeback for Calvin Ridley in 2023. Ridley will enjoy arguably the best quarterback play of his entire career catching passes from Trevor Lawrence, who took a huge step forward as one of the best young gunslingers in the game. The last time we witnessed Ridley on an NFL field, he was still one of the best in the game. In 2021, Ridley was seventh in target share (27.4%), fourth in air yard share (40.0%), and fifth in route win rate. Don't let faulty narratives like "rust" push you away from drafting Ridley in 2023. He could easily be one of the best values on the board and one of the highest-rostered players on Championship squads when it's all said and done.

SOLID OPTIONS

1. **DeVonta Smith, PHI:** After running Smith out there as their deep threat in 2021, the Eagles had a different plan in mind for last season. He carved out the role I hoped they would for him as an intermediate-volume beast. Smith saw 42.2% of his targets last year within nine yards of the line of scrimmage and thrived. He was 19th in target per route run rate and seventh in YAC. Any worries about Jalen Hurts' ability to support multiple pass catchers should have been dispelled last year, as Smith was the WR14 in fantasy points per game. He finished 14th in target share, ninth in receptions, and eighth in receiving yards. Smith remains a rock-solid WR2 in 2023.

2. **DeAndre Hopkins, FA:** DeAndre Hopkins is now a former Cardinal. Let's discuss Hopkins' talent and where he stands at this stage of his career. Last year he looked like a wide receiver still firmly in his prime. He was the WR9 in fantasy points per game, drawing a 29.4% target share (fourth-best) and a 43.5% air-yard share (second-best). Hopkins was 17th in yards per route run and fourth in route win rate. If he remains in Arizona, he resembles a volume-dependent WR2 that could finish top-12 if the touchdowns go his way. In most scenarios, if he gets dealt, he'll remain a WR2 because he still has the talent to draw a hefty target share.

3. **Amari Cooper, CLE:** Dallas gave Amari Cooper away last offseason for the price of a day-old ham sandwich. Cooper responded by having one of the best seasons of his career. He earned the highest target share (26.1%, 16th) and target per route run rate (26.1%) of his career. Cooper finished as the WR17 in fantasy points per game. His season could have been even better had Deshaun Watson's putrid play not tanked the back half of 2022. With Watson under center, Cooper only posted one week with a weekly fantasy scoring finish higher than WR30. Cooper remains a WR2 if Watson can get his career back on track. If in 2023, Watson is closer to last season's ghost; Cooper will be a volume-driven WR3.

4. **Tee Higgins, CIN:** Last season Higgins took a backseat to Ja'Marr Chase as the clear WR2 in the Bengals' passing attack. After Chase returned in Week 13, Chase saw a 29.6% target share and 38.3% air yard share, while Higgins lagged with 20.2% and 31.1% market shares. Higgins saw his fantasy impact diluted in the process as he finished the year as the WR26 in fantasy points per game. Higgins dealt with a hamstring strain, ankle sprain, and concussion last year. These injuries could have also played a role in his decline, but it could also be due to Chase ascending in his second year. Higgins is a low-end WR2/WR3 this season. He could bounce back with a top-15 season, but I'm not assuming that happens.

5. **D.K. Metcalf, SEA:** After exploding onto the NFL scene in his rookie season with a WR10 finish, Metcalf has nestled in as a low-end WR2 with WR20 and WR24 finishes in fantasy points per game over the last two years. Metcalf was a high-leverage target machine in 2022, ranking 12th in deep targets and second in red zone looks. He should continue to be a favorite of Geno Smith in both roles, but the addition of Jaxon Smith-Nigiba will impact his 141 targets (11th-most) and 25.5% target share (18th) from last season. How much 11 personnel versus 12 personnel will play a role here for Metcalf because he should be locked into an every-down role, but Smith-Njigba and Tyler Lockett could rotate perimeter snaps when Seattle is in heavy sets. Metcalf should still return WR2 results in 2023.

6. **Terry McLaurin, WAS:** Terry McLaurin experienced a Jekyll and Hyde season in 2022. With Carson Wentz under center, McLaurin withered, seeing a 16.3% target share and 26.4% air yard share. McLaurin's season would have been a dumpster fire had Wentz continued to draw starts, but as fate would have it, Wentz picked up an injury, and Taylor Heinicke rode in on his white stallion to save the day. McLaurin had a 29.8% target share with Heinicke and a 44% air yard share. As if last season's quarterback turmoil wasn't enough for McLaurin, Washington looks to be starting Sam Howell this season, with Jacoby Brissett waiting in the wings if he faceplants. McLaurin saw a 33% target share from Howell in their one game of action together last year. It's only one game, so we can't bank on that happening every week, but it's at least somewhat encouraging. McLaurin is a volume-based WR2.

7. **Tyler Lockett, SEA:** Tyler Lockett continues to scream at father time, "Not today!" We'll see if he can keep him at bay for another year, but last year's results offer hope. Last season he was the WR16 in fantasy points per game while ranking 26th in yards per route run and fifth in route win rate. Despite Lockett's age concerns, the worry is that he could take a hit with Jaxon Smith-Njigba's arrival. That could occur as Lockett wasn't a target hog last year with a 22.8% target share (26th) and 23.4% target per route run rate (36th). Lockett is best viewed as a WR3 with WR2 upside.

RED FLAGS

1. **Michael Thomas, NO:** The limited three-game sample we got with Thomas returning to the field last year was promising. Unfortunately, his season was cut short by another injury, but at least he resembled shades of his former self. Thomas had a 19.6% target share and a 33.3% endzone target share. Thomas wasn't a full-time player, though, as he saw only a 77.3% route run rate which could also speak to his health. If he weren't fully healthy at any time last year, it would make sense for the team to limit his snaps some trying to conserve him. Thomas managed a 22% target per route run rate and 1.73 yards per route run. Those aren't mind-blowing numbers, but they are solid. With a strong red zone role, he could still produce a WR3 season with those peripherals.

2. **Kadarius Toney, KC:** Kadarius Toney has a sky-high ceiling if he can ever put it all together. Toney was an efficiency darling in his rookie season, ranking seventh in target per route run rate and 17th in yards per route run. Those beautiful metrics carried over into 2022, with Toney garnering a 28.6% target per route run rate and 2.44 yards per route run. Now firmly implanted in Kansas City after a mid-season trade in

2022, Toney looks to step forward into a full-time role this year. Toney only eclipsed 40% of the snaps once last year with the Chiefs. He then missed time only to return to 30-32% snap shares in Weeks 16-18. Even in the playoffs, he couldn't surpass 29% of the team's snaps in any game. Toney is one of the most explosive players in the league with the ball in his hands, but his route running and overall game still need to be honed further. We'll see if he can make the necessary steps to access a full-time role in 2023. If his stars align, Toney is a WR4 that could evolve into a weekly WR2.

3. **Jameson Williams, DET:** The talented second-year receiver's star has dimmed some in the public's eye. Williams was sidelined for most of the 2022 season, and now he has been saddled with a six-game suspension. The runway is still wide open for Williams to blow it out in 2023 once he can return. Outside of Amon-Ra St. Brown, Detroit doesn't have a battle-tested high target share earner. There are plenty of candidates for the job opposite St. Brown, like Jahmyr Gibbs and Sam LaPorta, but Williams should still be considered the favorite to sit on this throne. Williams is still the same dude who was top 15 in yards per route run in his final season in college. Williams is a WR4 that could be a weekly WR2 once he returns.

4. **Elijah Moore, CLE:** After a promising start to his career in his rookie season, Elijah Moore had a rocky and underwhelming 2022. In the nine games, Moore played at least 70% of the snaps; he only saw a 13.2% target share, zero end zone targets, and a 14% target per route run rate. In that sample, he only mustered 1.00 yards per route run. Woof! Those are atrocious numbers for a ballyhooed second-year receiver touted as the next rocket ship to the moon type player. His quarterback play was abysmal, but some of the blame for his production woes also lies at his feet. Moore has the chance at a fresh start in Cleveland. The big question is will he be a full-time player in 2023? Cleveland ranked 22nd in 11 personnel usage in 2022, so worries are warranted. Cleveland will likely roll with Amari Cooper and Donovan Peoples-Jones when they go two wide, so the Browns' bump in 11 usage has to happen for Moore to actualize a ceiling.

5. **Rondale Moore, ARI:** Moore's abbreviated sophomore season was impressive. In his seven full games, he garnered a 22.7% target share producing 1.62 yards per route run. He handled a 22% target per route run rate in that stretch. In his full games played, he averaged 12.6 (PPR) fantasy points per game. That would have been good for WR32 (PPR) in fantasy scoring over the entire season. There are still dominoes to fall in the Cardinals' passing attack. Will DeAndre Hopkins get traded (he could already be by the time you read this)? Will Kyler Murray play more than half this season (if that)? Moore is a WR4/5 that could easily walk into WR3 production.

6. **Chase Claypool, CHI:** While consensus is ready to toss in the bag on Chase Claypool, I'm not. So quickly, everyone forgets that Claypool is an uber-athlete. His 90th percentile or higher speed and burst scores can create big plays at the drop of a hat. His rookie season marks of a 25.2% target per route run rate (15th-best) and 0.5 fantasy points per route run (14th-best) were the early signs of big-time talent. Has his value dropped further after a down 2022 season? Yep. That's exactly why his ADP has dipped to the basement where it resides. Claypool showed promise of fulfilling his rookie season promise in three games with the Bears, in which he played at least 63% of the snaps. In that small three-game sample, he saw a 22.1% target share, a 50% end zone target share, 1.77 yards per route run, and a 28% target per route run rate. Claypool is one of the best WR5 upside darts to toss this year.

UP AND COMING

1. **Chris Olave, NO:** Chris Olave heads into his sophomore season as a budding alpha wide receiver. Olave can cement his king status in this passing attack if he can continue to build upon last season's excellence. Olave's WR25 finish doesn't give him near the praise he deserves. Olave was 15th in target share (26.7%),

third in air yard share (40.8%), and tenth in yards per route run. This season, Michael Thomas' return to the huddle could invite some fantasy gamers to worry about Olave's standing as the number one in this passing attack. Thomas isn't the same player he was during his prime. If he can stay on the field and get open at an above-average clip, it should help Olave by keeping opposing defenses honest and reluctant to roll extra coverage Olave's way. Olave could easily be a WR1 in 2023 if Derek Carr can rebound from his disastrous 2022.

2. **Drake London, ATL:** Drake London might have disappointed fantasy GMs with his 2022 output (WR43), but his deeper metrics say LOUDLY that London's better days are ahead. London ranked fifth in target share (29.4%) and second in target per route run rate (32.4%) among wide receivers. These are alpha-level numbers. He was also 11th in yards per route run and 16th in yards per team pass attempt. London should be considered a WR2 with a ridiculous upside. London already gave us a peek at his WR2 floor for 2023 during last year's stretch run. In Weeks 13-18, he was the WR20 in fantasy, even though he failed to score a touchdown in this span. If he had spiked it once or twice for six points, London would have posted WR1 numbers in that span. Yes, Kyle Pitts wasn't available during that time frame. I won't use that fact to slight London, and you shouldn't either. Talent finds a way. London has the talent.

3. **Christian Watson, GB:** Watson has been my man crush since I watched him dominate every corner lined up against him at the Senior Bowl. Watson dealt with bumps in the road early on with injuries and the brooding Aaron Rodgers. He emerged from those setbacks to prove he was "that guy" as the season rolled along. In Weeks 10-18, Watson had six games in which he played at least 80% of the snaps. In those games, he earned a 23.4% target share, 42.9% end zone target share, and a 26% target per route run rate. If those numbers weren't impressive enough, he also churned out 3.07 yards per route run. All of these numbers are elite. Watson has the entire offseason to work on rapport with Jordan Love as the Packers' number one option. He's a WR2 with monster WR1 upside.

4. **Garrett Wilson, NYJ:** Every day is Christmas for Garrett Wilson now. Wilson gets a magical upgrade from the shenanigans of Zach Wilson, the backup-worthy play of Mike White, and the aged crusty arm of Joe Flacco. Aaron Rodgers might not be in his prime, but he operates in an entirely different zip code of quarterback play than those other three players. Last season in Weeks 8-18, Wilson had a 26.9% target share, a 37% air yard share, and 2.08 yards per route run. These are WR1-type peripherals. The only worry around Wilson is if the pace of this Nathaniel Hackett-led system will cap his raw target volume. Wilson is a high-end WR2 that could easily be a WR1 in 2023.

5. **Jerry Jeudy, DEN:** If you're looking for a bright spot from the Broncos' 2022 season, it's Jerry Jeudy's play. Jeudy turned in his best season as a pro with a WR19 finish in fantasy points per game. He commanded a 20.8% target share while ranking 16th in YAC and yards per route run. With Sean Payton at the controls, Jeudy could be primed for a breakout season in 2023. Considering what we saw unfold last year, it's painful to think about reinvesting in this offense, but with a proven offensive mastermind now pulling the strings; we could have been a year early. I'll draft players from Mile High with a clean slate and high hopes for this year.

6. **Brandon Aiyuk, SF:** Brandon Aiyuk is coming off a career-best season. He was the WR23 in fantasy points per game with a 23.5% target share (23rd) and 2.09 yards per route run (24th). He was uncoverable, ranking 16th in total route wins and 13th in route win rate. The 49ers' target hierarchy remains a headache, with Aiyuk dealing with Deebo Samuel, Christian McCaffrey, and George Kittle weekly. San Francisco's run-heavy offensive focus and target competition will cap Aiyuk's target ceiling. Last year's 113 targets could be close to his ceiling unless injury strikes this depth chart. It's sad because this volume level isn't in line with his talent level, but it's impossible to overlook his situation. Aiyuk should be viewed as a WR3 with WR2 upside.

7. **Christian Kirk, JAC:** The Christian Kirk breakout season that fantasy gamers waited so long to see finally came to fruition last season. Kirk blew away his previous career high water marks as he was the WR18 in fantasy points per game with 84 receptions (14th-most), 1,108 receiving yards (13th-most), and eight total touchdowns (11th-most). Kirk will be forced to share the spotlight with Calvin Ridley in 2023, which could hurt his raw volume, but help the efficiency department. Kirk played only 52% of his snaps in the slot last year. That number could rise in 2023 with Ridley and Zay Jones roaming the perimeter. Kirk has shown he can win outside, but putting nickel corners in spin cycles is his real calling. Kirk is a low-end WR2.

8. **Treylon Burks, TEN:** Outside of Chigoziem Okonkwo, Treylon Burks has no reasonable competition for the team lead in targets this season. The collection of Nick Westbrook-Ikhine, Racey McMath, Kyle Philips, Chris Moore, and company is arguably the worst collection of wide receivers in the NFL. At first glance, Burks' numbers last season don't look impressive. He handled a 17.6% target while sitting at 35th in air yard share and 32nd in yards per route run. When we dig deeper, there are reasons for hope. Burks was 31st in fantasy points per route run and 35th in route win rate. Burks entered the NFL as an unfinished product who struggled early in camp. With a full offseason to get his conditioning in line and refine his route running, he could post some surprising second-season stats as the Titan's de facto WR1.

9. **Rashod Bateman, BAL:** Bateman's bad run of injury luck continued last year as he was sidelined by a foot sprain in Week 4 and shelved for the rest of the season by Week 8. Bateman's raw talent is real, and the league got a glimpse of it in the first three games of the season. In that timeframe, Bateman was the WR34 in fantasy, drawing an 18.8% target share, a 30.3% air yard share, and producing 3.14 yards per route run. Bateman produced those numbers despite only being on the field for roughly 72% of Lamar Jackson's dropbacks. Bateman enters his third season with the most target competition he's ever faced in Baltimore, with Odell Beckham Jr. and Zay Flowers now in the fold. Bateman is a WR4 that could still establish himself as the number two option in this passing attack behind Mark Andrews.

10. **Jahan Dotson, WAS:** Dotson's overall rookie season numbers don't jump off the page. He was the WR38 in fantasy with a 15.9% target share (56th), a 24% air yard share, and 1.50 yards per route run (50th). None of these figures paint an accurate picture of his true upside. After he returned from injury, the season's final five games offered a clearer view of what a breakout sophomore season for Dotson could look like. In Weeks 13-18 of last season, Dotson ranked 20th in target share (24%), third in end zone target share (50%), 17th in weighted opportunity, and 13th in yards per route run. Sam Howell or Jacoby Brissett at the helm in 2023 doesn't inspire a ton of confidence, but Dotson is a skilled wide receiver well-versed from his college days in dealing with pitiful quarterback play. Dotson is a WR4/5 that could take a huge leap in his second season. I won't rule out him giving Terry McLaurin a run for his money for the team lead in targets this season. Investing in talented second-year wide receivers are strong bets to make.

11. **George Pickens, PIT:** Pickens had some standout moments in his rookie season, including highlight-reel catches and shadow realm run blocking reps. Still, overall if you were banking on him to be a major fantasy producer, you were probably disappointed. Pickens logged six weeks with top-24 fantasy finishes, but outside of those weeks, he was unstartable with also eight weeks of WR50 or lower fantasy production. With Allen Robinson on the roster, expect the Steelers to utilize three wide receiver sets heavily. In Weeks 1-8, with the team heavily deploying 11 personnel, Pickens had a 15.1% target share, a 26% air yard share, and 1.19 yards per route run. He barely eclipsed a 15% target per route run rate. These aren't the type of numbers you're hoping to see if you are a Pickens truther, but it's the reality of the situation. Pickens is a WR4/5 that could be the fourth option in a Kenny Pickett-led passing attack.

Like last year, there will be some spike weeks along the way, but it's murky at best if he will ever develop into a high target share earner and consistent fantasy asset.

VETERANS

1. **Courtland Sutton, DEN:** Courtland Sutton's 2022 season was tanked by injury and Russell Wilson's inaccuracies. Sutton performed well with what he can control, and that's getting open. Last year Sutton was 23rd in route win rate and tenth in win rate against man coverage. Wilson tanked his quarterback-dependent metrics, evidenced by his sub 2.00 yards per route run and 7.6 yards per target (55th). If Wilson can bounce back and Sean Payton can get this offense on track, Sutton could have the type of season we all hoped for a year ago. Enjoy the value. Draft Sutton late, and if he crushes this year, you're lapping the field with him as your likely WR3 or flex play.

2. **Marquise Brown, ARI:** Brown is a dice roll as I type this blurb. After being released in late May, DeAndre Hopkins is no longer with the Cardinals. With Hopkins gone, Brown could be one of the best values in fantasy this season. Last year without Hopkins, in Weeks 1-6, he was the WR7 in fantasy as he saw elite alpha-level love. He had a 26% target share, a 40.5% air yard share, and 2.00 yards per route run. That's the ceiling scenario. If Hopkins stays, Brown is likely a WR3/4 type, with Hopkins soaking up most of the volume on what could be a terrible offense. There's no certainty about Kyler Murray's availability this season. That leaves Colt McCoy as the quarterback. McCoy, under center, would downgrade every skill player as the offense will suffer in scoring potential and efficiency.

3. **D.J. Moore, CHI:** Last year was a familiar rerun for D.J. Moore. Suffering through pitiful quarterback play for the entire season leads to final stat lines that don't match up with the talent level. Moore was the WR33 in fantasy as he dealt with a target quality rating and a catchable target rate outside of the top 90 among receivers. The true testament to Moore's skill is his ability to earn targets at an extremely high rate. In 2022, Moore was 12th in target share (27.7%), 17th in target per route run rate (26.8%), and fourth in deep targets. Justin Fields is arguably the best quarterback that Moore has ever played with. Now Moore isn't fighting through wretched signal caller play, but his target volume is a big concern. Chicago was a run-centric offense last season, to put it mildly. If Chicago's passing volume can tick up some and Moore can earn targets at his previous rates, he should be fine to return value as a WR2/3 in fantasy.

4. **Michael Pittman, IND:** Pittman might not have lived up to the hype last year, but he didn't have a bad season by any stretch of the imagination. He was the WR21 in fantasy and nearly snagged 100 balls (99 receptions). Pittman was 17th in target share and top-ten in route win rate and win rate against man coverage. Talent is not a problem for Pittman. Matt Ryan failed him last season. New Colts' quarterback, Anthony Richardson, has a rocket arm, but the team's passing volume is a big question mark as Indy will look to ease Richardson in. Pittman looks like a solid WR3, but the capped target volume could keep him from sneaking back into WR2 territory unless he stacks touchdowns.

5. **Chris Godwin, TB:** Chris Godwin finished as the WR15 last season on sheer volume. Godwin, coming off an ACL/MCL repair, ranked tenth in targets and routes run last season. Without his weekly life blood volume, his season would have been quite different. He was reduced to a low aDOT (99th), and his yards per route run tanked (38th). Godwin's talent remains, though, as he ranked fifth in total route wins and 20th in route win rate last year. The Tampa Bay passing attack will take a hit without Tom Brady under center pushing the pace. Godwin is a volume-based WR3 that's probably tied to wretched quarterback play with either Kyle Trask or Baker Mayfield due to be the team's starter in 2023.

6. **Deebo Samuel, SF:** After an explosive 2021 season where Samuel was the WR3 in fantasy points per game with an 8.1 aDOT and 14 deep targets (0.9 per game), the team decided to neuter his depth of target and rob him of his high-value roles. Samuel finished last year as the WR28 with a 4.2 aDOT and only 0.4 deep targets per game. If the team doesn't get back to using him deeper down the field, he's likely to reproduce WR3 output in 2023. Despite commanding a 23.9% target share and a 27% target per route run rate with a fully integrated Christian McCaffrey (Weeks 10-13), he could only muster WR58, WR5, WR66, and WR33 weekly finishes. The arrow is pointing down for Samuel's 2023 fantasy value.

7. **Mike Williams, LAC:** It would be a small miracle at this point if Mike Williams could suit up for an entire season. It's not worth tossing pennies in that wishing well, though. At this point in his career, Williams isn't likely to suddenly turn in a clean bill of health for 17 games. He was able to take the field for 13 games last season. He was still very productive as the WR20 in fantasy points per game when he was out there. Williams was 42nd in target share (18.2%), 21st in air-yard share (31.1%), and 25th in receiving yards (895). He ranked 30th in yards per route run and 22nd in route win rate. Williams can't be counted on as a WR2 with his ever-present injury concerns, but as a WR3, he can put your team over the top at any time. With Kellen Moore calling plays, the Chargers could be a top-three scoring offense this season.

8. **Mike Evans, TB:** Evans has progressed to the back nine of his career. Last year his target share ranked 37th, his yards per route run fell to 33rd, and his route win rate sat below 45%. Evans' season-long numbers were falsely propped up by his Week 17 Madden score. That game accounted for 18.4% of his full season receiving yardage and 50% of his receiving touchdown total. If we remove this outlier game from the equation, Evans would fall from WR14 in fantasy points per game to WR33. Evans logged seven games in weekly scoring outside the top 36 wide receivers. This season doesn't look any more promising for Evans. Tom Brady is gone. The offensive pace and passing rate are sure to decline. Now add in Evans' eroding talent, and we have the perfect cocktail for an overvalued WR3.

9. **Diontae Johnson, PIT:** Diontae Johnson had a ridiculously unlucky season last year. He was the equivalent of 2021 Miles Sanders at the wide receiver position. Despite ranking 13th in target share, tenth in red zone targets, and the WR20 in expected fantasy points per game, Johnson finished the season with zero touchdowns. Kenny Pickett weathering the rookie season storm also plays a factor, but Johnson simply had a terrible run-out. Regression is coming for Johnson and this offense. Johnson still ranked 11th in total route wins, so no skill dropoff is involved here. It's just a case of legendarily bad luck. Johnson is in the WR3 with WR2 upside bucket.

10. **Brandin Cooks, DAL:** Last year, Cooks saw his fantasy value crater as Pep Hamilton tried to pigeonhole him into a low aDOT role early on, which crushed his productivity. After Week 8, Hamilton returned to his senses and transitioned Cooks to his field-stretching role. Once the switch was made, his yards per route run jumped from 1.39 to 1.86. His aDOT climbed from 8.6 to 15.3 during this time. Cooks might not be a young pup anymore, but his top-25 rankings in route win rate and win rate against man coverage last year dispel any notion that he's turned to dust. With Dalton Schultz gone and Michael Gallup being JAG, Cooks should return WR3/4 value with room for more if he gels quickly with Dak Prescott.

11. **Gabriel Davis, BUF:** Davis didn't live up to the deafening hype last year. He finished as the WR36 in fantasy with an 18.2% target share (43rd). He remains Josh Allen's deep threat of choice, ranking 12th in deep targets and sixth in aDOT among wideouts. Davis has proven that he isn't a high-end target share earner. He was 68th in target per route run rate last year. Davis remains tied to Allen's cannon of an arm, so spike weeks will come again in 2023. At this point, you're kidding yourself if you think he will turn into a consistent WR2 type of player. Davis is a WR3/4 that can win you a week when he's locked in.

12. **Jakobi Meyers, LVR:** Jakobi Meyers was a welcome addition to a Raiders' wide receiver room that looked thin outside of Davante Adams and Hunter Renfrow. Meyers will rotate slot work with Renfrow. Meyers played 69.5% from the slot last year (Renfrow 86.0%), drawing a 22.0% target share (29th), a 25.8% target per route run rate (22nd), and a 27.4% air yard share as the Patriots' number one option. Meyers has been the WR29 and WR35 in fantasy points per game over the last two seasons. Meyers' signing could signal the Raiders' plan to deploy more 11 personnel this season after ranking 18th in the use of three-plus wide receiver sets last year. Meyers is a low-ceiling WR3/4 that gets a small boost in PPR formats.

13. **Juju Smith-Schuster, NE:** Smith-Schuster had a solid season last year in one of the best offenses in the NFL, but it wasn't amazing, no matter how you slice it. He was the WR35 in fantasy points per game, drawing a 17.4% target share (46th) and 16.9% air yard share (70th). Smith-Schuster's ability to beat zone coverage is his calling card these days, so he should help New England's passing offense in this aspect. He should be the "new Jakobi Meyers" as a starter in two wide sets that flexes to the slot when they utilize 11 personnel. Smith-Schuster is an uninspiring WR4/5.

14. **Odell Beckham Jr., BAL:** The last time we saw Beckham Jr., he evoked thoughts of yesteryear when Beckham Jr. took the league by storm. While Beckham Jr. was on his way to possibly a stout Super Bowl before injury struck again, we're likely never seeing prime Beckham Jr. again. During his final seven regular season games with the Rams, Beckham Jr. saw a 15.1% target share, 20% target per route run rate, and produced 1.25 yards per route run. His five receiving touchdowns in this span help gloss over the fact that he was a mediocre receiver per efficiency numbers in that stretch. Beckham can continue to be a red zone weapon assuming full health in Baltimore with Lamar Jackson, but the days of valuing him as anything more than a WR4/5 are over.

ROOKIES TO KNOW

1. **Jaxon Smith-Njigba, SEA:** Jaxon Smith-Njigba was arguably the WR1 in this year's draft class. With his elite short-area quickness and surprising straight-line speed, he left college with a 75th-percentile breakout age. During his monster 2021 season, he commanded a 22.7% target share while sporting an 84.8% catch rate. The big worry for Smith-Njigba is how much Seattle will increase their usage of 11 personnel after ranking 28th in the usage of three-wide sets last year. Pete Carroll can say whatever he wants to the media, but I refuse to believe they spent a first-round pick on a receiver they intend to use as a part-time player. If that change comes to fruition, there should be enough passing volume to support all three studs. Last year Seattle ranked tenth in neutral script passing rate. If you're betting on talent, Smith-Njigba is a bet to make in fantasy for 2023. If everything lines up perfectly for him this season, he's a WR3/4 that could finish as a WR2.

2. **Jordan Addison, MIN:** Addison has the clearest path to a hefty target share and consistent playing time this season out of the four wide receivers selected in the first round of this year's NFL Draft. Addison can play the perimeter and slide into the slot when the team wants to take advantage of a soft nickel corner matchup. Addison is a smooth route runner with a varied release package. He reminds me of DeVonta Smith in some aspects while noting that Smith offers more play strength with his slighter frame than Addison. Addison should compete with T.J. Hockenson immediately for the second spot in the target pecking order behind Justin Jefferson. Last year the Vikings were fourth in neutral script passing rate and second in red zone passing rate. With the addition of Addison and a wretched defensive unit, the Vikings will again challenge for the league lead in passing attempts. Addison is a WR3 that can finish as a WR2 in fantasy if he can cement himself as the second option behind Jefferson.

3. **Quentin Johnston, LAC:** Quentin Johnston landed on what should be a high-powered Chargers' passing attack. His explosive RAC ability will be put to good use by an offensive coordinator who will feature a passing offense that should settle inside the top 5-10 teams in passing rate and neutral pace. Keenan Allen and Mike Williams aren't getting any younger, so it shouldn't surprise anyone if one or both of them is dinged up at some point in the 2023 season. This would leave Johnston as the team's de facto WR1. Johnston's big play ability, plus the possibility of getting some weeks as the clear focal point of the passing attack, should allow him to outkick his ADP and expectations this year. At the very least, Johnston should be the team's field stretcher in year one. The Chargers will throw deep early and often this season, so this role should be quite sexy for Johnston's fantasy upside. In Dak Prescott's two full seasons under Moore, he finished five and seventh in deep ball attempts. The days of dink and dunk under Joe Lombardi are over for the Bolts. Johnston is an upside WR3/4.

4. **Zay Flowers, BAL:** Flowers should immediately be starting in three wide receiver sets in Baltimore opposite Rashod Bateman and Odell Beckham Jr. in the Ravens' new-look passing attack under Todd Monken. With Greg Roman gone, Baltimore should usher in a new era of football with Lamar Jackson's arm doing the talking. The drastic changes incoming for the Ravens could open some eyes. The first could be the offensive pace and play volume, which means more passing attempts and targets for these receiving options. In three of Monken's last four seasons as an offensive mastermind, he's ranked inside the top 12 (eighth, 11th, fourth) in neutral script pace. Over that span, he was also top-five in passing attempts twice. If Beckham doesn't look like his old self and Bateman doesn't fully bounce back from last season's foot injury woes, Flowers could be the number two target in this aerial attack. Flowers can play inside and the perimeter as a receiver that can win at every level of the field.

5. **Marvin Mims Jr., DEN:** Sean Payton traded up in the second round of the NFL Draft to take the talented rookie from Oklahoma. Mims closes his collegiate career with a 94th percentile yards per reception and 96th percentile breakout age. Mims can work underneath and take the top off defenses with his 4.38 speed. He can also play above the rim with exceptional leaping ability and body control. Mims could be fighting for playing time with Tim Patrick from the outset, but it's possible he hops him on the depth chart and becomes a full-time starter immediately with a strong camp and preseason. Mims is a fantastic WR5 draft pick to stash on your bench. He could be a stretch-run hero and difference-maker in the fantasy playoffs if this offense bounces back from last year's pitiful showing.

6. **Jayden Reed, GB:** The Green Bay passing attack is wide open after Christian Watson. Reed will be a starter immediately and should have no problems hopping Romeo Doubs in the pecking order. Reed is a good fit for this offensive system with his strong lower half and YAC ability. He should allow easy completions for Jordan Love with the talent to do something with the ball in his hands. He flashed better route running chops at the Senior Bowl in Mobile than I gave him credit for after examining his college film. Grab him at the end of your drafts. He's worth a stash and hold to see how this Packer offense unfolds. He could easily be a weekly flex play that pays huge dividends as we move through the fantasy season.

7. **Rashee Rice, KC:** He is a talented rookie wide receiver drafted in the second round of the NFL Draft and now finds himself tied to Patrick Mahomes. Where have I heard this before? Oh, that's right. Skyy Moore stole my heart last year, only to be limited weekly by Andy Reid. Just because I (and many others) were burned last year doesn't mean I'm shying away from Rice. That worry and recency bias will keep many from pressing the button when on the clock in fantasy drafts. His risk will likely be baked into his ADP, so the worries should be factored in. I will say that it could only take a few training camp videos or positive blurbs to come out to create buzz and wipe the memories of fantasy GMs. Rice is a zone coverage destroyer who could take over for Chief Juju Smith-Schuster's role in this offense. He has experience playing both the perimeter and slot extensively. Rice produced a 64th percentile college dominator and

96th percentile collegiate target share at SMU. If Kadarius Toney and Skyy Moore aren't up to the task of operating as Mahomes' number two target, don't rule out Rice to seize the opportunity.

8. **Jonathan Mingo, CAR:** Jonathan Mingo stood out to NFL evaluators in a draft class that lacked a ton of tantalizing-size speed specimens. This helped him to secure second-round draft capital with the Carolina Panthers. Mingo's draft profile screams risk. He only managed a 40th percentile college dominator and 53rd percentile breakout age. These aren't exactly glittering production numbers that inspire confidence for a rookie season breakout, but the Panthers' depth chart isn't filled with insurmountable talent. Adam Thielen and D.J. Chark are solid veterans who should be locked into starting roles. Mingo will have to compete with Terrace Marshall for a starting spot. Mingo could emerge as a flex option if he can win the starting job this season.

9. **Josh Downs, IND:** The Colts selected the former North Carolina standout in the third round of the NFL Draft. Downs shouldn't have any problems beating out Isaiah McKenzie for the starting slot position in camp. Last year Shane Steichen directed a Philadelphia offense that utilized at least three wide receivers on the field for 73.6% (seventh-highest) of its snaps. The biggest worries for Downs will be the overall passing volume, with the Colts likely to lean on the run and ease in Anthony Richardson versus NFL competition. He could be the second target in the passing attack behind only Michael Pittman. Downs is someone to remember for the later rounds of PPR drafts. The ceiling isn't high, but he could be a solid WR3/flex in that format this season.

10. **Puka Nacua, LAR:** Yes, we're talking redraft fantasy football here, not dynasty. Puka Nacua could be in the weekly flex conversation this season if he can seize a starting role. Nacua didn't get any hype as a prospect from the national media, but he should have. Nacua stood out in yards per route run in his last two seasons at BYU, finishing inside the top ten each year. His size, body control at the boundary, and rushing utility (9.2 yards per carry at BYU) give him a varied skill set for Sean McVay to utilize. Assuming Matthew Stafford is healthy, he needs weapons to throw to not named Cooper Kupp and Tyler Higbee. Nacua could be the new Bob Woods in Los Angeles.

MATCHUP PLAYS

1. **D.J. Chark, CAR:** Are you an NFL team desperate to fill your starting lineup with serviceable veterans? Well, D.J. Chark is your guy. Chark heads to Carolina after only one year with the Lions. He should operate in a similar role with the Panthers he held last season. Chark will be asked to get open deep to create room for the running game and the underneath receiving options. Last year in the ten games Chark played at least 65% of the snaps, he drew a 14.3% target share, a 29.9% air yard share, and a 16% target per route run rate. He was fourth in aDOT last year (15.4) and 36th in deep targets among wide receivers. Chark is worth flexing this season when the Panthers face a secondary that struggles to defend downfield.

2. **Tyler Boyd, CIN:** After back-to-back seasons as a WR3 in fantasy, Boyd dipped to WR45 in fantasy points per game last year. Boyd's target share dwindled to 13.5% (71st) as he finished outside the top 60 wide receivers in yards per route run and route win rate. Boyd isn't a sexy name to plug in your starting lineup, but he remains tied to Joe Burrow, and when the Bengals get a soft matchup against a nickel corner, expect Burrow to feed him. Despite the down season, Boyd still had two weeks with WR1 fantasy finishes and eight games with WR36 or higher fantasy output.

3. **Donovan Peoples-Jones, CLE:** Peoples-Jones should have some spike weeks in the chamber this season if Deshaun Watson can get back on track. Peoples-Jones ranked 27th in aDOT and 21st in deep targets last

year. Similarly, as we look to D.J. Chark against defenses that struggle to stop deep passing, Peoples-Jones should be on your short list of players to flex or pick up off waivers when the opportunity presents to carve up a secondary downfield. Peoples-Jones had eight games with at least 60 receiving yards and 11 weeks of WR3 or better weekly fantasy production last year.

4. **Zay Jones, JAC:** Zay Jones finds himself in this lowly category after a WR31 season because the situation has changed with Calvin Ridley making his comeback. Ridley and Christian Kirk should occupy the top-two spots in the passing target tree, with Evan Engram slotting into the three spot. Zay Jones could be left to pick up the scraps, but Trevor Lawrence trusts Jones in the red zone. Last year he was 12th in red zone targets. Jacksonville faces eight teams inside the top ten for the most touchdowns allowed to wide receivers last season. Despite getting bumped down a rung during the offseason, Jones will still have spike weeks in 2023.

Chapter 6

Tight Ends

	TE1 PPR	RPV		TE2 PPR	RPV
1	Travis Kelce	67%	13	Dalton Schultz	10%
2	Mark Andrews	21%	14	Chigoziem Okonkwo	6%
3	T.J. Hockenson	15%	15	Greg Dulcich	6%
4	George Kittle	9%	16	Mike Gesicki	4%
5	Kyle Pitts	6%	17	Tyler Higbee	2%
6	Dallas Goedert	-8%	18	Juwan Johnson	-1%
7	Darren Waller	-14%	19	Zach Ertz	-1%
8	Pat Freiermuth	-16%	20	Irv Smith Jr.	-3%
9	Evan Engram	-17%	21	Tyler Conklin	-3%
10	Dalton Kincaid	-20%	22	Jelani Woods	-3%
11	Cole Kmet	-21%	23	Sam LaPorta	-7%
12	David Njoku	-22%	24	Michael Mayer	-11%

	TE1 STND	RPV		TE2 STND	RPV
1	Travis Kelce	58%	13	Dalton Schultz	29%
2	Mark Andrews	32%	14	Chigoziem Okonkwo	21%
3	T.J. Hockenson	23%	15	Greg Dulcich	13%
4	George Kittle	10%	16	Mike Gesicki	8%
5	Kyle Pitts	5%	17	Tyler Higbee	5%
6	Dallas Goedert	1%	18	Juwan Johnson	-3%
7	Darren Waller	-12%	19	Zach Ertz	-3%
8	Pat Freiermuth	-16%	20	Irv Smith Jr.	-11%
9	Evan Engram	-21%	21	Tyler Conklin	-11%
10	Cole Kmet	-21%	22	Jelani Woods	-11%
11	David Njoku	-30%	23	Sam LaPorta	-16%
12	Dalton Kincaid	-30%	24	Michael Mayer	-19%

Player Profiles and Overview

Scott Bogman

Like last season, TE is top-heavy with four big-time producers, three big upside plays, and then a 4th tier that could be anywhere from 9-13 deep. I've broken the tiers into names that reflect how I feel about drafting these guys.

Travis Kelce Tier - If there was ever a year that I would invest in Kelce in the 1st round, it's this season. Kelce is my #1 by a wide margin and is worth the investment early.

After Kelce Tier - Should you pass Kelce, I like picking out of the next tier to ensure I have a TE that has an advantage over at least eight teams in my league, and I know I don't have to waste a bench spot on a backup TE and I can save my FAAB to pick up other positions during the season.

Disappointment Tier - These 3 have the talent to turn in big seasons and are way cheaper, but there's something a little off about each. Goedert is the 4th or 5th option on his team, Waller can't stay on the field, and the offense in Atlanta didn't throw the ball last year. I'm generally pessimistic, but this tier has a chance to give you outstanding value and the opportunity to make you pull your hair out.

I gotta take 1 Tier - I've waited until the end of the draft, and now I have to roster a starter. With this group, it's about the upside, whether it's TD upside, target share upside, or talent upside. Just take whoever you feel best about because you'll probably be playing TE musical chairs this season.

Youth Movement Tier - Beyond the Top 15, I'll break the last few guys into young guys with upside and the old reliable vets. This Tier is where we are playing upside. If you're in a TE premium league, you can grab one of these guys to play or trade at the end of the draft if all other positions are exhausted. If you wait to take a TE in deeper leagues, pairing one of the young guys with one from the next tier could pay off.

Old Crust Vets Tier - The snaps will be there for these guys, but their upside is capped.

THE ELITE (AKA KELCE TIER)

1. **Travis Kelce, KC** - Kelce is the absolute tip of the spear at the TE position, and after last season it isn't close! Kelce led all TEs in Targets by 23, Receptions by 24, Receiving Yards by 424, and had the 2nd most TD receptions at any position with 12. PPR leagues saw Kelce lead TEs in points by over 100 points, and in .5 PPR, he still led TEs by almost 90. If we're talking Per Game (most other top-tier TEs outside of Hockenson missed games), he led by five over any other TE in PPR and 4 points per game better in half. Kelce also led all TEs in Target Share and was one of two TEs over 2 in Yards Per Route Run (my favorite advanced stat for receiving). Kelce has also been the first or second TE Per Game in points every year since 2016, and he's been #1 in three of the past four seasons. His 11 targets inside the 5-yard line were six more than anyone else. He led in red zone targets by 9. He lined up as a WR more than any other TE. Kelce is the #1 option on the best offense in football and one of the safest options in the draft.

TOP TALENT (AKA AFTER KECLE TIER)

1. **Mark Andrews, BAL** - I'll stick with Andrews at #2, but anyone in this tier can go at 2. Andrews is the only non-Travis Kelce to lead TEs in total points or PPG when he did both in 2021. Andrews suffered a knee injury late in the Week 6 game or practice that week that hobbled made him questionable for Week 7. Andrews played week seven but only had one catch for 4 yards after catching 5 TDs, averaging 9.5 targets, 6.5 catches, and 76 yards in the six weeks before that. Andrews then played Thursday night football in Week 8, suffered a shoulder injury to go on top of his knee injury, and missed a week before their bye. Andrews wasn't the same after that. He didn't catch one more TD or have a 10-target game after the knee

injury and averaged only 6.5 PPG (Half PPR) after averaging a better than Kelce 15.88 in those first 6. The Ravens are getting a new OC in Todd Monken coming over from Georgia. They are adding WR Odell Beckham Jr in Free Agency and Zay Flowers through the draft and 2021 first-round WR Rashod Bateman only played in 6 games last year so there could be a little more diplomacy with the targets. However, I still expect Andrews to lead and be closer to the 15 PPG than 6.5.

2. **George Kittle, SF** - Kittle had a weird 2022, starting with a groin injury in Preseason practice that cost him the first two games of the season. It wasn't until Week 7 that Kittle caught his first TD, and then he had a mid-season downturn when the 9ers traded for CMC and started dumping the ball off to him a lot. The addition of CMC took targets away from Kittle at the start, in Weeks 8-13 CMC out-targeted Kittle 38-20. Purdy took over at QB for the final 6 weeks of the season with Purdy as the starter Kittle averaged over 14 PPG and scored 7 of his 11 TDs. If we cut it to the final 4 weeks when he finally started out-targeting CMC, Kittle was averaging just over 19 PPG in half PPR. Unfortunately, Purdy is in question to start the season with an elbow injury, but recent updates are positive, and Shanahan wants Purdy to be the guy so if he's healthy he'll have every opportunity to win the job.

3. **T.J. Hockenson, MIN** - In one of the weirder trades I've ever seen Hockenson was flipped inside the NFC North from Detroit to Minnesota in the middle of the season. It resulted in career highs for Hockenson in targets by 28, receptions by 25, and tied a career-high in TDs with 6. Hockenson was rested Week 18 before the playoffs, but in the nine games with Minnesota before that, he averaged just under 11 PPG, and he should be the #2 receiving option behind Justin Jefferson.

DISAPPOINTMENT TEIR

1. **Dallas Goedert, PHI** - Goedert is going to be in the 2nd tier for a lot of rankers, but I think he belongs just below that. Goedert is going to be the 3rd option, and with the addition of RB D'Andre Swift, we should see more targets going to RBs, as the Eagles were dead last in 2022. Goedert missed five games between Weeks 11-15 with a shoulder injury, but he played admirably down the stretch and in the playoffs. Goedert has the talent to be in the higher group, but I think Brown, Smith, and the addition of Swift in Philly cap his upside.

2. **Darren Waller, NYG** - Waller was one of the best TEs in the league in 2019 and 2020, but in the last two seasons he's missed 14 games and looked like a different player. In his big seasons, he went over 1,000 yards twice which has only been done by 4 other players in the last 4 seasons Kelce, Andrews, Kittle, and Pitts. The trade to the Giants fascinates me, the Giants had the 2nd lowest target rate for TEs last season, but they were starting a rookie in Bellinger, and he missed 6 games, and Lawrence Cager was their next-best option. The reason I'm intrigued for this season is that the Giants receiving options at WR are still below average, but they added speedy rookie Jalin Hyatt to the mix who should be able to stretch the field, and Barkley is a nice option underneath. If Waller can stay healthy he could be in for a big year, not 19-20 big those days are done but a solid season should be expected.

3. **Kyle Pitts, ATL** - Pitts showed his elite talent with the Falcons in his rookie season. As a rookie, he put up over 1000 yards (as mentioned before, only 5 TEs have had 1,000 seasons in the last 4 seasons) but his 2022 ended in Week 11 when he suffered an MCL sprain and it was ugly before that. HC Arthur Smith, knowing his QB play was going to be bad and his OL was having a rough time protecting the QB decided to run the ball more times than any other team last season. The Falcons weren't dead last in pass attempts, but they were 31st (only the Bears had fewer passes 415-377) and trimmed 158 pass plays from 2021. Atlanta also drafted Drake London in 2022, and he led the team in target share by a mile, especially after Pitts's injury. The good news is that Ridder actually averaged more passes in his four starts than Mariota did and Pitts has more than enough time to recover from his injury. The Falcons still aren't going to pass a ton with a 1st-year starter in Ridder, and they drafted the best RB prospect since Saquon to lead this offense, but I think they have the talent to climb out of the gutter and Pitts could be at the front of it.

I GOTTA TAKE A TE TIER

1. **Dalton Kincaid, BUF** - Drafting rookie TEs is a gamble, but Kincaid is a gamble that could pay off handsomely. Diggs had the 7th highest target share of any WR in the league, and while that's expected from one of the best, it would be nice to take a little pressure off of him. Gabe Davis wasn't terrible last season, but it's pretty clear he wasn't ready to take the next step, and the Bills spent their 1st round pick on Kincaid. Dawson Knox isn't going to go away, but he will give up some of those slot snaps to Kincaid, who had the #1 PFF receiving grade among TEs in College last year and the 2nd highest yards per route run. This TE range is extremely close so I'll put the gamble here at 8 and know that if he doesn't work out that there will be someone comparable to pick up off the wire in a 12-team league.

2. **David Njoku, CLE** - This one is all about TD upside as Njoku was 2nd among TEs in red zone targets behind only Travis Kelce with 20 and he only scored 4 TDs. Njoku also saw the 2nd most targets of his career and averaged more PPG at 8.1 (half) than he ever has. The downside to Njoku is that he's boom-or-bust with 6 games in double-digits but also 6 games under 5 points last season and the Browns are adding Elijah Moore to the mix this season who should take targets away from DPJ and he could pluck some from Njoku also.

3. **Evan Engram, JAX** - Engram moves to Jacksonville and has career highs in catches and receiving yards! Engram has also shaken the injury-prone tag that he had early in his career by only missing two games in his last three seasons. My issue with Engram is that he was already behind Kirk and Zay on the Jags depth chart, and Calvin Ridley is going to have more targets than him too. Etienne could also get more than the 45 targets he saw last season as well, and Engram hasn't scored a ton of TDs in his career. Engram only has 20 TDs in his 6-year career, and 6 of those were as a rookie.

4. **Pat Freiermuth, PIT** - My man Freiermuth only added three catches to his total from his rookie season, but he improved his ADOT from 5.6 to 8.4 which added 3.4 yards per reception for him and 235 yards. Unfortunately, Pat still lost .4 PPG because he only scored two TDs with the combo of Trubisky and Pickett. The Steelers were 6th in TE Target share last season, and Pickett should have more than seven passing TDs in his 2nd year as a starter.

5. **Chig Okonkwo, TEN** - It's possible that we have just scratched the surface with Chig as a rookie with the Titans. Okonkwo was 3rd in TE snaps in Tennesse behind Hooper and Swaim, who both leave over 500 snaps behind. More importantly, the Titans brought in only Trevon Wesco, who only has eight receptions in four seasons, and 5th-round rookie Josh Whyle and both of these guys will be blocking TEs leaving the receiving job all to Okonkwo by himself. Chig only had four games with five or more targets last season, but he was #1 in YPRR among TEs last season and 2nd behind only Tyreek Hill. The only issues I see with Okonkwo are that he was not a very good blocker, he was just above average in pass blocking and WELL below average as a run blocker (83/101), and that needs to improve, or he has to really solidify himself as a top tier receiving TE to stay on the field. He's a risk for this season but a worthy one.

6. **Cole Kmet, CHI** - Kmet had a solid year, and while the Bears threw the ball to the TE at one of the better clips in the NFL (22.8% - 11th), they threw the ball so few times that the total targets for TEs were 28th. Kmet was tied for 3rd among TEs with seven receiving TDs, and they accounted for 34% of his production. The Bears might throw more this season, but I would guess that the majority of those targets go to new acquisition DJ Moore. I think he'll be about the same with more catches and yards but fewer TDs and stay right in this range.

7. **Tyler Higbee, LAR** - I feel more positive about Higbee than I probably should, but he was 4th in TE Targets last season with 104. The targets and total points (116 - 9th among TEs in half) were mainly attrition, he played all 17 games, and the Rams had injuries to Kupp, Allen Robinson and Skowronek, and most

importantly, Stafford. Kupp will be back to dominate targets, but the Rams will have the worst defense in the NFL this season and will be playing catch-up late, which should lead to some nice extra targets for Higbee. Luckily behind Kupp there is only Skowornek and Jefferson to compete with for catches and Higbee has a shot to be 2nd in targets for the Rams.

8. **Dalton Schultz, HOU** - Brand new team, brand new offense, and a rookie QB await Schultz in Houston. The possible range of outcomes is vast for Schultz, making him hard to project. Maybe he becomes the 'safety blanket' for his rookie QB, and he has career highs in everything, or, like Freiermuth, he loses TDs, and Stroud looks as bad as Zach Wilson. Schultz is smart and gets open (only 17 contested catch attempts on over 100 targets), so he'll be in the right spot, but I have a hard time trusting a rookie QB.

UP AND COMING (AKA YOUTH MOVEMENT TIER)

1. **Michael Mayer, LVR** - The Raiders moved on from Waller and took the most complete TE in the 2023 NFL in Mayer. Mayer is going to be a 'plug-and-play' who is a great receiving option (#1 in YPRR among TEs in CFB last year), and he was top 10 in run blocking last season. The Raiders also signed veteran Austin Hooper so while Mayer can be the day 1 starter, there is some stiff competition to start.

2. **Sam LaPorta, DET** - The Lions kicked Hockenson to the curb and drafted LaPorta in the 2nd to replace him, and I love this gamble. LaPorta is going to be a much better NFL player with some competent QB play. LaPorta has had 153 receptions in 4 seasons at Iowa, raising his targets and catches every year, and they only got him 5 TDs. LaPorta spent more time lined up between WR and the Slot last season, and with Brock Wright being the #1 graded pass-blocking TE and Zylstra the 5th best-graded run-blocking TE, LaPorta should be able to concentrate on catching the football. I wouldn't be surprised if he matched his four-year TD total at Iowa in his first season with Detroit.

3. **Greg Dulcich, DEN** - The Broncos are still looking for someone to replace Noah Fant since he was traded last season in the deal for Russell Wilson. Dulcich was the leading TE in target share in 2022, but he was under 10%. Dulcich did have the 5th highest snap% among TEs in the slot last season, with Mark Andrews, Logan Thomas, Isaiah Likely, and Darren Waller as the only ones higher than him. Dulcich does still have to win his job back under a new HC Sean Payton and OC Joe Lombardi. The good news is that the Chargers were top 10 and in the same neighborhood of TE targets last season, but they brought in veteran Adam Trautman, and he'll get a real shot to take the job away from Dulcich.

4. **Jelani Woods, IND** - Woods is a massive target at 6'7" and can be the main TE this season, as he out-snapped Mo Allie-Cox in two of the final four games for the Colts last season. Woods still has a long way to go as a blocker, and I think that ultimately caps his ceiling, but he's a dart throw with a lot of upside.

5. **Trey McBride, AZ** - Trey McBride was a one-man wrecking crew when he was at Colorado State. I hated his landing spot behind Zach Ertz in Arizona, but after Ertz went down for the season in Week 10, McBride led the Cardinals in snaps at the position by a wide margin. Unfortunately, there were too many mouths to feed with Hopkins, Brown, and Dortch in the pass-heavy offense and they should be moving to a slower-paced offense with Gannon taking over. The talent is there, but the opportunity might be limited especially if he doesn't get rolling before Ertz comes back.

6. **Cade Otton, TB** - Otton has the snaps for the Bucs, but he did last year and was still under 5 PPG (half). The Bucs brought in a receiving TE in Payne Durham in the 5th round and are downgrading from Tom Brady to Baker Mayfield at QB. Otton will have to score TDs to stay relevant, with Evans and Godwin still dominating targets.

7. **Isaiah Likely, BAL** - Likely is a Slot WR masquerading as a TE. I really think Likely could be a great option at TE, but unfortunately, he's buried behind not just Andrews but the players the Ravens added in OBJ and Zay Flowers. Target competition is going to be tough.

8. **Luke Musgrave and Tucker Kraft, GB** - Remember when the Ravens drafted Hayden Hurst and then Mark Andrews two rounds later, and Andrews became the receiving TE and Hurst was relegated to blocking? That's what Musgrave and Tucker Kraft could be in GB. These two are much closer in receiving talent, but I'm afraid that because Musgrave can block and Kraft is less likely to keep up in that regard, coming from a lower level of college competition. The same thing happened with Njoku for a while because he was able to block and Harrison Bryant couldn't. One of these guys should get targets because the Pack are likely to go with a rookie in Jayden Reed at the slot, and someone is going to have to space the middle of the field.

CRUSTY VTES TIER

1. **Gerald Everett, LAC** - Everett has averaged just under 7 PPG in half the past two seasons and been around 55-500-4 and I expect that to stick in the same area as long as he's healthy.

2. **Juwan Johnson, NO** - Johnson pushed Trautman out of the job and scored 7 TDs! The downside is that JJ was VERY TD-reliant (36.8% of his half PPR total) and with the Saints adding Foster Moreau and 2022 TD leader Jamaal Williams he could lose a little steam in 23.

3. **Mike Gesicki, NE** - I'm not as excited as most on Gesicki. He's primarily a Slot player, and the Patriots also signed Juju Smith-Schuster, who will take most of the Slot Targets for New England. The Patriots still have Hunter Henry, and as a better blocker, he'll probably see the field more. Gesicki should see more targets and production than he did in Miami, but I see more of a capped ceiling than most.

4. **Zach Ertz, AZ** - Ertz's goal is to be ready for Week 1, and if he is, I would put him at the bottom of the 'After Kelce Tier' because he's one of the more trustworthy TEs in the league. I think he starts the year on the PUP and may miss more time than expected. Probably just enough time to give us a flash of McBride and then bury him again.

5. **Hayden Hurst, CAR** - We can't get much more boring than Hurst as a starting TE, but he will see a ton of snaps in Carolina. Similar to Schultz in Houston, Hurst could become Bryce Young's favorite target quickly, but I think expecting more than 50-500-5 is pushing it.

Chapter 7

Kickers

Player Ranks and Profiles

Travis Sumpter

Tier 1

1. Justin Tucker, BAL, 13
2. Daniel Carlson, LV, 13
3. Evan McPherson, CIN, 7
4. Tyler Bass, BUF, 13
5. Harrison Butker, KC, 10

Tier 2

6. Brandon McManus, DEN, 9
7. Nick Folk, NE, 11
8. Jason Sanders, MIA, 10
9. Younghoe Koo, ATL, 11
10. Jake Elliot, PHI, 10
11. Matt Gay, IND, 11

Tier 3

1. Jason Meyers, SEA, 5
2. Riley Patterson, JAC, 9
3. Graham Gano, NYG, 13
4. Greg Joseph, MIN, 13
5. Greg Zuerlein, NYJ, 7
6. Dustin Hopkins, LAC, 5
7. Will Lutz, NO, 11
8. Matt Prater, ARI, 14

Rookies to Watch

1. Jake Moody, SF
2. Chad Ryland, NE
3. Anders Carlson, GB

Kickers? We talking about kickers? Blasphemous subject matter to most fantasy football enthusiasts and fantasy football analysts. Kickers are an essential part of real football and should also be considered essential in fantasy football. I completely get it from the perspective of all the randomness that the position can bring. Why can't we find ways to make it more fun, though? Try spicing things up depending on what platform you are on, and play around with the scoring settings to make it more predictable or even more unpredictable.

Ways to make it more predictable: keep it standard settings or even downplay the field goals to just being 3 points no matter the distance. Take away the same number of points that the field goal or extra point would have counted towards if made.

Ways to make it more unpredictable: make it weird! Only reward points for misses (3-5 points for missed field goals depending on distance, 6 points for missed extra points). Give kickers negative points for field goal makes (-3 to -5 depending on distance, -1 for extra points made). Just make it known a kicker must be started in your league. Feel free to play around with the settings and don't limit yourself to the confines of the standard scoring.

Drafting a kicker: There are all kinds of different ways you can draft a kicker. Some like to do it with the last pick of their draft, some a couple of rounds before to get an elite kicker a few rounds earlier. I will almost never actually draft a kicker unless I am required to do so. If required to draft one, do it in the very last round of your draft. The best way to do it is if you're not required to draft a kicker in your league, then DON'T.

If I can, I would rather spend that potential draft capital on another handcuff running back or sleeper wide receiver. I would rather hold out for potential stardom somewhere else on my roster than hold a kicker. Just drop a player before Week 1 and stream the position from there.

Stream the position:

When streaming your kickers, there are a few different approaches to take in this, and they are as follows:

1.   Play the waiver wire game. Were there any elite kickers or upcoming matchups that you feel good about that were dropped because of a bye week?

2.   Look at the teams your kicker is going up against. Do they generally give up a lot of points each week, and how many red zone opportunities do you believe will be afforded to them? Does the opposing team allow a lot of yards but not a lot of touchdowns? Think almost in terms of your kicker's team and their ability or inability to punch it into the endzone. It is always more beneficial for your kicker to be in a good offense that can move the ball up and down the field but struggles inside the red zone, 10, 5, or goal line. Also, the teams opposing defense and how they also perform on those areas of the field. Nothing is more advantageous than knowing the bend doesn't break defenses to maximize your chances of scoring well on a given week.

3.   If you're living the stream life, then drop your kicker every week for another waiver wire add that you think could break out or a potential handcuff or injury concern comes up for your own starting running back or someone else's running back. Then just rinse and repeat week after week and just stream the best kicker available as such.

4.   Watch the weather. Weather is a part of football in a little over 1/3 of all NFL stadiums. Lions, Falcons, Saints, Vikings, Raiders, Cowboys, Texans, Colts, Cardinals, Rams, and Chargers are those stadiums where weather is not a factor. I prefer my kicker to be playing at one of these weather-controlled environments because there is nothing worse than a kicker that is playing against 25-30 mile per hour winds, snow, or rain. More variances can come into play in which those environmental factors can have an impact on a kicker's weekly performance.

Week 1 Kickers to Stream:

•	 Joey Slye, WSH versus the Arizona defense that has been completely decimated by retirements in JJ Watt, the offseason, players wanting to be traded like Budda Baker and just the overall decimation of the roster the last few months. This should almost always be a defense to take a streamer against. A team like Washington may not be overly efficient in the red zone this year but could be a great Week 1 option for those of us that like to punt the position during our drafts.

•	 Riley Patterson, JAC on the road against Indianapolis in what could be a sneaky high-scoring affair Week 1. I am really loving Jacksonville's schedule this upcoming season and I always love my kickers attached to a good offense. Riley Patterson could be one of the kickers this year to make that jump into a top 5 kicker and might be worth holding onto beyond just Week 1.

•	 Michael Badgley, DET on the road in Kansas City. If last year's opener against the Philadelphia Eagles was any indication, then we should be in store for fireworks Week 1 at the Chiefs. Badgley could see plenty of work with his leg Week 1 in a game that might have a 55-plus point over/under by the time kickoff gets here.

Rankings and Settings: Most leagues make kickers score 1 for Points After Attempt or PAT and 3 for Field Goals or FG. Do what you want to do to keep it fun. In leagues that play with kickers, these are my preferred settings.

1.	1 point for PAT

2.	-1 point for missed PAT

3.	3 points for 1–39-yard FG

4.	4 points for 40–49-yard FG

5.	5 points for 50 yards or more

Chapter 8

Team Defense/Special Teams

Scott Bogman

I implore you to please give IDP a shot! IDP makes Fantasy Football more fun, in my opinion, because we don't have to rely on the weakest link of the team's defense that we drafted. If you are sticking with team defense, as we discussed in last season's Black Book, the best move from week to week is to go with whatever defense is playing the worst offense that week. Picking on the weak offensive teams isn't an exact science, as some defenses are so bad that they just can't get any points. But in general, it's a strategy that works. To start, my favorite strategy is to take whoever plays the worst offensive team Week 1. That is of course subjective so here are some good schedules for the first month of the season.

Cincinnati - @ CLE, vs BAL, vs LAR, @ TEN
New Orleans - vs TEN, @ CAR, @ GB, vs TB
San Francisco - @ PIT, @ LAR, vs NYG, vs AZ
Philadelphia - @ NE, vs MIN, @ TB, vs WAS
Jacksonville - @ IND, vs KC, vs HOU, vs ATL - skip the KC game, and this is beautiful.
Seattle - vs LAR, @ DET, vs CAR, @ NYG

Drafting a top-end defense is preferable, of course, but I usually like to draft position players and let D/ST and K fall to the last two rounds. In deeper leagues, I'm more willing to draft a top-tier defense because there are fewer available on a week-to-week basis.

Bogman's Top 12 Defenses

1. Philadelphia
2. San Francisco
3. Buffalo
4. New England
5. Baltimore
6. Dallas
7. Pittsburgh
8. NY Jets
9. Kansas City
10. New Orleans
11. Miami
12. Seattle

Arizona Cardinals
2022 Per Game Averages
Points Allowed Per Game - 26.4 (31st)
Passing Yards Allowed Per Game - 230.3 (24th)
Rushing Yards Allowed Per Game - 118.6 (14th)
Takeaways Per Game - 1.2 (21st)
Sacks Per Game - 2.1 (23rd)

Key Additions - IDL Kevin Strong, Edge BJ Ojulari, LB Kyzir White, CB Garrett Williams

Key Loses - J.J. Watt retired, IDL Zach Allen, LB Nick Vigil, CB Byron Murphy

Best Defensive Player Budda Baker has requested a trade

Why they get better - New HC Jonathan Gannon was the Philadelphia DC the past two seasons and will try to fix the leaks.

Why they get worse - The defensive line is starved for talent, Baker might hold out, and their best CB left in free agency. The offense will also likely be worse if Kyler Murray misses significant time.

Atlanta Falcons
2022 Per Game Averages
Points Allowed Per Game - 22.7 (21st)
Passing Yards Allowed Per Game - 231.9 (25th)
Rushing Yards Allowed Per Game - 130.2 (23rd)
Takeaways Per Game - 1 (26th)
Sacks Per Game - 1.2 (31st)

Key Additions - DL Calais Campbell, David Onyemata, OLBs Bud Dupree, Zach Harrison, LB Kaden Elliss, CBs Jeff Okudah, Clark Phillips, S Jessie Bates

Key Losses - LB Rashaan Evans, CB Isaiah Oliver, Rashad Fenton

Why they get better - The Falcons bring in former Saints DC Ryan Nielsen and have completely revamped this roster with at least six new starters. They should be better at every level and hopefully put way more pressure on the QB

Why they get worse - They can't get worse than last season with all of these additions

Baltimore Ravens
2022 Per Game Averages
Points Allowed Per Game - 18.7 (3rd)
Passing Yards Allowed Per Game - 229.4 (23rd)
Rushing Yards Allowed Per Game - 89.8 (3rd)
Takeaways Per Game - 1.4 (9th)
Sacks Per Game - 2.9 (5th)

Key Additions - LB Trenton Simpson, David Ojabo (healthy)

Key Losses - IDL Calais Campbell, Edge Justin Houston, Jason Pierre-Paul, CB Marcus Peters, S Chuck Clark

Why they get better - It's going to be tough to see the Ravens get better with a lot of new faces starting but a full season with Roquan and a fully healthy David Ojabo should help.

Why they get worse - Replacing five starters for any team is a lot to ask, so it's not a stretch to think that they get a little worse. Baltimore lost a starter at every position except ILB.

Buffalo Bills
2022 Per Game Averages
Points Allowed Per Game - 19.1 (4th)
Passing Yards Allowed Per Game - 214.6 (14th)
Rushing Yards Allowed Per Game - 104.8 (6th)
Takeaways Per Game - 1.6 (4th)
Sacks Per Game - 2.5 (13th)

Key Additions - LB Dorian Williams, S Taylor Rapp

Key Losses - LB Tremaine Edmunds

Why they get better - If Von Miller comes back sooner than expected and they offset the loss of Edmunds with some combo of Dorian Williams and Terrel Bernard they can get better. Tre White moving away from his big injury and Kaiir Elam going into his 2nd season should improve the Boundry CB spots.

Why they get worse - Tremaine Edmunds was one of the best players on this team and they are replacing him with either a 1st-year starter or a rookie. I'm not optimistic that Miller comes back early, he tore his ACL in Week 12 last season.

Carolina Panthers
2022 Per Game Averages
Points Allowed Per Game - 22 (17th)
Passing Yards Allowed Per Game - 227.5 (22nd)
Rushing Yards Allowed Per Game - 122.6 (18th)
Takeaways Per Game - 1 (26th)
Sacks Per Game - 2.1 (25th)

Key Additions - IDL Shy Tuttle, S Vonn Bell

Key Losses - IDL Matt Ioannidis, LB Corey Littleton

Why they get better - New HC Frank Reich brings former Broncos DC Ejiro Evero to switch this defense to a 3-4. Hopefully getting studs Brian Burns and Jeremy Chinn a little more room to work forces more pressure on the QB resulting in more sacks and turnovers.

Why they get worse - Switching to the 3-4 is a little harder than expected and the Panthers take longer than expected to get their feet under them in the new scheme.

Chicago Bears
2022 Per Game Averages
Points Allowed Per Game - 27.3 (32nd)
Passing Yards Allowed Per Game - 218.6 (18th)
Rushing Yards Allowed Per Game - 157.3 (31st)
Takeaways Per Game - 1.4 (14th)
Sacks Per Game - 1.2 (32nd)

Key Additions - IDL Andrew Billings, Gervon Dexter, Zacch Pickens, Edge DeMarcus Walker, LB Tremaine Edmunds, T.J. Edwards, CB Tyrique Stevenson

Key Losses - LB Nicholas Morrow, Joe Thomas

Why they get better - The Bears added a TON of talent through free agency and the draft, specifically to the DL with three big interior players and a better Edge than they have on the roster in Walker. The LBs allow the Safties to make more plays on the ball, too, without having to pick up so many tackles.

Why they get worse - Can't move down from the very bottom

Cincinnati Bengals

2022 Per Game Averages
Points Allowed Per Game - 19.6 (5th)
Passing Yards Allowed Per Game - 234.2 (26th)
Rushing Yards Allowed Per Game - 103.5 (5th)
Takeaways Per Game - 1.5 (8th)
Sacks Per Game - 1.9 (29th)

Key Additions - Edge Myles Murphy, CB DJ Turner, S Nick Scott, Jordan Battle

Key Losses - S Jessie Bates, Vonn Bell

Why they get better - I can't imagine that the Bengals are so bad at getting to the QB again this season, and it starts there. Cincy adding Myles Murphy should give them a chance to rest Hendrickson and have him gassed up to get to the QB on passing downs.

Why they get worse - The secondary is going through a lot of changes, including both starting Safety spots. And while Eli Apple was bad, he was experienced and leaves behind 1,100 snaps to replace.

Cleveland Browns
2022 Per Game Averages
Points Allowed Per Game - 22.4 (19th)
Passing Yards Allowed Per Game - 196.2 (5th)
Rushing Yards Allowed Per Game - 135 (25th)
Takeaways Per Game - 1.2 (21st)
Sacks Per Game - 2 (26th)

Key Additions - IDL Dalvin Tomlinson, Siaki Ika, Edge Za'Darius Smith, Ogbonnia Okoronkwo, S Juan Thornhill

Key Losses - Edge Jadeveon Clowney

Why they get better - The Browns did a great job of not only adding big guys to stop the run up the middle with Tomlinson and Ika but they also added Hurst and Hill for depth. Clowney was a big loss, but Smith and Okornkwo give the Browns more speed opposite of Garrett, and FS Juan Thornhill should push Delpit into the box to make tackles

Why they get worse - They shouldn't get worse, but the secondary needs to take advantage of the added pressure and get more takeaways.

Dallas Cowboys
2022 Per Game Averages
Points Allowed Per Game - 19.7 (6th)
Passing Yards Allowed Per Game - 207.8 (8th)
Rushing Yards Allowed Per Game - 124.4 (22nd)
Takeaways Per Game - 1.8 (1st)
Sacks Per Game - 3.1 (4th)

Key Additions - IDL Mazi Smith, LB DeMarvion Overshown, CB Stephon Gilmore

Key Losses - none

Why they get better - Adding an upper-echelon CB in Gilmore to go across from Diggs was such a great move. The Cowboys also added depth to the IDL and at LB. There's not a lot of room for growth but they can get slightly better if they can bottle up the run a little better.

Why they get worse - I think it would have to be injuries, the Cowboys are deeper or better at each position going into the start of the season.

Denver Broncos
2022 Per Game Averages
Points Allowed Per Game - 21.2 (12th)
Passing Yards Allowed Per Game - 210.2 (12th)
Rushing Yards Allowed Per Game - 109.8 (10th)
Takeaways Per Game - 1.4 (14th)
Sacks Per Game - 2.1 (23rd)

Key Additions - IDL Zach Allen, LB Drew Sanders

Key Losses - IDL Dre'Mont Jones

Why they get better - I don't think the Broncos can improve on defense unless the offense gets better and puts them in a better position in most games. New HC Sean Payton brings former Broncos HC Vance Joseph back to take over the defense, and Zach Allen and Drew Sanders are great additions

Why they get worse - Sometimes, a new coaching staff can experience growing pains by asking some established players to do new things. The Broncos should be close to what they did last season, as not much has changed in personnel, but Joseph shouldn't shake things up too much or we could see some regression.

Detroit Lions
2022 Per Game Averages
Points Allowed Per Game - 25.1 (28th)
Passing Yards Allowed Per Game - 245.8 (30th)
Rushing Yards Allowed Per Game - 146.5 (29th)
Takeaways Per Game - 1.3 (17th)
Sacks Per Game - 2.3 (17th)

Key Additions - IDL Brodric Martin, LB Jack Campbell, CB Cameron Sutton, Emmanuel Moseley, S Chauncey Gardner-Johnson, Brian Branch

Key Losses - CB Jeff Okuday, S DeShone Elliott

Why they get better - The Lions spent a lot of money and draft capital fixing the pass defense. They will have three players that replace duds in Sutton, Moseley, and CGJ; that doesn't even count the rookie Brian Branch! Jack Campbell fills a spot for the Lions that has needed to be fixed for a while. There's almost no way they don't improve to at least the middle of the pack on defense.

Why they get worse - They likely can't get worse but they didn't do much to fix the IDL and Edge rushers so that could remain pedestrian and hurt the overall growth.

Green Bay Packers
2022 Per Game Averages
Points Allowed Per Game - 21.8 (16th)
Passing Yards Allowed Per Game - 197 (6th)
Rushing Yards Allowed Per Game - 139.5 (26th)
Takeaways Per Game - 1.4 (11th)

Sacks Per Game - 2 (26th)

Key Additions - Edge Lukas Van Ness

Key Losses - IDL Jarran Reed, Dean Lowry, Edge Za'Darius Smith

Why they get better - It's hard to imagine the Packers getting better because they lost more than they gained on the defense and lost so much on offense, with Aaron Rodgers moving on to New York. If Jordan Love can get it together quickly, the Packers could be close to the same.

Why they get worse - The offense is going to put them in worse positions this year, and the already bad run D lost two big pieces in the middle with Reed and Lowry leaving. It's hard to be positive here.

Houston Texans
2022 Per Game Averages
Points Allowed Per Game - 24.7 (27th)
Passing Yards Allowed Per Game - 209.3 (10th)
Rushing Yards Allowed Per Game - 170.2 (32nd)
Takeaways Per Game - 1.6 (6th)
Sacks Per Game - 2.3 (17th)

Key Additions - IDL Sheldon Rankins, Edge Will Anderson, LB Denzel Perryman, Corey Littleton, S Jimmie Ward

Key Losses - Edge Ogbonnia Okoronkwo

Why they get better - The Texans' success will all start with improving the run defense, and they did that by adding Rankins, Ridgeway, and two LBs to give the Texans a decent rotation at each of those spots. Will Anderson should also put some added pressure on the QB.

Why they get worse - They can't get much worse on defense

Indianapolis Colts
2022 Per Game Averages
Points Allowed Per Game - 25.1 (28th)
Passing Yards Allowed Per Game - 209.9 (11th)
Rushing Yards Allowed Per Game - 124.1 (20th)
Takeaways Per Game - 1.2 (20th)
Sacks Per Game - 2.6 (9th)

Key Additions - IDL Adetomiwa Adebawore, Edge Samson Ebukam, CB Juju Brents

Key Losses - LB Bobby Okereke, CB Stephon Gilmore, S Rodney McLeod

Why they get better - The numbers weren't too awful except for the one that counts in PPG. If the offense can improve, the defense should get a little more time on the sideline and hopefully hold them out of the endzone.

Why they get worse - The offense is in transition with a new HC and QB, and the losses of Okereke and Gilmore outweigh the gains by a lot.

Jacksonville Jaguars
2022 Per Game Averages
Points Allowed Per Game - 21.4 (14th)

Passing Yards Allowed Per Game - 238. 2 (27th)
Rushing Yards Allowed Per Game - 113.8 (12th)
Takeaways Per Game - 1.4 (10th)
Sacks Per Game - 2 (26th)

Key Additions - None

Key Losses - Edge Dawuane Smoot, Arden Key, CB Shaq Griffin

Why they get better - They lost depth and didn't add any, the only way they get better is if Travon Walker takes a big leap and stacks up a lot of sacks.

Why they get worse - They were bad at getting to the QB last season and lost their depth pieces in Smoot and Key and then waited until the 5th round to draft a replacement.

Kansas City Chiefs
2022 Per Game Averages
Points Allowed Per Game - 22.2 (18th)
Passing Yards Allowed Per Game - 225.1 (20th)
Rushing Yards Allowed Per Game - 107.7 (8th)
Takeaways Per Game - 1.3 (19th)
Sacks Per Game - 3.2 (2nd)

Key Additions - Edge Charles Omenihu, Felix Anudike-Uzomah, LB Drue Tranquill

Key Losses - Edge Carlos Dunlap, Frank Clark, S Juan Thornhill

Why they get better - The Chiefs lost experience but gained speed at Edge rusher so they should keep pace in pressure. Thornhill was very experienced but I think Bryan Cook could be a better all-around Saftey.

Why they get worse - If one of Karlaftis, Omenihu, or FAU can't get rolling, it will be hard to match last year's sack numbers. The secondary is VERY young and they might need more depth at every spot that isn't LB.

Los Angeles Chargers
2022 Per Game Averages
Points Allowed Per Game - 23.1 (23rd)
Passing Yards Allowed Per Game - 204.4 (7th)
Rushing Yards Allowed Per Game - 144.2 (27th)
Takeaways Per Game - 1.6 (4th)
Sacks Per Game - 2.3 (16th)

Key Additions - Edge Tuli Tuipulotu, LB Eric Kendricks, Daiyan Henley

Key Losses - Edge Kyle Van Noy, LB Drue Tranquill, CB Bryce Callahan, S Nasir Adderley (retired)

Why they get better - The 2022 Free Agents play up to their contracts. Austin Johnson, Sebastian Joseph-Day, and J.C. Jackson were horrendous, but if they play up with the additions of Kendricks, Tuli, and, most importantly, the return of a healthy Joey Bosa, they almost have to get better

Why they get worse - They shouldn't be able to be much worse with all the investments they made, but never count the Chargers out for some big injuries.

Los Angeles Rams

2022 Per Game Averages
Points Allowed Per Game - 22.6 (20th)
Passing Yards Allowed Per Game - 226 (21st)
Rushing Yards Allowed Per Game - 115.1 (13th)
Takeaways Per Game - 1.3 (17th)
Sacks Per Game - 2.2 (21st)

Key Additions - IDL Kobie Turner, Edge Byron Young

Key Losses - IDL Greg Gaines, A'Shawn Robinson, Edge Leonard Floyd, LB Bobby Wagner, CB Jalen Ramsey, Troy Hill, S Taylor Rapp, Nick Scott

How they get better - They don't

How they get worse - The Rams lost their best player at every position except IDL, with Aaron Donald not retiring. There are going to be growing pains.

Las Vegas Raiders

2022 Per Game Averages
Points Allowed Per Game - 24.6 (26th)
Passing Yards Allowed Per Game - 242.9 (29th)
Rushing Yards Allowed Per Game - 122.8 (19th)
Takeaways Per Game - 0.8 (32nd)
Sacks Per Game - 1.6 (30th)

Key Additions - Edge Tyree Wilson, LB Robert Spillane, CB Duke Shelley, S Marcus Epps

Key Losses - IDL Andrew Billings, LB Denzel Perryman, CB Rock Ya-Sin, S Duron Harmon

Why they get better - Tyree Wilson is so good from the start that he and Maxx Crosby pair to make one of the best Edge duos in the league.

Why they get worse - Andrew Billings is a bigger loss than expected, and the Raiders continue to get no pressure while getting worse at LB and DB.

Miami Dolphins

2022 Per Game Averages
Points Allowed Per Game - 24.1 (24th)
Passing Yards Allowed Per Game - 239.3 (28th)
Rushing Yards Allowed Per Game - 103.2 (4th)
Takeaways Per Game - 0.9 (29th)
Sacks Per Game - 2.6 (8th)

Key Additions - LB David Long, CB Jalen Ramsey, Cam Smith, S DeShon Elliott

Key Losses - Edge Melvin Ingram, LB Elandon Roberts

Why they get better - With Jalen Ramsey coming to Miami and Xavien Howard getting back to his prime, the Dolphins improve the passing defense and force more turnovers.

Why they get worse - Howard is subpar again, and there's no improvement from Phillips or Chubb at getting to the QB.

Minnesota Vikings
2022 Per Game Averages
Points Allowed Per Game - 25.4 (30th)
Passing Yards Allowed Per Game - 266.9 (31st)
Rushing Yards Allowed Per Game - 124.2 (21st)
Takeaways Per Game - 1.4 (12th)
Sacks Per Game - 2.3 (20th)

Key Additions - IDL Dean Lowry, Edge Marcus Davenport, CB Byron Murphy, Mekhi Blackmon, Jay Ward

Key Losses - IDL Dalvin Tomlinson, Edge Za'Darius Smith, LB Eric Kendricks, CB Patrick Peterson, Duke Shelley, Cameron Dantzler

Why they get better - A completely remade CB corps greatly improves the Vikings pass defense to just 'middle of the road', and they give up way fewer points.

Why they get worse - The losses along the DL make the Run Defense worse, and they put less pressure on opposing QBs, opening the floodgates for a young secondary.

New England Patriots
2022 Per Game Averages
Points Allowed Per Game - 20.4 (11th)
Passing Yards Allowed Per Game - 216.5 (15th)
Rushing Yards Allowed Per Game - 105.5 (7th)
Takeaways Per Game - 1.8 (2nd)
Sacks Per Game - 3.2 (3rd)
Key Additions - Edge Keion White, LB Marte Mapu, CB Christian Gonzalez

Key Losses - S Devin McCourty (retired)

Why they get better - It's hard to move up from where they were last year, but they added depth everywhere except Saftey, and they were already extremely deep there.

Why they get worse - There's a bigger learning curve than expected without the play-caller McCourty on the field, who hasn't missed a game since 2015.

New Orleans Saints
2022 Per Game Averages
Points Allowed Per Game - 20.3 (9th)
Passing Yards Allowed Per Game - 184.4 (2nd)
Rushing Yards Allowed Per Game - 130.5 (24th)
Takeaways Per Game - 0.8 (31st)
Sacks Per Game - 2.8 (6th)

Key Additions - IDL Nathan Sheperd, Edge Bryan Bresee, Isaiah Foskey

Key Losses - IDL David Onyemata, Shy Tuttle, Edge Marcus Davenport, LB Kaden Elliss

Why they get better - The additions of Sheperd and Bresee help improve the run defense and playmaking Safties Mathieu and Maye start getting their hands on the football.

Why they get worse - The youth movement on the DL might take a little longer to develop than we hope, and Cameron Jordan has to slow down sometime, right?

New York Giants
2022 Per Game Averages
Points Allowed Per Game - 22.8 (22nd)
Passing Yards Allowed Per Game - 213.5 (13th)
Rushing Yards Allowed Per Game - 146.3 (28th)
Takeaways Per Game - 1 (26th)
Sacks Per Game - 2.2 (22nd)

Key Additions - IDL A'Shawn Robinson, LB Bobby Okereke, CB Deonte Banks, S Bobby McCain

Key Losses - S Julian Love

Why they get better - The run defense should see an immediate upgrade with Robinson dropping in the middle of it and Thibs, Ojulari, and Williams all healthy to start the season. With a healthy DL they start punishing the QB and funnel the run toward new tackle machine Okereke.

Why they get worse - The only thing that can make them worse is if the health issues crop up again.

New York Jets
2022 Per Game Averages
Points Allowed Per Game - 18.6 (2nd)
Passing Yards Allowed Per Game - 189.4 (3rd)
Rushing Yards Allowed Per Game - 121.6 (17th)
Takeaways Per Game - 0.9 (30th)
Sacks Per Game - 2.6 (7th)

Key Additions - Edge Will McDonald IV, S Chuck Clark

Key Loses - IDL Sheldon Rankins, Nathan Shepherd, Kwon Alexander

Why they get better - The secondary just needs to start going after the football for the Jets to get better they were already really good last year.

Why they get worse - Letting Rankins and Shepherd walk at the same time could be tough for an already middle-of-the-road run defense, and the secondary was so good last year that matching that is going to be tough.

Philadelphia Eagles
2022 Per Game Averages
Points Allowed Per Game - 19.8 (7th)
Passing Yards Allowed Per Game - 171.6 (1st)
Rushing Yards Allowed Per Game - 121.3 (16th)
Takeaways Per Game - 1.6 (7th)
Sacks Per Game - 3.9 (1st)

Key Additions - IDL Jalen Carter, Edge Nolan Smith, LB Nicholas Morrow, S Terrell Edmunds

Key Losses - IDL Javon Hargrave, LB T.J. Edwards, Kyzir White, S Chauncey Gardner-Johnson

Why they get better - It's hard to imagine they get better, but Carter softens the blow of Hargrave leaving, and they have Jordan Davis until he gets up to speed.

Why they get worse - It's hard to live up to what they did last year anyway, but I'm more concerned with the losses of both LBs and CGJ.

Pittsburgh Steelers
2022 Per Game Averages
Points Allowed Per Game - 20.4 (10th)
Passing Yards Allowed Per Game - 222.3 (19th)
Rushing Yards Allowed Per Game - 108.1 (9th)
Takeaways Per Game - 1.4 (14th)
Sacks Per Game - 2.4 (15th)

Key Additions - IDL Keanu Benton, LB Cole Holcomb, Elandon Roberts, CB Patrick Peterson, Joey Porter Jr, S Keanu Neal

Key Losses - IDL Chris Wormley, LB Myles Jack, Devin Bush, CB Cameron Sutton, S Terrell Edmunds

Why they get better - It all starts with the health of TJ Watt, the LBs are a slight upgrade from what they had last year, and Neal to Edmunds is a downgrade, but Benton could be a big boost for everyone on the line.

Why they get worse - I think the only way the defense goes south is if the new pieces take too long to gel. Watt, Highsmith, Ogunjobi, Fitzpatrick, and Wallace are the only returning starters meaning they are replacing over half of the significant snaps.

San Francisco 49ers
2022 Per Game Averages
Points Allowed Per Game - 17.2 (1st)
Passing Yards Allowed Per Game - 217.2 (16th)
Rushing Yards Allowed Per Game - 82.5 (2nd)
Takeaways Per Game - 1.7 (3rd)
Sacks Per Game - 2.5 (14th)

Key Additions - IDL Javon Hargrave, CB Isaiah Oliver, S Ji'Ayir Brown

Key Losses - Edge Charles Omenihu, Samson Ebukam, LB Azeez Al-Shaair, S Jimmie Ward

How they get better - The 9ers getting a healthy Arik Armstead to pair with newcomer Javon Hargrave and DPOY Nick Bosa will make this the most intimidating DL in the NFL outside of Philly. Ward was a big loss, but Brown is a nice replacement, and last year's 2nd round pick Drake Jackson will replace Omenihu as a starter.

How they get worse - The biggest loss for San Francisco might be DC Demeco Ryans leaving to take the Texans HC job. The CBs remain the weakness, so as long as they aren't horrific, I expect the same as last year.

Seattle Seahawks
2022 Per Game Averages
Points Allowed Per Game - 24.6 (25th)
Passing Yards Allowed Per Game - 217.7 (17th)
Rushing Yards Allowed Per Game - 151.9 (30th)
Takeaways Per Game - 1.4 (12th)
Sacks Per Game - 2.6 (10th)

Key Additions - IDL Jarran Reed, Dre'Mont Jones, Edge Derick Hall, LB Bobby Wagner, Devin Bush, CB Devon Witherspoon, S Julian Love

Key Losses - IDL Shelby Harris, LB Cody Barton, S Ryan Neal

How they get better - The depth of the DL takes some heat off Nwosu, and he can have more shots at the QB. Jamal Adams being healthy the entire season is probably too much to ask, but how about ¾'s of the season? Bobby Wagner back is the cherry on top this defense might be back to scary.

How they get worse - I hate them losing Shelby Harris, but they signed Reed and Jones to replace him, so as long as they can help improve the run defense, there's no way the Seattle defense is worse.

Tampa Bay Buccaneers

2022 Per Game Averages
Points Allowed Per Game - 21.6 (15th)
Passing Yards Allowed Per Game - 208.8 (9th)
Rushing Yards Allowed Per Game - 121.1 (15th)
Takeaways Per Game - 1.1 (24th)
Sacks Per Game - 2.6 (10th)

Key Additions - IDL Calijah Kancey, Greg Gaines, Edge Yaya Diaby, S Ryan Neal

Key Losses - Edge Carl Nassib, CB Sean Murphy-Bunting, S Logan Ryan

LB Devin White has requested a trade

Why they get better - Kancey, Diaby, and Tryon-Shoyinka combine to give the Bucs a got a better push up front with Barrett. Devin White stays and plays up to his potential, Neal replaces Love seamlessly, and the Bucs can stay in the neighborhood of what they did last season.

Why they get worse - Really, it's how often they're going to be on the field that will ultimately kill this defense. Tom Brady retiring and Baker Mayfield replacing him could send this offense back to the stone age, leading to a lot of 3-and-outs on offense and a gassed defense in the 4th quarter.

Tennessee Titans
2022 Per Game Averages
Points Allowed Per Game - 21.1 (12th)
Passing Yards Allowed Per Game - 274.8 (32nd)
Rushing Yards Allowed Per Game - 76.9 (1st)
Takeaways Per Game - 1.2 (21st)
Sacks Per Game - 2.3 (17th)

Key Additions - Edge Harold Landry (health), Arden Key, LB Azeez Al-Shaair, CB Sean Murphy-Bunting

Key Losses - IDL Kevin Strong, Edge DeMarcus Walker, Bud Dupree, LB David Long Jr, S Andrew Adams

Why they get better - Getting Harold Landry back is like adding a top 10 pick or a premium free agent, so that should help get pressure on the QB along with the addition of Arden Key. Hitting those opposing QBs should get the opposing offenses to run a little more, and the Titans were good, allowing the fewest rushing yards in the NFL last year. Sean Murphy-Bunting at least gives them a good CB on one half of the field, all their draft picks have fallen flat lately.

Why they get worse - Were the Titans good at stopping the run or just so bad at stopping the pass teams just threw? It's hard to imagine the worst passing defense being only 12th in points per game allowed two years in a row. I think they'll be better, but many starting spots are being replaced.

Washington Commanders

2022 Per Game Averages
Points Allowed Per Game - 20.2 (8th)
Passing Yards Allowed Per Game - 191.3 (4th)
Rushing Yards Allowed Per Game - 113.3 (11th)
Takeaways Per Game - 1.1 (25th)
Sacks Per Game - 2.5 (12th)

Key Additions - LB Cody Barton, CB Emmanuel Forbes, Cameron Dantzler, S Jartavius Martin

Key Losses - LB Cole Holcomb, S Bobby McCain

How they get better - Give the Commanders a healthy Chase Young, and this defense looks very different. They gave him a reason to put up crazy numbers by declining his 5th-year option and making him a UFA after this season. Washington brought in Forbes to go after the football for a team that was 25th in Turnovers forced last year, and he'll get burned, but they'll take those.

How they get worse - This secondary is very young, and it's hard to imagine them playing up to the standard they set last season. The offense could be worse under 1st-year starter Sam Howell who the Commanders seem set on starting.

Chapter 9

Individual Defensive Players IDP

Scott Bogman

IDP is WAY more fun than drafting an entire defense, and it's time for YOU and your league mates to take the plunge! Start with one at each position and add a flex so only three more roster spots (maybe two more bench spots), and now you get to enjoy both sides of the ball for Fantasy! Once you switch, you'll appreciate the defensive side of the ball way more, and you'll enjoy training camp and the NFL Draft more because you'll be able to think about these guys in context for Fantasy. Do it!

1.5 - solo tackle
.75 - assisted tackle
4 - INT / Sack
2 - FF / FR
1 - PD
6 - TD

There are leagues that offer more points for the 'splash plays' (INT/Sack/FF/FR) or add in TFL, QB Hits/Pressures or other variables, but I like to keep my leagues tackle-heavy. A basic or tackle-heavy scoring system keeps IDPs much lower than their offensive counterparts, keeping fellow managers from being intimidated by having to draft for the defensive side.

I feel like the sweet spot for IDPs on your roster is 7, 2 DL, 2 LB, 2 DB, and 1 Flex. If you are trying IDP for the first time, cutting it to 1 at each position and one flex to get a feel for it might be less daunting.

What to know if this is your first time drafting IDPs

1. Ensure you are familiar with your league's scoring; tackle-heavy and big-play-heavy scoring will have different rankings. Some IDP leagues try to match IDP scoring with their offensive counterparts, so IDPs will have to be drafted higher in those formats
2. Position Value

a. **DL** - Defensive Line offers the lowest PPG for IDP as they are usually sack dependent and have high swings in scoring on a week-to-week basis. If your league separates DE and IDL, you will need to prioritize getting an IDL, as there are very few options that are trustworthy on a week-to-week basis.

b. **LB** - This is where the majority of our production comes in IDP. MLB stack backers and are way less rotational than DL. The scoring I provided had 18 LBs with 10 or more PPG last season, and DL had none.

c. **DB** - Defensive Backs always have a high variance in scoring and should be prioritized last among IDPs. Strong / Box Safety usually give us higher tackle numbers as they are closer to the line, and Free Safeties are more likely to make a play on the ball as they can see a passing play develop in front of them and go after it. CBs are almost all boom-or-bust DB options as they depend on the ball coming their way to either make a tackle or play on the ball and are buried among DB rankings in most scoring formats.

3. IDPs have more variance outside of the very top of the positions than their offensive counterparts, so underperformers and injured players can be replaced quickly.

If you decide to dive into IDPs, I guarantee most of the managers in your league will enjoy it more than drafting a whole team defense. It will make weekly transactions more interesting, AND IDPs can be used to even out trades! It's time to make the plunge!

Defensive Line

1. **Maxx Crosby, LVR** - We already knew that Crosby was an excellent pass rusher, but he added a high tackle total as well in 2022 which vaulted him to #1 on my board. Like any other DL, he has some variance, but he had 8 games over 10 points and only 2 under 5 points. Even though Bosa had 6 more sacks in a tackle-heavy scoring format, Crosby outscored him by 24 points last season because of his tackle total.

2. **Nick Bosa, SF** - Bosa is the pinnacle for sack-heavy formats, but in regular high tackle scoring formats, he still clocks in as the #2 DL. Bosa has been fairly healthy over the last two seasons and just won the DPOY; he's a top IDP option and has room to grow.

3. **Myles Garrett, CLE** - Garrett has averaged at least 7.5 points over the last five seasons and peaked at just over 9 in 2022. I'm particularly interested to see how the additions of Dalvin Tomlinson, Za'Darius Smith, and rookie Siaki Ika to the Browns DL will impact Garrett's production. This could be his best season yet!

4. **Brian Burns, CAR** - Burns is another ascending DL who had career-highs in Sacks and Tackles last season! The Panthers are switching to a 3-4 this season, and hopefully, that will give Burns a little more space to work on Pass Rush Attempts as he was significantly lower in Pass-Rush Win% than the top 3 guys on the list. Burns still has 'meat on the bone' to grow but is firmly 4th on the DL list to me.

5. **Alex Highsmith, PIT** - I know that I appreciate Highsmith more than others because I watch him play every week as a Steelers homer, but I feel like TJ Watt takes a little shine off of him as well. Highsmith set a career-high 14.5 sacks last season, with Watt missing seven games. I'm excited to see what he looks like with a fully healthy Watt across from him and improved interior depth! The best part is you probably won't have to take him anywhere near this high in IDP drafts.

6. **Christian Wilkins, MIA** - Wilkins is the only guy on this list for a while that is not likely to get double-digit sacks, but he had the most tackles among DL (Fantrax eligibility) by a WIDE margin. Wilkins had 98, Crosby had 89, and only 4 others had 70! Wilkins only has 12.5 sacks over his four seasons, but two years in a row, he's had over 90 tackles, so the floor is VERY high.

7. **Aidan Hutchinson, DET** - In his rookie season, Hutch ended inside the top 20 in Total Points and PPG among DL, and there is still a lot of room for growth. Hutch had a ton of swings his rookie season, with seven games of 5 points or less and five games over 10 points. With as much talent as this guy has, I think we'll see a big jump this season, and he ends up as a DL1.

8. **Danielle Hunter, MIN** - Hunter definitely took a step back in 2022, but the floor is still pretty high. Hunter was one of only 8 DL with 60+ tackles and 10 or more sacks in 2022. The Vikings did lose some strength along the line with Dalvin Tomlinson leaving in Free Agency and the trade of Za'Darius Smith to Cleveland, but they have good depth on the interior and signed Marcus Davenport. Hunter isn't a sexy pick, but his floor is higher than a lot of DL ceilings.

9. **Cameron Heyward, PIT** - Heyward is about to enter his 13th season in the NFL, we might have thought he was slowing down in 2020, but 2021 was his highest-scoring season, and 2022 was his 3rd highest-scoring season! The Steelers have added depth and talent to DL and should have a fully healthy TJ Watt going into next season. Heyward will have high tackle totals and flirt with double-digit sacks, so the floor is still VERY high!

10. **Joey Bosa, LAC** - 2022 was rock bottom so far for Joey Bosa as he missed 12 games after tearing his groin in Week 3. Bosa only ended up playing in 5 games and averaged just over 5 PPG. In the previous six seasons for Bosa, he averaged between 9.6-7 PPG and was a DL1 (PPG) every season except 2018, when he missed it by one spot! Bosa has missed games in the past, but with so much variance along the DL, these numbers are too strong to pass up!

11. **Aaron Donald, LAR** - Donald had a stretch of 5 seasons of double-digit sacks come to an end last season. During the five-year stretch for Donald, he averaged between 10.6-7.2 PPG, and while last season he missed the last six games, he still averaged 7.5 PPG, so the talent isn't missing from him. The Rams lost A LOT of talent around him, specifically with A'Shawn Robinson, Greg Gaines, and Leonard Floyd leaving, and it's going to be harder to generate pressure. Donald's still one of the best but with the worsening talent around him on both sides of the ball, he's moving down the list.

12. **Jaelan Phillips, MIA** - Phillips had a top 10 PFF Pass Rush Grade in 2022 but a bottom 10 tackle grade. Phillips is going into his 3rd season, and I expect him to take a jump and put it all together. Phillips was tied for 5th among Edge/DL in QB hits, and I can't imagine the tackling gets worse, so I feel like his arrow is pointing up, and he could be a deal in drafts this season.

13. **Quinnen Williams, NYJ** - Williams flipped a switch in his 4th season for Gang Green by adding five sacks to his previous high of 7 for 12 to go with 55 tackles and a career-high 7.9 PPG. Williams is holding out for a new contract and missed OTAs, so as long as that issue is solved before the season starts, Williams is going to be a hot commodity. Quinnen is starting to peak, and with the Jets adding one of the best passers of all time, the offense might put the defense in a position to chase down the QB more often this season. Williams' floor is already high, and his point ceiling is higher than ever.

14. **DeForest Buckner, IND** - Buckner is as steady as they come on the DL, specifically for an IDL, as he's averaged between 8.5-6.2 PPG in each of his seven seasons. Buckner had a career-high in tackles last season with 74 and has had at least seven sacks in each of his last five seasons. Buck is a high-floor IDL who is less valuable in sack-heavy leagues.

15. **Demarcus Lawrence, DAL** - I think the double-digit sack days are probably done for Lawrence, but in 2022, he proved he can stay healthy and on the field for a full season again and set a career-high in tackles. Playing opposite Micah Parsons could net him more sacks, as Parsons had the most QB Pressures in the league, and Lawrence was tied for 16th. Lawrence is making money getting tackles with run plays coming his way and double teams going to Parsons.

16. **Kayvon Thibodeaux, NYG** - This ranking isn't all optimism, but I really like the way that Thibs ended the season, and there is a lot of room left for improvement for him from his rookie season. Thibodeaux averaged over 13 PPG over his last four games, and even if we took away his TD, he's still well over double-digits. Before that stretch, Thibs only had one game over 6.5 points and one sack. He finished averaging just under 6.5 PPG and had four sacks total. I don't want to project him in the Top 5 off of his big finish, but the ceiling is way higher than 6.5 PPG!

17. **Javon Hargrave, SF** - Hargrave is coming off career-highs in Sacks and PPG playing with the NFC Champs in Philly last season, and SF is one of the few places he could have landed and not lost much steam in my eyes. Philly worked because everyone on the line was really good, and they had depth. With the 9ers, Hargrave will be playing on the line with DPOY Nick Bosa and a healthy Arik Armstead. SF doesn't have the depth Philly does, but no one does! Hargrave should get the same 60-ish tackles, and he might not hit 11 sacks like last season, but it is attainable in SF.

18. **Chris Jones, KC** - I want to put Jones so much higher, but I think we can't get much higher than last season for Jones, and that was with 15.5 sacks. 15.5 tied a career-high sack total for Jones with his 2018 total, and that was the 4th most in the league last season, but the low tackle total limits his ceiling, and 44 was a career-high for him last season. Jones was a DL1 last season in total points and just missed it in PPG, but as my favorite overused saying goes, there's not a lot of 'meat on the bone' to add from last year. The Chiefs will put him in a position to get after the QB, but I don't know that we should lock in 15 sacks, and I don't know where more tackles come from in his 8th season.

19. **Sam Hubbard, CIN** - I thought we might get a little boost from Hubbard last season, and I was a little too high on him, and I almost did the over-correction, but this is about right in line with where he should be going. Three seasons in a row, Hubbard has averaged around 6.5 points, and the last two seasons are almost identical at 60 tackles and 7.5 sacks. Hubbard is good to miss a couple of games (only one full season in his 6-year career) and could have rookie Myles Murphy eat into his snap percentage a little bit. The floor is still pretty high for Hubbard, but the ceiling isn't far off.

20. **Will Anderson, HOU** - The Texans were so excited to draft Will Anderson that they traded back up after getting their QB in CJ Stroud to get Will Anderson to be the Defensive Leader under new HC Demeco Ryans (who is also an LB from Alabama drafted by the Texans). The Texans defense has a long way to go, but Anderson is going to put pressure on the QB immediately. With Ryan scheming things up, no one to threaten Anderson for playing time, and an improved offense, I think he's going to get a lot of on-the-job experience, which is great for us IDPers!

21. **Uchenna Nwosu, SEA** - The Seahawks unlocked something with Nwosu, who spent his first 4 seasons with the Chargers never even getting to 5 PPG, and then he exploded to 7.8 last season with career-highs in tackles (66, his previous high was 40) and sacks (9.5, his previous high was 5) and they added help to the DL. Seattle added vets Dre'Mont Jones, Jarran Reed and spent a 2nd (Derrick Hall), 4th (Cameron Young) and 5th (Mike Morris) draft pick to boost this line. Nwosu hitting his stride and getting more help could see him boost his lofty numbers from last year.

22. **Cameron Jordan, NO** - Jordan is going into his 13th season and is definitely on the 'Back 9' of his career, but his ceiling still seems to be pretty high. According to PFF, Jordan had the lowest Pass-Rush and Tackle grade of his career and his lowest overall defensive grade since 2014. Despite that, Jordan still finished as a high-end DL2 in PPG and Total. The Saints adding Bresee and Foskey should help him out a bit and keep him in this range, but the ceiling isn't far from the floor in year 13 for Jordan.

23. **Chase Young, WAS** - Can he stay on the field? That's the obvious question for Young, who played in 15 games his rookie season, 9 in his 2nd, and was down to only three last season. Young is relatively unknown at this point, but this is right about where I would want to gamble, and with Sweat, Allen, and Payne still on the Washington line, it's not like he'll have to do it himself. This season means so much to him because the Commanders declined his 5th-year option, so he needs to prove the ACL/MCL tear in 2021 hasn't ruined his career. I'll throw a dart if I have a solid DL1 already.

24. **Jeffery Simmons, TEN** - Simmons put up identical back-to-back seasons with 54 tackles and 7.5 sacks (8.5 in 2021), but in 2021, the Titans were solid, and last season, they were awful and lost one of the premier pass-rushers in the NFL before the year even started. I think with what has to be an improved offense and Landry back in the fold, Simmons can improve on a solid season last year and is a borderline DL2/3 type of guy.

25. **Kwity Paye, IND** - Paye took a big step forward in 2022, so this ranking might be a little bit hopeful, but Paye is a solid tackler with room for growth as a pass rusher. I'll pay for some high-floor traits with what should be a career-high in snaps and more chances at the QB.

26. **Jonathan Allen, WAS** - I have a similar feeling with Allen that I do with Chris Jones in that I don't know how much more we can expect from a season with career-highs in PPG. Allen was a DL1 in PPG and DL2 overall, but I'll take a risk on some other Edge guys that I feel are riskier but have a higher ceiling in most cases. Allen is solid to pair with a risky pick if you've waited on DL and drafted Thibodeaux, Anderson, or Young early, and you need some floor.

27. **Dexter Lawrence, NYG** - It almost makes my skin crawl to rank a true NT this high, but Lawrence is the real deal as a pass rusher. Lawrence had the 2nd highest PR grade behind Parsons last season and was top 10 in PR attempts. 7.5 sacks as a Nose Tackle is a lot, but there is room for growth, and this young core of

the Giants line is only getting better. Lawrence also had 68 tackles last season, which keeps the floor pretty high.

28. **Josh Allen, JAX** - Josh Allen is similar to Sam Hubbard for me as I had him a little too high last season and was tempted to do the over-correction, but I feel a mid-range DL3 is about right. Allen might not get 10 sacks, but he's had 7 with at least 50 tackles the last two seasons. There's room to grow, but I expect more of the same with Allen, and I'll be happy if there's significant growth.

29. **Greg Rousseau, BUF** - I expected a bigger jump in snaps for Rosseau in 2022, but with three missed games, he was a little lower and only slightly higher in per-game percentage. Hopefully, this is the season that Rosseau marries his 50-tackle rookie season with his 8-sack 2nd season and vaults himself higher than this. If Von Miller is back quickly, Rosseau could be in for career highs in both.

30. **Josh Sweat, PHI** - I might be a little more nervous with the Eagles losing Hargrave, but they drafted a monster in Jalen Carter, and Jordan Davis getting more snaps shouldn't be much of a downgrade. Reddick is the #1 Pass-Rusher for Philly, but Sweat is the clear #2, and the offense is still very strong, so I see a similar season coming for Josh Sweat.

31. **Azeez Ojulari, NYG** - Ojulari had an injury-plagued 2nd season missing 10 games with an ankle injury, returning to play over 50% of the snaps in only three games before injuring his quad and limping to the finish line. In the three games, Azeez was healthy and played at least 50% of the snaps, he averaged over 10 PPG. The good news is he's still only 23, and if he can get his legs under him, his ceiling is enormous. It's kind of scary to think of the Giants line if Ojulari and Thibodeaux can play a full season with Lawrence and Williams anchoring inside.

32. **Travon Walker, JAX** - The #1 Overall pick in the 2022 draft didn't quite live up to expectations, but the good news is that his cost is probably going to be even lower than this in a lot of drafts, and he's only 22 with a lot of room to grow. Walker was disappointing, but the Jaguars will give him every opportunity to improve this season, and he's going to be nice and cheap.

33. **Leonard Williams, NYG** - Williams suffered through 3 different injuries in 2022, leading to a disappointing 2.5 sack campaign. The good news is that Williams played over 90% of the snaps in the Giants two playoff games and should be good to go to start the season. Williams finished as a DL1 in total points the previous two seasons and should come cheap this year.

34. **Montez Sweat, WAS** - Sweat's best season was in 2020 with a healthy Chase Young, who is (hopefully) healthy going into this season and has something to prove going into a contract year. Sweat has room to grow in tackle totals and sacks, so he's a nice upside play if you already have a solid contributor.

35. **Daron Payne, WAS** - To say I'm not buying a career-high in sacks for Payne might be an understatement. 11.5 for Payne in 2022, when he had averaged just over 3.5 in his first four seasons, seems like too big of a jump to be believed. Payne did also have a career-high in tackles, but he's been between 64-54 all 5 seasons he's played. The line is the strong point of Washington's defense, but I think expecting the same type of numbers Payne put up last year is probably asking too much.

36. **Zach Sieler, MIA** - Sieler isn't going to get many sacks as he only has 10 in 5 seasons, but he's had 60 tackles two seasons in a row and improved his PPG every year of his career. The floor and the ceiling are close, but Sieler plays a high snap% on a very good line.

37. **Trey Hendrickson, CIN**
38. **Zach Allen, DEN**
39. **Grover Stewart, IND**
40. **Marcus Davenport, MIN**

41. **Darrel Taylor, PHI**
42. **Brandon Graham, PHI**
43. **George Karlaftis, KC**
44. **Arden Key, TEN**
45. **Deatrich Wise, NE**
46. **Denico Autry, TEN**
47. **Tyree Wilson, LVR**
48. **Chandler Jones, LVR**

Almost all DLs need to get to the QB to give us some points, but guys like Allen, Stewart, Taylor, Graham, Wise, and Autry are going to be 'high floor' without a huge ceiling, 'steady-Eddie' types. Hendrickson is a PR specialist that won't get tackles; same for Davenport (although I'm excited to see him on a new team); Karlaftis finished the year well and hoped to bring that momentum to a starter's role. Arden Key should see a significant increase in snaps moving to Tennessee, Tyree Wilson is the Raider's big rookie, and while the ceiling is enormous, vet Chandler Jones isn't handing his spot to him just yet!

Carl Granderson, NO
Bradley Chubb, MIA
Drake Jackson, SF
B.J. Hill, CIN
Charles Omenihu, KC
David Ojabo, BAL
Arik Armstead, SF
Carl Lawson, NYJ
Bryan Bresee, NO
Jonathan Greenard, HOU
Kenny Clark, GB
Ogbonnia Okoronkwo, CLE

The DL5 group should see steady production from Granderson, Hill, Armstead, and Clark, but the rest of these guys have wild swing potential. Bradley Chubb underperformed statistically in Miami after being traded; Drake Jackson has huge upside as a starter for SF in his 2nd season, and Ojabo would have been a top 15 pick in last year's draft had he not been injured at his Pro Day and miss the majority of the season. Lawson might be more rotational with young guns Will McDonald and Jermaine Johnson breathing down his neck, Bresee needs to prove his College injuries are behind him, and Greenard needs to prove he's worthy of a starting spot after the calf injury cost him so much in 2022. There's lots of upside but tons of risk in this group and beyond!

Linebackers

1. **Foye Oluokun, JAX -** Oluokun has led all IDPs in scoring for two consecutive years and ranked 11th overall in 2020. He has had back-to-back seasons with over 180 combined tackles and shows no signs of slowing down! His consistency is impressive too, having had only one game under 10 points in 2022 and just four in 2021. He sets the standard for IDPs!

2. **Roquan Smith, BAL -** Roquan is the only other plausible choice for the #1 IDP player this season. Even with the learning curve associated with a new defense in the middle of the season, Roquan still averaged over 13 PPG! He has maintained an average of over 11 PPG in each of his five seasons and scored more points last season than ever before. He is one of the players with the highest floors, and still has 'room for improvement' to achieve even more.

3. **Nick Bolton, KC -** This marks the end of the 'elite' tier. Bolton, being the newcomer, put up 180 tackles last season and led the league in Defensive Snaps with over 1300! Bolton merely needed the snaps to

perform, and he's receiving them. He should continue to be one of the most productive LBs in the league this year.

4. **Bobby Wagner, SEA -** Wagner is back in Seattle after a season with the Rams, and he steps right back into his former role as the main guy. Brooks has been fantastic for the last two seasons, and had he been healthy, I might have given Wagner some competition. However, Brooks tore his ACL in Week 17. Carroll expressed optimism that Brooks can return for Training Camp, but caution might be a better approach. Even if Brooks was active, Wagner IS the superior LB, and they would both be close to 100% snap players. Wagner has averaged at least 11.6 PPG every season since 2016, and I expect this pattern to continue.

5. **Fred Warner, SF -** Fred Warner is as reliable as an LB1 can get. Warner hasn't missed any games and has ranged between 137-118 tackles in all five seasons he's played. He ranked third in snaps for LBs, behind Bolton and Oluokun. While Warner may not have a lot of room for growth, there are no players with a higher floor, barring the four guys ranked above him.

6. **Bobby Okereke, NYG -** Okereke is moving to a team that DESPERATELY needs an LB: the Giants. He should step in and play all the snaps for them from the get-go. While I wouldn't classify him as a great LB like those ahead of him or some below him, he can tackle and is, by far, the best LB on the Giants roster. Okereke exceeded 200 points last season, and I predict he will have many more snaps this season, solidifying his LB1 status.

7. **Logan Wilson, CIN -** Wilson is another 100% snap LB playing for a team with a potent offense. Wilson has averaged over 11 PPG in each of the last two seasons and has an extraordinarily low missed tackle rate. The only downside I see is that he has missed at least one game in each of the three seasons he's played, with only one absence last season being a career low after missing three in his second season and four in his rookie year. His floor is 100 tackles and around 10 PPG, but he has the potential to improve as he's only going into his fourth season.

8. **Devin White, TB -** Devin White is an anomaly because, compared to most of the other guys on this list, he's not a very good player. Based on PFF grades, he's quite underwhelming, and he MISSES some tackles, but he just keeps posting good IDP numbers. The tackles may be too far downfield, but the Bucs keep deploying him, and he keeps amassing them. White requested a trade in April, but GM Jason Licht stated they have 'no interest' in trading him. White should continue to rack up an abundance of tackles too far downfield, further boosting points for our IDP teams.

9. **C.J. Mosley, NYJ -** This ranking almost feels too low for Mosley! He is going into his 10th season, and while players tend to start slowing down at this stage, no one seems to have informed him. After tearing his groin in 2019 and opting out of 2020, he set a career-high in tackles in 2021. He surpassed 200 points for the third time in his career last year and finished 9th among LBs in total points and PPG. Mosley may be entering his 10th season, but he's one of the high-floor LBs and should score 200 points again if he stays healthy.

10. **Josey Jewell, DEN -** Jewell suffered a pectoral tear in the second game of 2021, missing the rest of the season. Then a calf injury sidelined him for the first two games, followed by a knee injury on TNF in Week 5, causing him to miss two more games. However, he went on an absolute rampage after that. Jewell ended up averaging the fourth most PPG among LBs, trailing only Foye, Roquan, and Bolton! While Jewell has had some injuries, he consistently accumulates points when on the field.

11. **Tremaine Edmunds, CHI -** Edmunds has been disappointing for IDP managers, but the Bears gave him $50 million guaranteed, and that money says he's going to be on the field for every snap. He's had at least 103 tackles in all of his five seasons and has a high floor, but there is a chance he adds a little in a new spot. Chicago's putrid offense should keep him on the field for more tackle opportunities!

12. **Zaire Franklin, IND -** Franklin set the Colts' single-season tackle record last season with 167 tackles. Franklin had been a depth guy for the Colts, but when Leonard went down, he stepped in and started tackling everybody. Similar to Devin White, I wouldn't call Franklin a great LB in terms of missing tackles and being well below average in coverage, but Leonard is a huge injury risk, and there is no one with experience behind him on this Colts roster. Franklin doesn't have to be great; he just has to be on the field, getting tackles for us.

13. **T.J. Edwards, CHI -** I almost want to put Edwards ahead of Edmunds, and I wouldn't be surprised if Edwards outscores him, but the ceiling is probably higher for Edmunds. Edwards can call plays immediately for Chicago and has improved his tackle totals in each of his four seasons in the NFL. Edwards probably doesn't have a ton of room to grow with 159 tackles last season, but I think he's going to be underrated in most drafts, and I'll snap him up and let him stack tackles for me.

14. **Cole Holcomb, PIT -** The Steelers punched the reset button on their ILB this offseason. They let Devin Bush walk and cut Myles Jack, then signed Holcomb and Elandon Roberts. Holcomb finished the season on IR with a foot injury but played 100% of the snaps in 6 of 7 games for Washington and averaged over 11 PPG. Holcomb is a high-floor tackle machine that has averaged double-digit PPG the last two seasons and at least 9.1 PPG in each of his 4 NFL seasons.

15. **Dre Greenlaw, SF -** Greenlaw has been a little nicked up over the last two seasons, but the 49ers are really depending on him this season with Al-Shaair walking for Tennessee. Last season, Greenlaw played in 15 games and finished in this exact spot in PPG at LB15. Greenlaw's ceiling is capped with Fred Warner next to him, but he'll put up solid tackle totals as long as he's healthy.

16. **Eric Kendricks, LAC -** Maybe I should have Kendricks higher as he's one of the highest floor players in the league. Kendricks has averaged double-digit points since 2018, and 9.3 PPG in 2017 was his lowest average. Plus, he's had 100 tackles every season after his rookie campaign. The Chargers have been a little snake-bitten with LBs recently, but Kendricks should shake that quickly, and the high floor makes him an easy buy.

17. **Lavonte David, TB -** Lavonte David is the Terminator. This dude is going into his 11th season and has scored over 10 PPG in 9 of his first 10 seasons. David maybe has a little more variance from game to game, but he's still going to stack tackles and be on the field for 100% of the snaps.

18. **T.J. Watt, PIT -** We finally get to an OLB who, for whatever reason, only qualifies at LB with TJ Watt. Let's be clear: if Watt qualifies as a DL or if you use Edge, his value vaults into the Top 5 players because of the lack of double-digit producers on the line (only Crosby last season). Watt suffered pec and knee injuries early that kept him out for seven weeks, and when he came back, he clearly wasn't 100%. I don't think it's reasonable to expect 22.5 Sacks and a DPOY like 2021, but somewhere in the neighborhood of 15 sacks and 60 tackles should have him flirting with a double-digit average.

19. **Micah Parsons, DAL -** Parsons is in the same deal as Watt, if he qualifies at DL, his value skyrockets. In most leagues, Parsons will be an LB only. I don't really understand that, as he played way more snaps on the line than in the box last season (859-195), but that's above my pay grade. Parsons is great wherever the Cowboys put him, but for IDP leagues, he's better getting the tackles. His points per game (PPG) fell from 10.8 in 2021 to 8.8 in 2022 because he dropped nineteen tackles and only added half a sack, playing on the line way more. Parsons said he's been bulking up to play more Edge this season, but Dan Quinn recently called him a pass-rushing LB, so we'll see.

20. **Shaq Leonard -** Leonard was one of the best IDP LBs I've ever seen, and I have him here because if he is healthy, he can be back in the top five LBs. But I don't know how to justify taking a guy who only played three games last season because of a neck injury as an LB1. Leonard has said his surgically repaired ankle will probably never be the same, and he's missed time with back and neck injuries. He's a little too dicey

for me to invest in, and I'll let someone else take the risk and potentially reap the rewards.

21. **Alex Singleton, DEN -** If you listened to the IDP show on FP with Joe and me, you know that we always wondered why Singleton wasn't getting more snaps in Philly. Singleton earned it in Denver last season, and he played much better, lowering his missed tackle rate to 6.5% when it had been well over ten percent in his first two seasons with the Eagles. Denver did draft Drew Sanders in the third round, and he could push Singleton if he's ineffective, but Sanders is a bit of a 'tweener' at LB and Edge and has a lot of work to do to earn a starting NFL spot. Singleton should have this job all year and continue to stack tackles.

22. **Jordan Hicks, MIN -** The Vikings are leaning on Hicks to be the three-down LB with Kendricks gone and Asamoah being a first-year starter. Hicks has averaged at least 9.7 PPG in each of his last four seasons and eclipsed 115 total tackles in each of those seasons. He's steady, not sexy.

23. **Pete Werner -** Werner started the 2022 season on FIRE! He averaged over twelve points per game (PPG) through the first eight games of the season, but hamstring and ankle injuries saw him limp to the finish line and cede snaps to a fully healthy Kaden Elliss. Even missing four games and receiving less than his fair share of snaps, he still ended the year with over nine PPG. With Elliss now in Atlanta, Werner should come into the season healthy. He has a ton of upside, entering only his third year.

24. **Matt Milano, BUF** - Milano and Hicks find themselves in the exact same scenario. Edmunds' departure for Chicago designates Milano as the three-down linebacker (a role he fulfilled last year, anyway), alongside a first-year starter. Bernard, Williams, and Dodson will compete for this position during camp. Despite only achieving hundred-tackle seasons twice in his six-year career, I would anticipate Milano setting personal bests in snaps and tackles this season.

25. **De'Vondre Campbell, GB** - Campbell is a big question mark to me. I want to like him, but he's been all over the place in productivity. In the last six seasons, Campbell only missed games in 2022. He averaged as much as 13.3 PPG in 21, only 7.7 in 18, and was at 9.6 last season. His PFF grades hovered between 56-49 from 2018-2020 and then spiked to 85 in his awesome 2021 season. I expect close to 10 PPG and over 100 tackles but who knows?

26. **Jordyn Brooks, SEA** - Brooks had the 5th most points of any LB and averaged the 6th most PPG in 2022, but he tore his ACL in Week 17. I don't know what to expect, I know guys are recovering quicker than ever, but that's A LOT to ask. I wouldn't be surprised if Brooks starts the year on the PUP and misses the first month. Feel free to move him up the list with more good news as we get closer to Week 1, but I'll drop him in as an early LB3 for now.

27. **Shaq Thompson, CAR -** There was a little rumbling that Shaq might be a cap casualty this offseason, but he ends up staying in Carolina and should be a 100% snap LB. Thompson didn't miss one defensive snap after Week 9 last season and put up a career-high 135 tackles. Luvu will be asked to do more blitzing than Thompson, so his ceiling is a bit capped, but the floor is very high.

28. **Quay Walker, GB** - Walker ended the year on a sour note after being ejected for making contact with a Lions training staff member (weirdly happened in the game against the Bills, too), but he performed admirably in his rookie season outside of those issues. Walker ended up leading the Packers LBs in snaps with Campbell missing games, and he had over 120 tackles, and there's room for growth. My concern is that only two players graded worse against the run in Christian Harris and Kenneth Murray, and they were both moved to rotational with some signings. Walker doesn't have anyone on the roster to challenge him, but plenty of vets are still lurking around in Free Agency. If he's a starter, this ranking could be a little low, but he makes me nervous.

29. **Frankie Luvu, CAR -** Luvu proved to be a significant asset for Carolina! He racked up over one hundred and ten tackles and seven sacks! The only linebackers with more pass rush opportunities on this list so far are Watt, Parsons, and Devin White. Luvu could fare better in the new three-four, but I believe expecting a similar performance is more reasonable. Jeremy Chinn's undefined role is a concern for everyone except Shaq Thompson, but I think Luvu could shift to an outside linebacker role during the snaps when Chinn steps down to a linebacker position.

30. **Jack Campbell, DET -** Despite the draft pundits' disdain for the Lions choosing a linebacker in the first round, Campbell is set to be the immediate number one linebacker and should sideline either Anzalone or Rodriguez. Of course, Campbell has yet to experience a full NFL season, but he's an old-school, tackle-heavy linebacker with two hundred and sixty-five tackles over his last two seasons at Iowa. He could potentially be the play caller from day one.

31. **Demario Davis, NO -** Davis is entering his twelfth season and has achieved over one hundred tackles in each of the last six seasons. Davis isn't expected to set any personal records, but he should be close to the nine-point four points per game he's averaged over the last two seasons. Davis played every single defensive snap the Saints had last year.

32. **Willie Gay, KC -** Gay had a commendable year for the Chiefs, averaging just under ten points per game, and established himself as the number two linebacker for the Chiefs behind Bolton. The only apprehension I have about Gay is that the Chiefs drafted Leo Chenal last year and signed an experienced veteran in Drue Tranquill. As Bolton isn't expected to lose snaps, it could be Gay who does.

33. **Cody Barton, WAS -** Barton experienced a fluctuating season with the Seahawks last year. He started the season as a principal player and was a favored sleeper target by many, including myself. Despite facing coverage issues and losing snaps for about a month, Barton regained his position and put up notable numbers. Even with this minor setback, he averaged over eleven points and now transitions to a Washington team desperately in need of linebacker support following Holcomb's departure. Barton is anticipated to be a three-down linebacker for them from the start.

34. **Matt Judon, NE -** Judon is another frustrating Edge Rusher who, for some reason, only qualifies as a linebacker in certain formats. Once again, if your provider classifies him as Edge/DL, his position on the board rises. Judon managed fifteen and a half sacks, but his value is capped in tackle-heavy formats due to his lack of tackles. Last season, Judon surpassed his previous career-high sack mark with fifteen and a half and was one shy of his highest tackle total at sixty. He contributes more significantly to the NFL than to fantasy football.

35. **Ernest Jones, LAR -** Last season, we thought the stars were aligning for Jones, but perhaps this year will be his moment. Jones achieved one hundred and fourteen tackles last season with no sacks, and he averaged the same points per game as Matt Judon with fifteen and a half sacks and sixty tackles. Without Bobby Wagner, Jones is expected to be a three-down linebacker. Currently, Christian Rozeboom, who has ten snaps in his first two seasons, is listed next to him on the depth chart at inside linebacker. Jones didn't have any games with one hundred percent of the snaps and hovered around seventy-five percent last season. This reflects a bit of the 'someone has to catch passes' argument, but someone also needs to make tackles, even if they're way downfield.

36. **Denzel Perryman, HOU -** Perryman is joining Houston with the expectation of being the lead middle linebacker and significantly improving the run defense that surrendered two hundred and twenty more yards than any other team last season. Perryman is entering a convoluted linebacker situation with Kirksey, Harris, Carter, and rookie To'oTo'o. Perryman concluded last season on the injury reserve but should be ready for camp and to take on the role of Houston's number one linebacker.

37.	Jeremiah Owusu-Koramoah, CLE
38.	David Long, MIA
39.	Jerome Baker, MIA
40.	Devin Lloyd, JAX
41.	Zaven Collins, AZ
42.	Haason Reddick, PHI
43.	Isaiah Simmons, AZ
44.	Quincy Williams, NYJ
45.	Azeez Al-Shaair, TEN
46.	Ja'Whaun Bentley, NE
47.	Nicholas Morrow, PHI
48.	Kyzir White, AZ

The LB4 tier boasts some potential high-performers in JOK, Devin Lloyd, and Al-Shaair. JOK needs to maintain his health as he's missed eight games in his first two seasons. Devin Lloyd needs to elevate his performance because Chad Muma can replace him if he doesn't step up, and Al-Shaair has a clear path to snaps in Tennessee, which should be all he needs to be reliable. Long, Baker, Bentley, Morrow, and White offer limited upside but should yield solid tackle totals. The Cardinals are still deliberating whether Collins should play more as an Edge or Inside Linebacker, so he could rise or fall depending on the clarity we get. It's unclear why Simmons still qualifies as a linebacker, given that he played 409 Slot Cornerback snaps and 297 Box snaps. Reddick should qualify as DL, but for some reason, he's still only a linebacker in most formats. Last year, he managed sixteen sacks while playing 863 DL snaps and only thirteen times in the box.

49.	Harold Landry, TEN
50.	Leighton Vander Esch, DAL
51.	Jamin Davis, WAS
52.	Kaden Elliss, ATL
53.	Germaine Pratt, CIN
54.	Elandon Roberts, PIT
55.	Mykal Walker, ATL
56.	Nakobe Dean, PHI
57.	Divine Deablo, LVR
58.	Patrick Queen, BAL
59.	Anthony Walker, CLE
60.	Za'Darius Smith, CLE

I love Harold Landry, but he's coming off knee surgery and missed the entire 2022 season. Landry's a tweener that can get sacks and tackles, but he has a lot of rust to knock off. LVE, Pratt, Roberts and Anthony Walker are vets that should be steady but have little room for growth. Kaden Ellis followed his former Saints DC Ryan Nielsen to Atlanta. Elliss is probably going to get time at LB and DL, which limits his upside. Jamin Davis, Mykal Walker and Patrick Queen are guys we expected a little more from; this might be their last chance. I don't think Deablo is very good, but he's definitely the best LB the Raiders have and averaged over 10.5 PPG last season. Smith should give us more of the same on the other side of Garrett with a little bit of upside baked in.

Defensive Backs

1. **Derwin James, LAC -** Derwin's skill is so commendable that anything up to five missed games is tolerable. James averaged over twelve PPG and was the fifth highest-scoring Defensive Back (DB) despite missing three games. Derwin will make plays on the ball, but his consistency stems from his ability to tackle. He's had three out of four seasons with more than one hundred tackles, and I expect this to continue as long as he's healthy.

2. **Budda Baker, AZ -** Baker has requested a trade from the Cardinals, but as of now, Monti Ossenfort said the Cardinals have 'no interest' in trading him. Baker is another Box Safety that is going to compile high tackle numbers. He's had at least ninety-eight in each of the past five seasons and peaked at one hundred forty-seven in 2019. Defensive backs are so hit-and-miss that high-tackle Safeties are going to be the first ones picked, and Baker is as consistent as they come.

3. **Jaquan Brisker, CHI -** That sound you hear is me congratulating myself for correctly predicting these next two DB picks from last season. Brisker put up over one hundred tackles and sacked the QB four times. Brisker still has a lot of room to grow, and I expect him to do just that this season and provide us with a high floor at DB.

4. **Jalen Pitre, HOU -** Pitre's numbers outperformed any other DBs last season. He averaged just under thirteen PPG and had two hundred eighteen and a half total points, which was first among DBs and fifth among all IDPs. The reason I don't rank him higher is because I'm somewhat concerned about him losing playing time if he continues missing tackles. Pitre had one hundred forty-seven tackles last season, and he missed over twenty percent! His missed tackle rate was tied for fourteenth worst among qualified players and third worst among DBs. Pitre also shouldn't have to do that much tackling with improvements in the LB core and Defensive Line (DL) in front of him. Demeco Ryans should be able to get the best out of him though, and I'm banking on that.

5. **Antoine Winfield, TB -** Winfield has hovered right around 100 tackles but is yet to get there in his three seasons, but this could easily be the year. Winfield was on pace last season but missed four games with two different injuries (ankle, concussion). Winfield was also the highest-graded Pass Rushing DB and took down the QB 4 times. The floor is extremely high, and he has room to grow going into just his 4th season.

6. **Minkah Fitzpatrick, PIT -** This is probably a homer ranking, but I don't care Minkah is an absolute joy to watch, and he's a stud DB for IDP. Fitzpatrick isn't going to rush the passer, but he's averaged well over 100 tackles the last two seasons and has eight picks, six last season. INTs are less dependable than sacks, but Minkah has averaged 3 per season, and he seems to get better every year.

7. **Talanoa Hufanga, SF -** Hufanga burst onto the scene last season and just missed 100 tackles, had 4 INTs, and two sacks! There is a ton of room for growth, too, with Hufanga only going into his 3rd season. With DB getting deeper every year, this is the gamble I'm looking for. Hufanga was a DB3 in PPG, but with all the injuries at DB, he was a DB1 in total. I think he's going to be a DB1 in pace and total this year.

8. **Kyle Hamilton, BAL -** Hamilton spent the majority of his rookie season as a Slot CB, but with Chuck Clark being moved to the Jets, that should open up the Box S spot for Hamilton, and he should put up some good tackle numbers for Baltimore. Hamilton is going to play all over the place like all of the best Safeties, and his ceiling is crazy high, but he should establish himself with high tackle numbers and a few big plays.

9. **Donovan Wilson, DAL -** Wilson was the #1 Free Agent Priority for Dallas; they gave him the bag, and it's because he can do everything. Wilson built a solid floor with over 100 tackles and then added five sacks, 2 FF, and 1 INT and FR. There's even room for growth with Wilson if he can clean up his missed tackle rate, which has been well over 10% the past three seasons.

10. **Harrison Smith, MIN -** Harrison Smith is an old standby that might be on the 'Back 9' of his career, but he's averaged over 10 PPG in 3 of the last four seasons. Smith is going into his 12th season, and he averages 86 tackles, 3 INTs, 2 Sacks, 1 FF, and 8 PDs. If we cut that sample size to the last four seasons, all those numbers come up except sacks by a half. This floor is higher than a lot of DBs ceilings

11. **Kyle Dugger, NE -** Dugger has been patiently waiting for some snaps to open up in the big Safety rotation in New England. Devin McCourty retiring creates room for 1000 extra snaps to be picked up between Dugger, Phillips, Peppers, and Mills. If those snaps are split evenly, Dugger will be pushing right around 1000 snaps

himself (and potentially more if they aren't split evenly). Adding 25% more to Dugger's totals would easily put him in double-digits on average, and the potential for making a big play expands. There are too many good DBs not to speculate somewhere.

12. **Richie Grant, ATL** - The Falcons signing Jessie Bates should push Grant into the primary Box Safety role where he can stack tackles behind a questionable LB trio in Walker, Anderson, and Elliss. Grant played a decent amount in the Slot and will still get some snaps there, but the Falcons brought in Mike Hughes and drafted Clark Phillips for the majority of those snaps. Grant has a nice opportunity this season, and I'll be snapping him up if he gets too far down the board.

13. **L'Jarius Sneed, KC** - I'm generally against taking a CB this high, and I refuse to put any of them as a DB1 in a 12-team league, but Sneed is a great IDP option. Sneed was the most targeted player in the NFL last season, which led him to get over 100 Tackles, the only CB in the league to do it. Chiefs opponents get down and are forced to pass late, and that's where Sneed makes his money. Sneed is going to get INTs being targeted that often, he came down with three last year, and he can rush the QB a little bit as he was credited with 3.5 sacks last year as well. Sneed is the perfect CB to get points in IDP.

14. **Jordan Poyer, BUF** - It's weird not to have Poyer in the DB1s, but he missed four games last season after not missing a single game in the previous four seasons. More concerning than the injuries is the fact he only put up double-digit totals in 4 games last season. His production slipped a little bit, and I wonder if the mileage is getting to him. He's better than he was last season, but the ceiling is closing quickly.

15. **Jevon Holland, MIA** - Holland is the 2nd true FS behind Minkah on this list and I love his potential. Holland is going into his 3rd season and I think he can improve his missed tackles and he should be given more chances to blitz. He should improve this season, and I wouldn't be surprised if it was exponentially.

16. **Jessie Bates, ATL** - Bates sunk like a stone last season, and it's kind of hard to see why. He missed fewer tackles than he has in the past, he was targeted the 2nd most in his career, and Vonn Bell had fewer tackles as well. My guess is that Logan Wilson and Germaine Pratt had 30 more tackles than they had in the previous season, and BJ Hill having 18 more, were the culprits. Fewer plays were making it to him, and I guess the good news is that he's back to questionable LBs in Atlanta. Bates should be back up to stacking them and making a play on the ball with some rough QBing in the NFC South!

17. **Jeremy Chinn, CAR** - I'm worried about Chinn's role in a new defense. The Panthers signed Vonn Bell, and he's pretty specific as a Safety, so most of those snaps are taken. It could be that he just moves to LB more, but they are going to a 3-4, which means there are only two LB spots inside, and those are going to be occupied by Shaq Thompson and Frankie Luvu. I think he's primarily a Slot CB with Nickel LB duties on 3rd and longs. I'm just not sure what to expect from him if that's the case; I was kind of hoping he'd be traded during the draft, but no such luck.

18. **Jamal Adams, SEA** - "We want to be really careful with this. It's been two years in a row where he's been banged up now." That was the quote from Seahawks GM John Schneider on Jamal Adams when asked about him in mid-May. Adams is an incredible talent that hasn't been able to stay on the field; he tore his quad in week 1 of last season and ended 21 with shoulder surgery. If he can stay on the field, he'll put up high tackle numbers and a ton of sacks as a DB, but that's a big if. He's worth a shot if you've waited too long

19. **Jalen Thompson, AZ** - Jalen has put up over 100 tackles in each of the last two seasons for the Cardinals. Thompson has a Top 10 Tackle Grade among all defensive players, according to PFF, and that is where his bread is buttered. They've never asked him to blitz, and INTs are not very reliable, so the upside is a bit limited for him.

20. **Grant Delpit, CLE** - The Browns didn't sign Thornhill to drop him down into the box, so Delpit is going to be closer to the line and should be able to improve his tackle totals. Delpit will hopefully work on his blitzing skills, and with an improved DL for Cleveland, maybe he can sneak in there a few times. The upside is in the tackle totals, but there's meat on the bone here to add some versatility to the 4th year Safety.

21. **Kevin Byard, TEN** - If you have taken a risk early, then taking Byard as a high-floor DB is a very smart move. Byard hasn't missed a game in his career and has averaged between 10.2-8.6 PPG in each of the past 5 seasons. There's not a lot of room for growth, but the Titan's defense could see the field more than they ever have before, with the offense looking well below average.

22. **Kamren Curl, WAS** - Curl has been a steady producer for the Commanders for the past three seasons and should continue to be the primary Box Safety for them. Curl opened the year missing the first two weeks with thumb surgery and missed the last three games with an ankle injury, but neither were considered long term so he should be good to hover around a 9-10 PPG average again in his 4th season.

23. **Tyrann Mathieu, NO** - Mathieu set a personal best with 91 tackles in his first season in New Orleans! He has also had at least 3 INTs in each of his last four seasons and is a 'chess piece' meaning he lines up everywhere. The Saints used him as the primary Box Safety, but he also played over 300 snaps at FS and over 100 as a Slot CB. Mathieu should put together more of the same this season and sit somewhere in the neighborhood of 8.5-9 PPG with room for some growth going into his 2nd season in New Orleans.

24. **Darrick Forrest, WAS** - Forrest took over as the primary FS for Washington and got 100% of the snaps from Weeks 10-17 and averaged 9.5 PPG. That should be his role for the entire season in 2023, and I expect him to continue to be a very solid contributor. The Commanders did draft Jartavius Martin, a Safety out of Illinois, in the 2nd round, but he's going to be the primary Slot CB. Forrest is probably going to be a bit cheaper than this on draft day but keep him in mind for the 2nd DB spot on your team.

25. **Vonn Bell, CAR** - Bell had a career-low in tackles last season with only 79, he had 114 in 20 and 97 in 21, but we already looked at the Bengals tackle numbers and know the guys in front of him, and Bates took a lot of them. Bell can line up all over the place for Carolina with over 2500 snaps at Box and FS and over 1000 as a Slot CB, but his role should most likely be as their primary Box Safety. Bell took advantage of not having to make as many tackles and had a career-high 4 INTs after only 2 in his previous six seasons. I expect him to be closer to 10 PPG than under eight like last season.

26. **Eddie Jackson, CHI** - I LOVE watching Eddie Jackson play! He's a ball-hawking FS that can score when he gets an INT, and with Brisker being able to play in the Box, Eddie can roam a little more, and it led to the 2nd highest tackle total of his career while missing five games with a Lisfranc injury. The injury didn't require surgery, and he's on track to be ready for OTAs but remember, the Bears added Edwards and Edmunds up front, and they should take a good amount of those tackles for Eddie. Jackson will be boom or bust, but if you want a DB that can win you a week by coming down with an INT, he's your guy!

27. **Rayshawn Jenkins, JAX** - Jenkins makes me a little nervous because he was not very good last season. For IDP managers, he was solid; he averaged over 10 PPG for the first time and some enormous games. The problem for me is that he's the worst-graded DB by a fair margin and was particularly bad in Coverage and Tackle grade, which is exactly what a Safety is supposed to do. Jenkins had an enormous game against Green Bay where he scored over 30 points, and that was over 17% of his total production. If we take that game away, he dips back to under 10 PPG, just over 9. The Jaguars also drafted Antonio Johnson, who could take snaps. Jenkins has a decent floor, but I'll let someone else take the gamble.

28. **Chauncey Gardner-Johnson, DET** - CGJ, played better than this ranking last season, but I think his role will change a little bit in Detroit. With Philly, he moved around, going from FS, where he spent half of his snaps, to a quarter at Slot CB and a quarter at Box safety. The Lions have some musical chairs they can do with a lot of

their DBs, but I think Walker and Joseph are the primary Safeties, with the rookie Branch getting a mix of S and Slot CB snaps with CGJ sticking primarily as the Slot CB. He spent the majority of his snaps at Slot CB in his previous three seasons and never averaged more than 7.3 PPG.

29. **Ryan Neal, TB** - Neal should be the primary Box Safety for the Bucs this year and emerged as a winner after the draft as the Bucs didn't draft competition for him. Winfield will get a fair amount of Snaps in the Box as well, but he's more of a 'chess piece,' and they'll move him into the Slot and probably more at FS with Mike Edwards leaving in Free Agency. Neal should have a career-high in snaps and put up his best IDP numbers yet in Tampa Bay because he probably won't be rotated out nearly as often as he was in Seattle.

30. **Julian Love, SEA** - Love had a career year for the Giants in 2022, putting up over 120 tackles with 2 INTs and a sack, but I'm a little concerned about what his role will be in Seattle. Jamal Adams has had an extensive injury history, but if he's good to go, then Adams is the primary Box Safety, and Diggs should still be the primary FS, and Love will have to roam a bit. The good news is that Love has experience at every secondary spot except as a boundary CB. If/When Adams goes down, Love's value should vault but even with the other two Seattle Safeties healthy, he'll still be on the field enough to contribute.

31. **Kareem Jackson, DEN** - The crusty old vet sticks with Denver going into his 14th season in the NFL! Jackson had his worst IDP output since 2013 last season with Denver, mainly because it was only the 2nd time in his career that he didn't have a sack or INT. I don't think that will happen again, but he's long in the tooth, and Caden Sterns is pushing him; as long as he's on the field, he should be a decent IDP contributor.

32. **Marcus Williams, BAL** - Williams missed a big chunk of the season with a nasty wrist injury after Week 5, which kept him out until Week 14. Williams is going to be the primary FS for Baltimore this season and is in line to see a career-high in snaps with Chuck Clark gone to the Jets. Williams averaged over 10 PPG but was over 20 points in Week 1 and 2, and only playing 10 total games boosted his average. I think he'll be better than his previous Career averages, but he's INT-dependent and will likely continue to be a weekly boom-or-bust option, so pair him with a steady tackler.

33. **Marcus Maye, NO** - Marcus Maye had a rough 2022 season missing seven games with rib and shoulder injuries and had some off-the-field issues as well. Maye could be looking at a short suspension to start the year because of the off-the-field stuff, but as of now, he's going to be healthy and the primary FS for the Saints. Maye gets the majority of his production from tackles but averages half a sack and 1 INT. He's a high-floor player with room for upside, but I don't expect much more than 8 PPG.

34. **Terrell Edmunds, PHI** - I'm torn on Edmunds; he's in a great spot moving to Philly, who just lost their top 4 tacklers in free agency, leaving a lot to be picked up. Edmunds should step in and be the primary Box Safety and sit right behind Morrow and Dean to pick up tackles but watching Edmunds with Pittsburgh, I know that he's rough in coverage, and the Eagles did draft a replacement in Sydney Brown out of Illinois. Edmunds will be on the field as a Nickel LB even if he does end up giving snaps to the rookie, so I have to put him as at least a DB3. Edmunds is a gamble with a high ceiling but could bottom out by losing snaps.

35. **Chuck Clark, NYJ** - Clark is a smart Safety; he wore the green dot communicator helmet and called plays for the Ravens, which is why they didn't want to trade him even after drafting Kyle Hamilton last season. The Ravens pulled the trigger and sent Clark packing to the Jets, where he is slated to be the starting SS. Clark is another S that makes his money getting tackles, and he went over 100 for the first time in his career last season and should have the chance to do the same with the Jets.

36. **Brandon Jones, MIA** - Jones is a risk because he tore his ACL in late October, but he said he's 'way ahead of schedule' in mid-May and that he expects to be ready in Week 1. Obviously, we'll have to keep that in mind but in the eight games that he's played over 90% of the snaps in, he's averaged well over 10 PPG. DeShon Elliott should also see time, so Jones is a risk because of the injury, and a 90% snap rate might be a little high,

but he's extremely productive given the snaps and worth the risk right in this range.

37.   Jayron Kearse, DAL
38.   Dax Hill, CIN
39.   Kerby Joseph, DET
40.   Trevon Diggs, DAL
41.   Taron Johnson, BUF
42.   Xavier McKinney, NYG
43.   Jalen Ramsey, MIA
44.   Xavier Woods, CAR
45.   Tracy Walker, DAL
46.   Tariq Woolen, SEA
47.   Jordan Whitehead, NYJ
48.   Andre Cisco, JAX

In the DB4 range, we have the last of the Safeties that I trust, most are FS that will be more dependent on INTs and get the last shot at tackles like Kearse (more chess piece that will move around for Dallas), Dax Hill, Kerby Joseph, Xavier McKinney (Box), Jordan Whitehead and Andre Cisco. We also have our first boundary CBs in Diggs, Ramsey, and Woolen. I hate rostering boundary CBs because they are boom or bust, all these guys are good enough to not be thrown at a lot if they get hot but most teams don't care who is guarding their #1 WR they are going to throw at them no matter what. CBs are just too INT-dependent to be reliable from week to week and year to year. A strong example would be Trevon Diggs going from 8.5 PPG in 2021 with his 11 INTs to 6.5 last season with only 3. Diggs got better in Coverage Grade, was only targeted 10 fewer times (101-91, top 10 in the league both years), missed fewer tackles, and still lost over 25 points still from his total. Diggs was a better real-life player as are most CBs.

49.   Adoree' Jackson, NYG
50.   Jonathan Jones, NE
51.   Amani Hooker, TEN
52.   D.J. Reed, NYJ
53.   Nick Scott, CIN
54.   Marlon Humphrey, BAL
55.   Sauce Gardner, NYJ
56.   Kenny Moore, IND
57.   Keanu Neal, PIT
58.   Carlton Davis, TB
59.   Patrick Peterson, PIT
60.   Rasul Douglas, GB

The DB5 tier is getting into more CBs that will cover #1 WRs like Jackson, Jones, Humphrey, Sauce, Davis, and Peterson. Sauce is on the border of being unrankable because teams started throwing away from him which could make fellow Jets CB Reed even more valuable. Kenny Moore and Rasul Douglas both are solid tackle options at CB. Hooker, Scott, and Neal are Safeties that currently have a starting job but aren't guaranteed to stick but probably will.

I have the rookie CBs down in the 70s, guys like Devon Witherspoon, Christian Gonzalez, Deonte Banks, Joey Porter Jr, Emmanuel Fores, Tyrique Stevenson, and Juju Brents are all projected to be starters but rookie CBs are often pulled on and off the field. If one of these guys sticks, the Rookie CB rule of QBs targeting them can provide a high floor for them. Drafting them is tough without a guarantee but if you take risks anywhere it needs to be at DB/CB.

Chapter 10

Dynasty '23 Rookies & UDFA

"Top 25 College Prospects"

Ranks, Overview and Player Profiles

Thor Nystrom

QUARTERBACKS

Following a year in which only one quarterback was selected in the top-70 picks, things returned to normal for Superflex owners in the 2023 NFL Draft. Quarterbacks were the first two picks off the board, and three of the top four. Five quarterbacks went in the top-70.

Bryce Young, CAR (Round 1 - Pick 1, Alabama)
Player comparison: Russell Wilson

Young thinks quickly, moves quickly, and has a very quick release. He is so very dangerous in chaos. His right arm isn't a bazooka, but it's twitchy and more than strong enough. Young weighed in at 204 at the NFL Combine but will likely be smaller by the time the season starts, as he was at Alabama. But pre-draft concerns about his durability were overblown. He missed only one game at Alabama, an AC joint sprain to his throwing shoulder injury that usually keeps college quarterbacks out double that time. In Young's return, he threw for 455 yards and two TD with zero INT against Tennessee. Young doesn't needlessly put himself at risk because he senses the pass-rush as good as any quarterback who's entered the NFL the past few years. His preference for staying in the pocket also limits the damage he takes.

Dynasty Value: Carolina probably does not have Young's future WR1 on the roster yet. The better that receiving corps gets in the future, the more dangerous Young will be and the more fantasy value he will provide in kind. Young's full-field vision and ability to create consistently gives his WR corps advantageous YAC opportunities. Young's fantasy ceiling is capped by his preference to stay in the pocket – he will never provide much rushing utility – but he'll start putting up enormous passing numbers once his supporting cast is up to the task.

CJ Stroud, HOU (Round 1 - Pick 2, Ohio State)
Player comparison: Justin Herbert

Stroud is a new-age pocket-passing prototype similar to Justin Herbert. He's well-built. He's got a smooth, juicy arm. Stroud attacks all levels of the field. His combination of touch and placement was the best in the 2023 quarterback class. He's the pitcher who can throw any pitch in any sequence at any time and fit it through a keyhole. Stroud's game — the accuracy, touch and timing — maximizes yards after catch (YAC) opportunities. During the 2022 regular season, the difference between Stroud's work in clean pockets (93.4 PFF grade) and under pressure (42.0) was staggering. He flipped the script in the CFP game against Georgia. Continuing to use his legs to help him solve problems under duress will help inform how far he ultimately gets along his developmental curve.

Dynasty Value: Stroud is going to start from Day 1, but I'd rank him QB3 in this class in terms of dynasty. Stroud's pocket game isn't as good as Young's. And Stroud's lack of running value means his fantasy ceiling is beneath Anthony Richardson's. But Stroud could become a top-10 fantasy QB as Houston adds weapons around him in future years.

Anthony Richardson, IND (Round 1 - Pick 4, Florida)
Player comparison: Daunte Culpepper

Prior to this spring, only 11 players in the history of the NFL Combine who weighed 244-plus pounds had run better than a 4.45 forty – none of them were quarterbacks. Richardson became the first with his 4.43. Richardson also broke the combine record for quarterbacks in both the vertical and broad jumps. He generates easy, natural velocity, and his ability to heave the ball 70-plus yards downfield incentivizes defenses to keep extra help deep, thinning out boxes for the running game. Of course, he's also a one-year starter who wasn't dominant during that one season. A stable environment should help his development. Across Richardson's three years on campus, he played for two head coaches, one interim HC, three offensive coordinators, and three QB coaches. He spent the offseason prior to his lone year as a starter learning an entirely new offensive system under a new staff.

Dynasty Value: When you're on the clock in your fantasy draft, you're going to have to ask yourself the same question the Colts did in late April: Do you feel lucky? More specifically, ask yourself this: Are Richardson's inconsistencies as a thrower, at least to some degree, a function of his overall inexperience and the lack of coaching and system continuity his entire time at Florida? Or are they endemic to his game?

Will Levis, TEN (Round 2 - Pick 33, Kentucky)
Player comparison: Carson Wentz

Levis is a big, strapping quarterback with solid athleticism and an enormous right arm. Levis is experienced at full-field reads after playing in a pro-style system under former Rams OC Liam Coen. He has strong accuracy when his mechanics are sound. But especially when he's under duress, Levis eschews those, leading to maddening bouts of inaccuracy. His decisions under pressure also need to improve. The rushing element of his game waned last year, likely due to injuries, but Levis should be expected to leave the pocket more in the NFL. Levis has less work to do on his mechanics than Anthony Richardson, but some of these complicating factors may prevent him from getting there. Levis is also far less comfortable and accurate throwing left than right due to the truncated follow-through on his compact motion in that direction. NFL defenses will pick up on that quirk quickly and exploit it – much as they did to Mitch Trubisky, who had a similar peccadillo coming out.

Dynasty Value: The arm and athletic profile imbue a reasonable ceiling. But don't underestimate the work that needs to be done, and don't overrate the athleticism when considering his fantasy import – he's no Josh Allen in that area. Levis is an upright, north-south runner who doesn't break many tackles. In the NFL, Levis is going to have to learn to surrender, or he's going to get hurt from the big collisions his style leads to. Especially because I worry he's going to be taking damage in the pocket, at least initially.

Hendon Hooker, DET (Round 3 - Pick 68, Tennessee)
Player comparison: Jordan Love

Hooker is a fun combination of dual-threat utility and deep-ball acumen. He is very cognizant of his base when throwing — diligence that led to improved accuracy throughout his career. Light came on after transferring to Knoxville. But that was under ideal circumstances. Josh Heupel is one of the sport's best play-callers. The Vols' scheme cleaved the field in half for Hooker. Boy was Hooker confident reading his half of the field — but you very rarely saw his head move from one side of the field to the other. While he's a strong runner, Hooker is strangely very little threat to actually throw while on the move. Per PFF, Hooker completed only seven passes over 151 dropbacks the past two years when moved off his spot. NFL scouting reports will zero in on that tendency and instruct defenders to trigger downhill the instant Hooker moves off his spot until he proves he can throw on the run.

Dynasty Value: Hooker will turn 27 during his second season – and his rookie season is a wash on account of the late start he'll get while finishing off his ACL rehab. Hooker is a studious learner who improved every year in college – but he's entering the unknown, having played in a see-it, throw-it offense in college that offered advantageous first-read throws on a silver platter. Stay away.

Jake Haener, NO (Round 4 - Pick 127, Fresno State)
Player comparison: Brock Purdy

Haener's weaknesses – lack of size, athleticism, arm strength – are eerily similar to Purdy's. But so too are his strengths, from the accuracy, to the experience, to leadership qualities, to how teammates rave about him, right down to the football-Mensa S2 scores. Both are zippy rhythm throwers who command every huddle they step into.

Dynasty Value: Limited upside, but Haener is worth a stash if your league's rosters are big enough. If everything breaks right, Haener is Purdy – a caretaker who could produce numbers if surrounded by an elite collection of skill players.

Others who were drafted:

Stetson Bennett, LAR (Round 4 - Pick 128, Georgia)
Player comparison: Ian Book

Aidan O'Connell, LV (Round 4 - Pick 135, Purdue)
Player comparison: Mike White

Clayton Tune, ARZ (Round 5 - Pick 139, Houston)
Player comparison: Josh McCown

Dorian Thompson-Robinson, CLE (Round 5 - Pick 140, UCLA)
Player comparison: Tyler Huntley

Sean Clifford, GB (Round 5 - Pick 149, Penn State)
Player comparison: Colt McCoy

Jaren Hall, MIN (Round 5 - Pick 164, BYU)
Player comparison: Shea Patterson

Tanner McKee, PHI (Round 6 - Pick 188, Stanford)
Player comparison: Mike Glennon

RUNNING BACKS

For the first time since the 2018 draft, a running back was selected in the top-10. And for the first time since 2010, two running backs were selected in the top-12. The 2023 RB class was lauded both for its high-end talent and also its depth, and that was the story on Draft Weekend: Seven different RB were selected in the top-90 (three last year), and, while things slowed down briefly for the position in Round 4, the only RB selected that stanza has a chance to start immediately (Roschon Johnson). This RB class is a grand buffet for fantasy players.

Bijan Robinson, ATL (Round 1 - Pick 8, Texas)
Player comparison: Edgerrin James

Robinson is a good-sized back with incredible feet and a diverse skillset. Last year, he broke PFF's single-season record with 104 missed tackles forced. Robinson is a slalom runner who is at his freakiest when he's stringing together moves in space. He slices this way and that, and jet-pack accelerates out of those cuts to put the entire defense on a balancing platform. The movement makes it exceedingly difficult for defenders to square him up, and the horsepower helps him shirk off-angle attempts, leading to the prolific broken tackle numbers. Robinson's added value in the passing game is what cemented his draft day value – and what makes him such an exciting fantasy asset. He's a clever route-runner who is very difficult to stay with in the open field, especially when he's flash-bang accelerating out of those violent cuts. His hands are extremely reliable. Over 77 career targets, Robinson dropped only four balls – including zero last season.

Dynasty Value: It's been several years since a fantasy prospect this exciting entered the NFL. Robinson can do it all. He can handle heavy usage as a runner. And he'll help turbo-charge your passing-game out of the backfield, in the slot, and even out-wide. He's the toy you want to play with all the time, and because of that, he suffered multiple nagging injuries in college. If you're lucky enough to draft him, be wise enough to prioritize the acquisition of Tyler Allgeier as a cheap insurance policy on your investment.

Jahmyr Gibbs, DET (Round 1 - Pick 12, Alabama)
Player comparison: Dalvin Cook

Gibbs is a horror-movie slasher in the open field – he's so very difficult to touch. And he's even more difficult to catch. His 4.36 speed ranked second among running backs at the NFL Combine behind Devon Achane (4.32). He's got a special ability to access that pronto. Gibbs is a forward-thinking route-runner who keeps his cards close to the vest until the time comes to leverage his movement to shake his man, hit the jets, and separate. His size wasn't an impediment to catching balls in traffic in a limited sample in college. Last year at 'Bama, Gibbs took 87 snaps in the slot or out wide – expect more of that at the NFL level. He is also a skilled returner who should see plenty of special teams work at the next level.

Dynasty Value: Gibbs is an exciting talent – but he's also a usage-specific player. He disappointingly weighed into the NFL Combine at 199 pounds. His touches need to be monitored at the next level – and they will be… Detroit will platoon him with David Montgomery. Gibbs will likely be peppered with targets, jacking up his PPR value. But he likely won't get much goal line work, cutting down on his conventional fantasy utility.

Zach Charbonnet, SEA (Round 2 - Pick 52, UCLA)
Player comparison: Todd Gurley

Charbonnet is a muscular north-south thumper with a twist. He's always attempting to get defenders to over-commit in the beats before contact, and he has a deep bag of tricks to evade them once they do. He was top-20 in the nation in elusive rating last year. Charbonnet is a surprisingly reliable receiver for a back of his ilk. Over 90 collegiate targets, Charbonnet had only five drops. He's a taller back with long arms – the catch radius is atypically large for a running back, and he's reliable with anything you can drop into that net. He averaged over 10 yards after catch (YAC) last year, and posted a career mark of 9.1. Charbonnet ranked No. 13 last season in PFF receiving grade among all qualifying FBS running backs.

Dynasty Value: Charbonnet's dynasty value was severely complicated by his landing spot in Seattle. He and Kenneth Walker's games have some overlap – both are strong runners who don't have much interest in pass-blocking. Charbonnet is the clearly superior receiver, and Seattle's administration spoke immediately after drafting him about its desire to improve the screen game. But then the Seahawks took Kenny McIntosh late in Day 3 – a pure receiving back. On situation alone, he needs to be downgraded from a fantasy perspective.

Kendre Miller, NO (Round 3 - Pick 71, TCU)
Player comparison: Jamaal Williams

Miller is a hard-charging runner with a fearless bent to his game. He's not an elite athlete, but Miller makes more defenders miss than most backs his size. It'll be interesting to see how much receiving value he ultimately provides at the next level. TCU simply didn't use him in this area a ton (29 catches over three seasons). At the next level, Miller needs to work both on broadening his route-running possibilities, and also tighten up his ball security (one fumble every 60 carries in college).

Dynasty Value: Miller absolutely has NFL-starter ability if he can fix the ball security issue and prove he can run routes out of the backfield. In New Orleans, he'll start out behind Alvin Kamara and the player I comped him to, Jamaal Williams. Miller has a year to prove to New Orleans that he indeed can start at the next level.

Tyjae Spears, TEN (Round 3 - Pick 81, Tulane)
Player comparison: Travis Etienne

Spears is a natural. He consistently turns defenders into Keystone Cops in the open field with his explosion, cuts, and deceleration. Defenders' feet tend to get stuck to the turf or tied into knots as Spears introduces his newest Guitar Hero flurry. Was his hit-and-miss work as a receiver in college a usage thing? Spears was dangerous after reeling the ball in – but he dropped four balls the last two years on 43 targets despite a -0.6 aDOT.

Dynasty Value: What'll be interesting to see is if Spears can polish off his receiving skills to get on the field on passing downs early in his career, because obviously he'll be on a roster with Derrick Henry next season. The other interesting thing to monitor his rookie year will be whether he can impress enough in his looks to incentivize the Titans to move on from Henry after the 2023 season. Spears' medical concerns are real, but I'm bullish on his talent.

Devon Achane, MIA (Round 3 - Pick 84, Texas A&M)
Player comparison: Jahvid Best

Achane has devastating, game-breaking speed. The defense is aware of his whereabouts at all times because of that. He's so very dangerous when he turns the corner and hits the jets. Unique for a smaller back in that he doesn't dance around much. Achane was underutilized by A&M as a receiver. He's an underrated receiver. Soft hands. Too often, when used in this phase in college, Achane was the last-resort checkdown. May have dormant potential in this area. Natural return ability. Goes down on contact.

Dynasty Value: The majority of Achane's touchdowns in the NFL will likely be long ones. Your concern as a dynasty owner is that his per-game touches will be limited, and he won't see many goal line touches. Achane weighed into the NFL Combine at 188 pounds, but he'll likely play around 185. The touches need to be carefully chosen because the frame can only sustain so much contact each game before his special-sauce movement begins to depreciate.

Tank Bigsby, JAX (Round 3 - Pick 88, Auburn)
Player comparison: Sony Michel

Bigsby boasts a plus-plus combination of vision, instincts, lateral agility, and contact balance. Bigsby is a fabulous inside runner who takes what is given when it's there. Upfield ethos. Varies tempo. Not only runs through soft contact, but doesn't get knocked backwards by hard contact – he's taking the extra yards each run by falling forward. The big question here is Bigsby's hands. He had eight drops for a non-ideal 11.6% drop rate on catchable balls at Auburn despite an aDOT of -1.7. And while Bigsby improved as a pass-blocker last season – into the "adequate" range – he mightily struggled in this phase over his first two seasons.

Dynasty Value: Bigsby is a legitimate threat to Travis Etienne on early-downs from Day 1. And perhaps that's the entire point. You can bet that Bigsby is going to vulture touchdowns early-on, as well. Whether he ultimately develops into a bell-cow will come down to whether he can ever offer anything on passing downs.

Roschon Johnson, CHI (Round 4 - Pick 115, Texas)
Player comparison: Brian Robinson Jr.

Power runner with a versatile skillset. A tall back, Johnson gets a good vantage point of the line of scrimmage, and he uses that for a full-spectrum shot of his options. Strong short-area burst for a big fella, hits the hole with authority. Johnson doesn't have the wear-and-tear that other collegiate backs enter the NFL with due to his situation behind Bijan Robinson. Johnson showed a little more as a receiver in 2022, but at this time, he's only a dump-off and run-after-the-catch guy in that regard. Johnson's real utility on passing downs is in pass-pro. He'll throw his body around and drop a linebacker.

Dynasty Value: What a perfect landing spot! Not only does the Bears landing spot afford Roschon the opportunity to potentially start from Day 1, it by extension offers the chance to establish himself as the long-term starter.

Israel Abanikanda, NYJ (Round 5 - Pick 143, Pittsburgh)
Player comparison: Tevin Coleman

Upright sprinter with good vision who is looking to hit home runs every time he steps to the plate. Abanikanda is young – he won't turn 21 until October – and he's an explosive athlete with 4.44 wheels whose pedal-to-the-metal game evokes Tevin Coleman, for better or worse. Both players pick down the line looking not for small profits, but for long slants of daylight they can accelerate through like a tall-running Sonic the Hedgehog.

Dynasty Value: Long-term – and perhaps even at some point during his rookie campaign – I like Abanikanda's odds of usurping Bam Knight and Michael Carter on the Jets' hierarchy behind Breece Hall. Abanikanda can return kicks, and he's a passable receiver. But it's hard to see him ever being more than a situational-touch RB2 behind the bellcow Hall, needing the sort of injury Hall suffered last year to step into a significant role.

Chase Brown, CIN (Round 5 - Pick 163, Illinois)
Player comparison: Myles Gaskin

Brown is a burner who can create issues for the defense when he gets a crease with space in front of him. But Brown doesn't break many tackles, and he's not overly-gifted at making defenders miss in the hole. More problematically, as he transitions to the NFL, Brown is a mediocre receiver, and he's a poor pass-blocker. Something is going to have to change in that regard for Brown to carve out a long NFL career.

Dynasty Value: Brown exited the draft as a popular sleeper due to landing spot. But he's a one-note runner whose game lacks nuance. Unless he finds that, his situation is irrelevant.

Eric Gray, NYG (Round 5 - Pick 172, Oklahoma)
Player comparison: Clyde Edwards-Helaire

Very elusive with unpredictable movement patterns. Gray strings together combo moves and surprises defenders with his next step. Doesn't let you square him up. Strong receiver with a nice set of hands. Don't keep him back in pass-pro or your quarterback will get flattened. Also lacks pop as a runner. Can be finished by one defender – if they can hit him square, which is a chore.

Dynasty Value: I like Gray's game. But I don't see an RB1. Still, Gray will almost assuredly be a valuable NFL platoon back.

Evan Hull, IND (Round 5 - Pick 176, Northwestern)
Player comparison: Joseph Addai

Myths about Hull's speed were dispelled at the NFL Combine – Hull ran a 4.47 and checked in as a 92nd-percentile size-adjusted athlete. He's an extremely skilled receiver. Last year, he was near tops in this class in targets, receptions, aDOT, and snaps in the slot or out wide. Detail-oriented route-runner regardless of deployment. Hull has slick, reliable hands. As a runner, he's a muscle-packed back with one-cut suddenness. Hull's cuts are sudden, and he has the contact balance to absorb blows and stay on his feet. Hull quickly deciphers if the initial plan is viable. when it's not, has the ability to flatten down the line of scrimmage and steal the edge.

Dynasty Value: Hull projects as a strong complimentary back for the Colts – and he might even develop into a little more down the road. Short-term, I think Hull is going to force his way onto the field situationally as a rookie because of his receiving skill.

Chris Rodriguez, WAS (Round 6 - Pick 193, Kentucky)

Player comparison: Benny Snell

Rodriguez isn't trying to deceive you. He isn't trying to outrun you. He's a built-Ford-tough grinder with good vision and power who always takes a profit – but doesn't have the athleticism to pilfer anything more than that.

Dynasty Value: Rodriguez was a bellcow at Kentucky who won you over with his reliability and efficiency – not only did he keep the offense on schedule, but he very rarely fumbled. He could hang around as a grinder, but he'll never have much fantasy utility.

Deuce Vaughn, DAS (Round 6 - Pick 212, Kansas State)
Player comparison: Tarik Cohen

Vaughn popped up at the same school that produced Darren Sproles and produced almost as much nostalgia as he did all-purpose yardage the past-three seasons. It's not instructive to think of him as Sproles, a historic outlier. He's more like Tarik Cohen. And there's reason to think he could hang in the NFL. Despite his size, Vaughn handled enormous usage while never missing a game.

Dynasty Value: Very nice landing spot, on a Cowboys team that really only has Tony Pollard above him. I think Vaughn carves out the same sort of situational role as a rookie that he's going to have for the duration of his rookie contract.

Zach Evans, LAR (Round 6 - Pick 215, Mississippi)
Player comparison: Player comparison: Elijah Mitchell

Bursty back who gets through holes quickly to challenge the second-level. But despite Evans' pedigree, he's never equaled the sum of his parts. Evans runs high and without a sense of tempo, seemingly divorced from the rest of his teammates. He's also an inconsistent receiver – flashes interspersed with too many drops to make them worth it – a non-factor blocker, and he has little experience on special teams, meaning that he has to make it as a runner.

Dynasty Value: Dynasty owners are excited about Evans, having read about his pedigree, and knowing full well the advantageous situation he's entering. I'd offer a bit of a buyer-beware. Both colleges that brought Evans in ended up being thoroughly underwhelmed by his services.

DeWayne McBride, MIN (Round 7 - Pick 222, UAB)
Player comparison: Tyler Allgier

Power runner with oodles of make-you-miss ability. Tackle-breaking machine. Now-you-see-me-now-you-don't foot-in-the-dirt cuts. Always fighting for yards upfield. Bounces away from off-angle shots and keeps trucking upfield. Fearless north-south runner. Shows the patience and vision to allow his blocks to set up, the feet to quickly change paths into a more enticing hole, and the power and contact balance to power through arm tackles. Just may never provide anything on passing downs. If there's good news, it's that his work in pass-pro has improved. Last season, McBride got 28 more reps in that phase than he had the two seasons combined before it. McBride responded by improving his PFF pass-pro grade from 47.7 to 64.4.

Dynasty Value: Better than several guys drafted above him. Because – at least coming out of college – he's a better early-down back than Alex Mattison and Ty Chandler. With one caveat: McBride must cut down on fumbling. A part of that comes from his never-say-die running style, which allows defenders to poke balls out while he's extending plays. McBride won't catch many balls – a warning for PPR owners – but he should make up for it around the goal line.

Others who were drafted:

Lew Nichols, GB (Round 7 - Pick 235, Central Michigan)

Player comparison: Brandon Bolden

Kenny McIntosh, SEA (Round 7 - Pick 237, Georgia)
Player comparison: Mewelde Moore

WIDE RECEIVERS

All spring, draft pundits panned this receiver class. On the last weekend of April, the NFL took its turn, not selecting the first one until the 20th pick. That was the latest the first receiver had been selected since the 2019 draft – the last time a receiver class had been so widely pillaried. The only first-rounders in that 2019 class were Hollywood Brown and N'Keal Harry. And while plenty of duds came later, Day 2 also provided several gems: Deebo Samuel, A.J. Brown, D.K. Metcalf , Diontae Johnson, and Terry McLaurin. We'll find out if this eye-of-the-beholder class can similarly provide bonanza value to dynasty owners who choose correctly on draft day.

Jaxon Smith-Njigba, SEA (Round 1 - Pick 20, Ohio State)
Player comparison: Adam Thielen

Smith-Njigba lacks deep speed and burst, but is a next-level route-runner with legitimate joystick agility. He tosses throwing windows wide open in rhythm with the quarterback's drop-back off violent route breaks in the intermediate area – many of his receptions are uncontested layups. JSN has natural ball skills. Reels it in clean on the move and like he's on a treadmill, with no speed lost. He's an underrated source of YAC despite his lack of juice, because JSN often gets the ball in space, where he returns the joystick moves, along with a preternatural feel for bodies in space.

 Dynasty Value: Opposing coordinators are going to have to pick their poison, much as they did when JSN was at Ohio State, working inside Garrett Wilson and Chris Olave: Do we give our outside corners over-the-top help on DK Metcalf and/or Tyler Lockett? If we do, JSN has oodles of intermediate space to clown his overmatched defender one-on-on in. If we don't, we're exposed to one-on-one shots downfield whenever Seattle wants them. Smith-Njigba could climb into the top-12-15 dynasty wide receiver ranks by the end of his rookie season.

Quentin Johnston, LAC (Round 1 - Pick 21, TCU)
Player comparison: Taller Brandon Aiyuk

A muscled-up 6-foot-3 long-strider with a 40.5-inch vertical and a 6-foot-8 wingspan, Johnston is a natural deep threat who is a proven winner in jump-ball situations, reeling in at least seven contested targets every year he was on campus. Johnston's ability to pop-the-top opens up his intermediate machinations. He's a fearless runner with arm-tackle-breaking muscle and one-cut shake.Johnston ranked No. 11 in missed tackles forced and No. 6 in YAC per reception last season. This aspect of his game wasn't discussed nearly enough during the pre-draft process – but the Chargers were keenly aware of it, discussing it immediately upon drafting him.

Dynasty Value: Johnston was my WR1 in this draft class. He's not a perfect prospect, but he had the highest ceiling in the class. He won't catch the same amount of balls as JSN – but the yardage and touchdowns could ultimately be higher.

Zay Flowers, BAL (Round 1 - Pick 22, Boston College)
Player comparison: T.Y. Hilton

Flowers is a lightning-in-a-bottle mover. If you whiff trying to jam Flowers off the line, you've put yourself in a hole that you aren't going to be able to dig yourself out of. Over the last three seasons, Flowers 47.3% of Flowers' receiving yards (1,285) came on receptions occurring 20+ air yards downfield. He made 16 contested catches over those three years. He adjusts to balls well downfield, and he attacks the ball in the air. Flowers consistently succeeded in college despite coming from a rancid offensive environment, and you can play him anywhere.

Dynasty Value: I'm bullish on Flowers' ability to stress NFL defenses, my only question, from a fantasy perspective, is expected volume these next few years – because of that, he'd be my dynasty WR4.

Jordan Addison, MIN (Round 1 - Pick 23, USC)
Player comparison: Tyler Lockett

Addison won the Bilitnikof at Pitt in 2021 as a slot before transferring to USC for a season on the boundary with Caleb Williams at USC last season. He isn't big, he isn't a burner (4.49), and he's only a decent athlete. He controls his body like he's playing himself in a video game. Addison knows to shake corners free. He needs to, because he struggles in traffic. Last year, his first on the boundary, he went just 2-for-9 in contested circumstances.

Dynasty Value: This was a bonanza of a landing spot – Addison is never going to leave the field, he's always going to draw the CB2, and he's never going to draw double-coverage nor extra-help. There are limitations in the profile that will prevent Addison from becoming an NFL superstar. But he should be an outstanding second-fiddle – exactly what Minnesota drafted him to be.

Jonathan Mingo, CAR (Round 2 - Pick 39, Mississippi)
Player comparison: Chase Claypool

Mingo soared up my board along with everybody else's following a sensational pre-draft process. That was necessary after he never equaled the sum of his parts at Ole Miss. Mingo tested as a superb athlete in a huge physical package. At 220 pounds, Mingo ran a 4.46, with broad and vertical jumps that both checked in 94th-percentile-or-better when adjusted for size. And he has experience both inside and outside – last year, the Rebels gave Mingo 261 snaps in the slot.

Dynasty Value: Long-term, I see him as a No. 2 receiver with the versatility to win inside or outside. Mingo's ability to mix-and-match will give the Panthers plenty of options in finding compliments for him in Bryce Young's future receiving corps.

Jayden Reed, GB (Round 2 - Pick 50, Michigan State)
Player comparison: Skyy Moore

Short, quick-footed boundary receiver who plays ticked-off. He knows how to run a route and get free. I appreciate how he attacks the ball downfield. And also how he tries to start lunchroom brawls with his man every blocking assignment. But he has physical limitations that may make his transition difficult – even Big 10 press-corners could impede him off the line. He also has mediocre hands and isn't much of a YAC guy.

Dynasty Value: My eval didn't leave me as high on Reed as others – certainly not as high as the Packers. But Green Bay has signaled that it views Reed as an immediate starter in its swiss cheese receiving corps.

Rashee Rice, KC (Round 2 - Pick 55, SMU)
Player comparison: Nate Burleson

He has experience both in the slot and the outside — 69.0% of his college snaps came on the boundary. Rice is not the shiftiest. As he himself stated by omission during his draft process by skipping the 3-cone. A staple of his game is the north-south explosion to get downtown (92nd- and 98th-percentile jumps). Rice's long arms come in handy in the sky. Rice converted 32-of-66 (48.5%) contested-catch opportunities in college.

Dynasty Value: Tremendous landing spot – both short-term and long-. Rice has the starter kit to develop into a legitimately dangerous NFL WR2. In this case, that means second-banana to Travis Kelce on Patrick Mahomes' Merry Band. There's a legitimate path to that here – and early.

Marvin Mims, DEN (Round 2 - Pick 63, Oklahoma)

Player comparison: Santonio Holmes

Despite having 36% or more of his usage coming on throws 20+ yards downfield all three seasons of his career — for a bloated career 16.7 aDOT — Mims dropped only seven balls on 177 career targets (5.4% drop rate). Mims very clearly lacks play strength. And at Oklahoma, he got free releases. In the NFL, he will be tested in this regard. Corners will play up and try to get their hands on him. Will being jarred along the route be a fly in the ointment against bigger, stronger NFL corners?

Dynasty Value: He's too athletic and too skilled not to be a long-time, solid starter. Some people didn't love his landing spot. But he'll force his way into that lineup. Watch.

Nathaniel Dell, HOU (Round 3 - Pick 69, Houston)
Player comparison: Hollywood Brown

Pint-sized slot with lightning-in-a-bottle movement skills. NFL corners will try to bully Dell off the line. If they can't, they're in a world of trouble – nobody can stick with him in space. His jumbo production at Houston was no fluke. Across five games against P5 bowl teams and Cincinnati's CFP team the past two years, Dell posted a 39-582-3 receiving line.

Dynasty Value: Dell has the footwork to get off the line and the ball skills to win downfield, despite his size. The thing to keep an eye on will be if he can get off the line against high-end NFL press corners. If he can, he will succeed early, often, and for a long time. I'm buying in fantasy.

Jalin Hyatt, NYG (Round 3 - Pick 73, Tennessee)
Player comparison: John Ross

Hyatt is a one-trick pony and a one-year wonder. His production in college was mostly isolated to five games against poor competition and/or after Cedric Tillman got injured. Hyatt was never pressed off the line in college. He is an unproven route-runner. He's going to have to learn how to win downfield in contested situations, and his raw route-running game is going to have to be fleshed out to force defenders to respect him in the intermediate area.

Dynasty Value: Ultimately, Hyatt went in the draft where he always should have gone. If nothing else, when he's on the field, NFL defenses will have to respect his speed. Everything else about his game is a leap of faith that the Giants will have to try to flesh out on the practice field. Let another owner spend the capital that it will acquire to buy him.

Cedric Tillman, CLE (Round 3 - Pick 74, Tennessee)
Player comparison: Courtland Sutton

Tillman is big, strong, long, springy, sure-handed, and north-south explosive. He is a proven downfield home-run hitter against the best competition college football had to offer over the past two years. Of his 101 catches between 2021-2022, 19 were contested. Tillman was insanely efficient on his force-fed targets, dropping a mere 4.4% of catchable career targets. Tillman wasn't hiding. He was the clear WR1 alpha on the boundary. He's not the most elusive receiver, with mediocre agility. But his route breaks are crisper than he's given credit for because of his attention to footwork and his plus body control.

Dynasty Value: Tillman is going to be a prototypical NFL WR2. His downfield utility speaks for itself and will translate due to Tillman's body control and ball skills in traffic, and he's going to move chains at the next level.

Josh Downs, IND (Round 3 - Pick 79, North Carolina)
Player comparison: Sterling Shepard

Downs is a competitive, feisty presence out of the slot. He's super quick off the blocks and brings 4.4 wheels on the back end. Downs has choppy feet, and the acceleration/deceleration combination of a SeaDoo. This gets him into-and-out-of breaks lickity-split. He's assuaged size concern by winning in congested quarters, converting 13-of-18 contested-catch opportunities last year.

Dynasty Value: Downs got dinged during the process because he's confined to the slot – he's tiny, and you can jam him off the line. But he's an extremely reliable player who is going to start immediately in the NFL and handle heavy usage for a long time.

Michael Wilson, ARZ (Round 3 - Pick 94, Stanford)
Player comparison: Braylon Edwards

Wilson boasts a premium mix of size, strength, movement, body control, and hands. It's rare to see a receiver his size decelerate with the force and precision that Wilson does. His profile is very quick and explosive, with a 97th-percentile 10-yard split and 84th-percentile vertical. But he's a modest long-strider who ran a 4.58.

Dynasty Value: The opportunity is there. Can Wilson kick the injury bug to take advantage of it? He would have gone higher in April had he not struggled to stay on the field in college due to a variety of nagging injuries.

Tre Tucker, LV (Round 3 - Pick 100, Cincinnati)
Player comparison: Calvin Austin III

Pure-speed receiver who the Raiders undoubtedly prioritized on Friday due to Tucker's added special teams utility. I was surprised he was drafted as high as he was because I question Tucker's ball skills.

Dynasty Value: The Raiders intend to have Tucker return kicks next season – that's a spot in the NFL that has lost its luster in recent years. A road onto the field as a regular is more precarious. Stay away.

Derius Davis, LAC (Round 4 - Pick 125, TCU)
Player comparison: Kavontae Turpin

Davis is an undersized speed merchant who explodes to top-gear very quickly. Unfortunately, he has very inconsistent hands. He's also a one-note route-runner who is full-throttle all the time. He was drafted where he was because he's a very-skilled return man with five career punt-return TD in college.

Dynasty Value: Davis' speed and return utility give him NFL value. But for him to ever have any fantasy value, he's going to have to flesh out the rest of his game. Leave him for someone else.

Charlie Jones, CIN (Round 4 - Pick 131, Purdue)
Player comparison: Hunter Renfrow

Extremely good route-runner who doesn't waste any time getting to work, or any motion during his routes. Won at all three sectors last year over heavy usage. Jones' biggest weakness is his lack of play strength – Penn State CB Joey Porter Jr. showed that you can disrupt his entire game when you can harass him off the line. But Jones' game should translate smoothly to the slot at the next level.

Dynasty Value: It seems pretty obvious that the Bengals drafted him to be Tyler Boyd's replacement. Boyd will be an unrestricted free agent following the 2023 season.

Tyler Scott, CHI (Round 4 - Pick 133, Cincinnati)
Player comparison: Corey Coleman

Scott was surprisingly drafted after his collegiate teammate Tre Tucker despite possessing ball skills that Tucker doesn't. Scott is small and lacks strength, but he's a burner with a jetpack off the line. He can be interrupted by contact, but when he frees himself to open catch-points, his hands are reliable.

Dynasty Value: While Tucker went higher than expected, Scott dropped lower than experts predicted. That said, this is a decent landing spot. The Bears no longer have a vacant starting WR spot after trading for DJ Moore.

Justin Shorter, BUF (Round 5 - Pick 150, Florida)
Player comparison: Equanimious St. Brown

One of the bigger receivers in this class, checking in at 6'4/229 with 82 ⅜" wingspan. Shorter is a downfield jump-ball guy. He has solid speed (4.55) and explosion for his size, and he has hops and a very long arm when he goes to the sky for a rebound. The rest of Shorter's game is unrefined — he and underwhelmed in college.

Dynasty Value: I get that he's a former five-star recruit who is big and reasonably athletic. But he's a one-trick downfield guy who was chosen to be Gabe Davis insurance. You can do better in dynasty drafts.

Dontayvion Wicks, GB (Round 5 - Pick 159, Virginia)
Player comparison: Van Jefferson

Last year, Wicks' 23.1% drop rate and 21.4% contested catch rate were both among the worst in this entire receiving class. Neither were issues the year before. I think he was undervalued this spring during the draft process. Wicks is an underrated athlete (9.17 RAS) because the thing he lacks is speed (4.62). He's an awesome route-runner.

Dynasty Value: Sleeper alert. The Packers have very little in the receiver room. Circumstances conspired against Wicks last year. But he has an NFL-caliber frame, and his route-running is going to play at the next level.

Puka Nacua, LAR (Round 5 - Pick 177, BYU)
Player comparison: Discount Deebo

Similar to Michael Wilson, Nacua was underappreciated in the spring and went under-drafted because his career was dogged by nagging injuries. BYU had great fun using Nacua's diverse skillset on gadget plays — end-arounds, screens, quick-throws, and plays that decoyed off those ones. Nacua is more dangerous with the ball in his hands than most receivers in this class who are this size. When the Rams' coaching staff called Nacua to inform him they were picking him, they gushed about their intention to get similarly creative with him.

Dynasty Value: This was a perfect landing spot for one of my favorite sleepers in this entire draft class. Nacua is extremely skilled, if not a touched-by-god-athlete. Therefore, he needed both a smart offensive staff that knew how to use him, as well as an opportunity to show his stuff on an NFL field. Check and check, going to the Rams.

Parker Washington, JAX (Round 6 - Pick 185, Penn State)
Player comparison: Amari Rodgers

Those that do NFL Draft evaluation have "types" at every position, and, by extension, whatever the opposite of that is. The latter is Parker Washington, for me — a manufactured-touch slot. Washington came into the process hailed as a Day 2 pick. I railed against that in the spring. I ranked him WR28 — No. 204 on my board overall. The NFL ended up agreeing with me, with Washington going No. 185.

Dynasty Value: I'm not a believer in Washington's game. Even if I was, he would need Kirk off Jacksonville's roster to get a shot, and his upside would remain capped because he doesn't win downfield.

Kayshon Boutte, NEP (Round 6 - Pick 187, LSU)
Player comparison: Robert Woods

Boutte burst onto the scene as a Freshman All-American during the truncated 2020 COVID season. That year, he looked like the second-coming of Stefon Diggs, a kinetic mover with superb ball skills. But the next year, he wasn't playing as well prior to suffering a season-ending broken ankle in October. Last season, returning from that, he neither moved around on the field as he had previously, nor appeared as engaged. Then Boutte went out and posted a rancid 4.99 RAS during pre-draft testing.

Dynasty Value: Total shoot-the-moon shot on upside – just like New England's pick on him. Is Boutte's lethargic movement on the field last year and poor pre-draft testing explainable by the after-effects of his 2021 ankle surgery? Or was he an overrated athlete to begin with who now has durability and work-ethic questions?

Trey Palmer, TB (Round 6 - Pick 191, Nebraska)
Player comparison: Jalen Reagor

I've seen Palmer before, I know his game well – he's Jalen Reagor. Palmer is an inch taller, and Reagor is 10 pounds heavier. But everything else jives – including an identical 6.18 RAS. Both are explosive, sleek athletes with speed and explosion for days. Both showed tantalizing flashes with the balls in their hands in college. Both imbue you with they-can-take-it-to-the-house-from-anywhere dreams. But both categorically lack ball skills. Palmer's mission in the NFL: Fix the thing that Reagor hasn't been able to.

Dynasty Value: This goes back to the thing above – can Palmer's hands and overall ball skills improve? If they can, he's going to be a home run-hitting NFL starting receiver. The far more likely outcome – as we saw with Reagor – is that they don't, which'll render Palmer something similar... a backup receiver and special teams returner.

A.T. Perry, NO (Round 6 - Pick 195, Wake Forest)
Player comparison: Devante Parker

Perry is a true outside receiver with proven downfield chops to go up and get it. Perry's 6-foot-9 wingspan was more than five inches longer than the aggregate average of the rest of the pre-draft top-20 receivers on my board. Perry labors to quickly change directions — his 46th-percentile short shuttle was easily his worth test — and is only so-so in contested situations, which he'll see more of in the NFL.

Dynasty Value: Perry was unfairly nitpicked because of the offense he came out of. But because of that, it's true that he'll probably need a year to acclimate into an NFL system while polishing off his route-running technique and adding a few more branches to his route tree. He's a good dynasty buy.

Xavier Hutchinson, HOU (Round 6 - Pick 205, Iowa State)
Player comparison: Jakobi Meyers

Hutchinson's game is all based on physicality. He has a bully-ball ethos after the catch, breaking tackles and fighting for extra yards. Iowa State manufactured him a lot of touches simply so he could convert them into manufactured yards via upfield fight. This is why his touches were always manufactured, downfield, or on slants.

Dynasty Value: There are a lot of things to like about Hutchinson — the biggest of which is his YAC ability. But as a big slot without an explosive element, what sort of value is he bringing to the table?

Andrei Iosivas, CIN (Round 6 - Pick 206, Princeton)
Player comparison: Breshad Perriman

At the FCS level, Iosivas was a threat to take it to the house from anywhere on the field if you hit him on the hands in stride. Two areas the Bengals will get to work on with Iosivas immediately: route-running and physicality.

Iosivas' breakneck speed toggles significantly down out of breaks before requiring multiple steps to build back up. Iosivas also needs to work on his release package.

Dynasty Value: Long-term stash. Iosivas has all the physical ability in the world, he'll be working with one of the league's best quarterbacks, and he should be locked onto a roster spot in the short-term, considering Cincy's lack of WR depth.

Others who were drafted:

Demario Douglas, NEP (Round 6 - Pick 210, Liberty)
Player comparison: Jaelon Darden

Antoine Green, DET (Round 7 - Pick 219, North Carolina)
Player comparison: Steve Breaston

Colton Dowel, TEN (Round 7 - Pick 228, Tennessee-Martin)
Player comparison: Justin Watson

Jalen Brooks, DAL (Round 7 - Pick 244, South Carolina)
Player comparison: Isaiah Ford

Ronnie Bell, SF (Round 7 - Pick 253, Michigan)
Player comparison: Freddie Mitchell

Grant DuBose, GB (Round 7 - Pick 256, Charlotte)
Player comparison: Cody Lattimer

TIGHT ENDS
Dalton Kincaid, BUF (Round 1 - Pick 25, Utah)
Player comparison: Todd Heap

A late-bloomer who played only one season of high school football, Kincaid announced his arrival by erupting for a 70-890-8 receiving line and third-team All-American honors last season. Kincaid is big, rugged, fluid, skilled-to-the-gills, and he boasts one of the surest sets of hands at the position to enter the NFL over the past five years. He's a route-running natural, with nimble feet and a natural feel for spacing, tempo, leverage. He threatens deep so quickly. Where Kincaid truly stands out is the ball skills. Last fall, Kincaid posted PFF's No. 1 receiving grade and No. 3 hands grade in this tight end class. Kincaid logged a miniscule 2.8% drop rate in 2022 while going 9-for-18 on contested catches. Only two tight ends in the 2023 TE class had bigger mitts than Kincaid's 10 1/4-inch hands. And last year, Kincaid finished No. 2 in this TE class with 16 missed tackles forced.

Dynasty Value: After the wide receiver run in Round 1 of the NFL Draft, the Bills pivoted and simply selected arguably the best "pass catcher" on the board. I think Kincaid will be Buffalo's second-most-targeted receiver next season. Don't worry about Dawson Knox. Dawson Knox will remain inline. Kincaid is going to take over the slot, and also be deployed situationally out-wide.

Sam LaPorta, DET (Round 2 - Pick 34, Iowa)
Player comparison: Owen Daniels

LaPorta converted 74 of 111 catches into first downs or touchdowns (66.7%) the past two seasons in the worst offensive environment that you can possibly imagine. LaPorta's special sauce comes when he has the ball in his hands, a tank with riding-mower agility. Last year, LaPorta was No. 1 among all FBS tight ends with 20 missed tackles forced, the fifth-highest single-season TE total over the nine seasons PFF has tracked the stat. For a 240-plus pounder with plus-play strength, LaPorta is shockingly agile and sudden. Both with the ball in his hands, and also along his route path. LaPorta is an extremely versatile weapon. Last year, his snaps were distributed as evenly as any tight end in this entire draft class – 30.1% slot, 20.5% wide, and 48.4% inline. I'd use him predominantly in the slot. But he isn't going to embarrass himself inline, and he can also swing out-wide work.

Dynasty Value: I banged the drum for Sammy Ballgame all process. He was TE3 on my board with a bullet – in my industry, I was out on a limb. Turns out, the Lions were even higher on him than me. Now it's time for you to believe the hype. His athletic profile compares favorably to George Kittle, the last under-drafted Hawkeye tight end to who turned into a fantasy juggernaut. WR Jameson Williams is suspended for the first six games, and the Lions' TE room behind LaPorta is a wasteland. Prioritize LaPorta in your draft – be okay "overpaying". It won't be an overpay once the season begins.

Michael Mayer, LV (Round 2 - Pick 35, Notre Dame)
Player comparison: Jason Witten

Mayer is considered the greatest tight end in Notre Dame history. Mayer's body positioning at the catch point could be a Tom Emanski video, the quintessential basketball rebounder boxing out his man. A marked-man who was often double-teamed in Notre Dame's offense last season, Mayer went 17-of-26 (65.4%) in contested catch situations while posting a strong 5.6% drop rate. The issue with his game is that he lacks downfield athletic oomph, and he doesn't easily create separation.

Dynasty Value: Michael Mayer may have slipped to the second round of the NFL Draft, but that does little to dim his fantasy outlook. Jimmy Garoppolo, already familiar with Rob Gronkowski, doesn't need to be taught how to throw to tight ends who prefer defenders close when the ball is delivered. Mayer's receiving ceiling may be capped, but his floor is quite high.

Luke Musgrave, GB (Round 2 - Pick 42, Oregon State)
Player comparison: Cole Kmet

Musgrave is a very good athlete who ran a 93rd-percentile 4.61 forty with 96th-percentile-or-higher splits and 90th-percentile-or-higher jumps during the pre-draft process. But Musgrave made only 13 collegiate starts with just 47 catches over five years on campus. Musgrave suffered a season-ending knee injury in Week 2 last year. Musgrave is big, he's athletic, and he's a skilled receiver downfield. But he posted a career drop rate of 16.1% in college, including a career 7-for-18 in contested situations, he doesn't break tackles (a mere two over his entire career), and Musgrave's average agility doesn't buy him much separation in the intermediate area – especially since his route-running mechanics remain raw.

Dynasty Value: Musgrave is a moldable, athletic ball of clay for the Packers' coaching staff. Green Bay's tight end depth chart was a joke before the Packers doubled-up at the position with Musgrave and Tucker Kraft. Musgrave has a great opportunity here. But the profile is too risky for my blood. I'd let someone else take the risk.

Luke Schoonmaker, DAL (Round 2 - Pick 58, Michigan)
Player comparison: Dalton Schultz

Schoonmaker has an ideal build, and he surprised during pre-draft testing by checking in as a 98th-percentile size-adjusted athlete. He's a true inline tight end who blocks his tail off. His athleticism as a receiver on tape is sporadically apparent, mostly in Schoonmaker's leveraging of it to try to get free. But his ball skills are wildly inconsistent, and he has a poor feel for timing along his route path, which contributed to losing trust from his quarterbacks at Michigan.

Dynasty Value: After the Cowboys were sniped by the Bills for Dalton Kincaid in the first round of the NFL Draft, they deferred the tight end need to the second round by reaching for Schoonmaker. I get what they saw. Schoonmaker is experienced. He's from a tight end factory. He's big. And a strong athlete. And he's a true inline guy. But he's got a long way to go as a receiver – and he'll be 25 in September. I'd let someone else draft him.

Brenton Strange, JAX (Round 2 - Pick 61, Penn State)
Player comparison: Jonnu Smith

Strange is a sawed-off, muscled-up move-TE who started three years at Penn State. Strange is a very good blocker no matter where he's deployed, which is going to help keep him on an NFL field regardless of situation. He was underutilized as a receiver in Penn State's system, never eclipsing even a 10% target share in any single season at Penn State. But Strange did show very strong hands in his opportunities, with a miniscule drop rate.
Dynasty Value: Strange ran a 4.7 forty with an 86th-percentile burst score. He's a linear athlete that has heavy feet in close quarters – the complication to the "fix his route-running" plan. The other complication is Evan Engram. If Engram signs a long-term deal to stay in Jacksonville, Strange's dynasty value is nuked. Don't overpay.

Tucker Kraft, GB (Round 3 - Pick 78, South Dakota State)
Player comparison: Dawson Knox

Kraft weighed into the NFL Combine at 254 pounds and posted 73rd-percentile-or-higher showings in every single pre-draft test. He's a coiled spring off the snap. He used his combination of strength and acceleration to earn separation in college, which happened so often he actually got dinged for it in the spring. Kraft isn't a nuanced route-runner. He never had to be. He's going to need to learn to leverage his brain and feet as much as his athletic powers to gain NFL separation. If he learns to do that, the Packers stole him in Round 3.

Dynasty Value: Don't be surprised if this Green Bay draft class becomes the second coming of Hayden Hurst and Mark Andrews, with Kraft becoming the better NFL player. Kraft will drop into the third round or later of most dynasty rookie drafts. At that point, take the shot on and stash him on your taxi squad. The upside is real.

Darnell Washington, PIT (Round 3 - Pick 93, Georgia)
Player comparison: Martellus Bennett

Washington is a true "third offensive tackle" as a blocker. That part of his eval was unimpeachable. The other part – the part relevant to fantasy owners – is filled with holes. Washington caught only three career balls 20+ yards downfield. The argument is that he played with Brock Bowers. My counter is that if Washington was good at it, he would have gotten more looks. Beyond that, Washington had a 10.0% career drop rate in college, which is concerning for an intermediate safety blanket that doesn't win downfield. And for all Washington's athletic gifts and power as a blocker, he's not overly hard to tackle.

Dynasty Value: If Washington can't win downfield, and if he isn't going to gain many yards after the catch… he simply must cash in the opportunities he's presented with over the middle of the field to at least cash in freebie yards. I want to be clear: We aren't even there yet. Yes, Darnell Washington tested like an alien. But his reported "medicals" aren't the only reason he dropped. He's going to go higher in your dynasty draft than his actual worth due to name value.

Cameron Latu, SF (Round 3 - Pick 101, Alabama)
Player comparison: Kaden Smith

Latu isn't a great athlete (4.78 forty), and he's on the smaller side. But on the field, he's an efficient mover with a crafty game. Latu's brains were confirmed when his leaked S2 score of 98 matched Bryce Young's herculean showing. Latu needs to continue working on the technical aspects of his craft that he can control, as well as clean up his concentration drops (seven drops, 56 catches the past two years).

Dynasty Value: Latu immediately becomes TE2 on San Francisco's roster behind Mr. George Kittle. Last year, Tyler Kroft assumed that role, and was mostly used as a blocker. Latu should eventually open up more possibilities for a 49ers' offensive braintrust that fetishizes multiplicity. Latu is a dynasty flier with some potential long-term upside if he can convince the 49ers in the next year or two that he has what it takes to be Kittle's heir apparent.

Others who were drafted:

Josh Whyle, TEN (Round 5 - Pick 147, Cincinnati)
Player comparison: Coby Fleener

Will Mallory, IND (Round 5 - Pick 162, Miami)
Player comparison: Michael Egnew

Payne Durham, TB (Round 5 - Pick 171, Purdue)
Player comparison: Gavin Escobar

Davis Allen, LAR (Round 5 - Pick 175, Clemson)
Player comparison: Cole Turner

Elijah Higgins, MIA (Round 6 - Pick 197, Stanford)
Player comparison: DeAndre Smelter

Zack Kuntz, NYJ (Round 7 - Pick 220, Old Dominion)
Player comparison: Mike Gesecki

Brayden Willis, SF (Round 7 - Pick 247, Oklahoma)
Player comparison: Josiah Deguara

2023 Defensive Rookie Rankings

IDL

1. Jalen Carter | Eagles | Pick: 1.9
Georgia | 6031/314 | RAS: N/A | Comp: Ndamukong Suh

2. Calijah Kancey | Buccaneers | Pick: 1.19
Pittsburgh | 6005/281 | RAS: N/A | Comp: John Randle

3. Bryan Bresee | Saints | Pick: 1.29
Clemson | 6055/298 | RAS: 9.59 | Comp: Jerry Tillery

4. Adetomiwa Adebawore | Colts | Pick: 4.110
Northwestern | 6015/284 | RAS: 9.72 | Comp: Osa Odighizuwa

5. Mazi Smith | Cowboys | Pick: 1.26
Michigan | 6026/323 | RAS: N/A | Comp: B.J. Raji

6. Keeanu Benton | Steelers | Pick: 2.46
Wisconsin | 6034/312 | RAS: 8.9 | Comp: Maliek Collins

7. Siaki Ika | Browns | Pick: 3.98
Baylor | 6032/335 | RAS: 2.75 | Comp: Damon Harrison

8. Zacch Pickens | Bears | Pick: 3.64
South Carolina | 6035/300 | RAS: 9.22 | Comp: Nick Fairley

9. Gervon Dexter Sr. | Bears | Pick: 2.53
Florida | 6055/310 | RAS: 9.52 | Comp: Montravius Adams

10. Moro Ojomo | Eagles | Pick: 7.249
Texas | 6024/293 | RAS: 9.16 | Comp: Amobi Okoye

Edge

1. Will Anderson Jr. | 1.3 | Pick: HOU
Alabama | 6036/253 | RAS: N/A | Comp: Von Miller

2. Tyree Wilson | 1.7 | Pick: LV
Texas Tech | 6061/271 | RAS: N/A | Comp: Chandler Jones

3. Lukas Van Ness | Packers | Pick: 1.13
Iowa | 6046/272 | RAS: 9.39 | Comp: Trey Hendrickson

4. Myles Murphy | Bengals | Pick: 1.28
Clemson | 6045/268 | RAS: 9.71 | Comp: Rashan Gary

5. Nolan Smith | | Pick:
Georgia | 6021/238 | RAS: 9.23 | Comp: Haason Reddick

6. Keion White | Patriots | Pick: 2.46
Georgia Tech | 6046/280 | RAS: 9.92 | Comp: Carlos Dunlap

7. Will McDonald IV | Jets | Pick: 1.15
Iowa State | 6034/241 | RAS: 9.67 | Comp: Julian Peterson

8. Felix Anudike-Uzomah | Chiefs | Pick: 1.31
Kansas State | 6031/255 | RAS: 8.73 | Comp: Harold Landry

9. Isaiah Foskey | Sants | Pick: 2.40
Notre Dame | 6047/262 | RAS: 9.61 | Comp: Marcus Davenport

10. Derick Hall | Seahawks | Pick: 2.37
Auburn | 6026/252 | RAS: 9.4 | Comp: Sam Williams

LB

1. Jack Campbell | Lions | Pick: 1.18
Iowa | 6045/249 | RAS: 9.98 | Comp: Leighton Vander Esch

2. Drew Sanders | Broncos | Pick: 3.67
Arkansas | 6041/235 | RAS: 8.97 | Comp: Anthony Barr

3. Daiyan Henley | Chargers | Pick: 3.85
Washington State | 6003/225 | RAS: 8.07 | Comp: Dre Greenlaw

4. Trenton Simpson | Ravens | Pick: 3.86
Clemson | 6021/235 | RAS: 9.84 | Comp: Jeremiah Owusu-Koramoah

5. Nick Herbig | Steelers | Pick: 4.132
Wisconsin | 6021/240 | RAS: 7.75 | Comp: Joe Schobert

6. Dorian Williams | Bills | Pick: 3.91
Tulane | 6006/228 | RAS: 8.82 | Comp: Telvin Smith

7. Henry To'oTo'o | Bills | Pick: 5.167
Alabama | 6010/227 | RAS: 6.82 | Comp: Reuben Foster

8. Yasir Abdullah | Jaguars | Pick: 5.136
Louisville | 6010/237 | RAS: 9.63 | Comp: Josh Uche

9. Ivan Pace Jr. | Vikings | Pick: UDFA
Cincinnati | 5105/231 | RAS: 5.71 | Comp: Denzel Perryman

10. DeMarvion Overshown | Cowboys | Pick: 3.90
Texas | 6026/229 | RAS: 8.18 | Comp: Divine Deablo

CB

1. Devon Witherspoon | Seahawks | Pick: 1.5
Illinois | 5114/181 | RAS: N/A | Comp: Darius Slay

2. Joey Porter Jr. | Steelers | Pick: 2.32
Penn State | 6024/193 | RAS: 9.71 | Comp: Sauce Gardner

3. Christian Gonzalez | Patriots | Pick: 1.17
Oregon | 6013/197 | RAS: 9.95 | Comp: Dominique Rodgers-Cromartie

4. Deonte Banks | Giants | Pick: 1.24
Maryland | 6000/197 | RAS: 10 | Comp: Eli Apple

5. Cam Smith | Dolphins | Pick: 2.51
South Carolina | 6006/180 | RAS: 9.68 | Comp: Alterraun Verner

6. Emmanuel Forbes | Commanders | Pick: 1.16
Mississippi State | 6006/166 | RAS: 9.26 | Comp: Jack Jones

7. Julius Brents | Colts | Pick: 2.44
Kansas State | 6026/198 | RAS: 9.99 | Comp: Joshua Williams

8. Clark Phillips III | Chargers | Pick: 4.113
Utah | 5090/184 | RAS: 5.6 | Comp: Mike Hilton

9. DJ Turner | Bengals | Pick: 2.60
Michigan | 5110/178 | RAS: N/A | Comp: Johnathan Joseph

10. Darius Rush | Colts | Pick: 5.138
South Carolina | 6020/198 | RAS: 9.81 | Comp: Alontae Taylor

S

1. Brian Branch | Lions | Pick: 2.45
Alabama | 5115/190 | RAS: 5.27 | Comp: Tyrann Mathieu

2. Antonio Johnson | Jaguars | Pick: 5.160
Texas A&M | 6020/198 | RAS: 4.79 | Comp: Ronnie Harrison

3. Jartavius Martin | Commanders | Pick: 2.47
illinois | 5110/194 | RAS: 9.29 | Comp: L'Jarius Sneed

4. Jordan Battle | Bengals | Pick: 3.95
Alabama | 6010/209 | RAS: 5.9 | Comp: Adrian Amos

5. Jammie Robinson | Panthers | Pick: 5.145
Florida State | 5110/191 | RAS: 6.07 | Comp: Quandre Diggs

6. Sydney Brown | Eagles | Pick: 3.66
Illinois | 5100/211 | RAS: 9.68 | Comp: Nick Scott

7. Ji'Ayir Brown | 49ers | Pick: 3.87
Penn State | 5110/203 | RAS: 5.95 | Comp: Calvin Pryor

8. Marte Mapu | Patriots | Pick: 3.76
Sacramento State | 6030/221 | RAS: N/A | Comp: Bernard Pollard

9. JL Skinner | Broncos | Pick: 6.183
Boise State | 6040/209 | RAS: N/A | Comp: Jayron Kearse

10. Jason Taylor II | Rams | Pick: 7.234
Oklahoma State | 6000204 | RAS: 8.91 | Comp: Gerald Sensabaugh

2024 NFL Draft fantasy look-ahead:

QB

1. Caleb Williams, USC
2. Drake Maye, UNC
3. Shedeur Sanders, Colorado
4. Michael Penix Jr, Washington
5. Quinn Ewers, Texas
6. Michael Pratt, Tulane
7. JJ McCarthy, Michigan
8. Bo Nix, Oregon
9. Spencer Rattler, South Carolina
10. Joe Milton, Tennessee

RB

1. Raheim Sanders
2. TreVeyon Henderson
3. Braelon Allen, Wisconsin
4. Blake Corrum, Michigan
5. Will Shipley, Clemson
6. Trey Benson, Florida State
7. Donovan Edwards, Michigan
8. Devin Neal, Kansas
9. Kendall Milton, Georgia
10. MarShawn Lloyd, USC

WR

1. Marvin Harrison Jr., Ohio State
2. Emeka Egbuka, Ohio State
3. Xavier Worthy, Texas
4. Malik Nabers, LSU
5. Rome Odunze, Washington
6. Johnny Wilson, Florida State
7. Troy Franklin, Oregon
8. Mario Williams, USC
9. Jacob Cowing, Arizona
10. Oronde Gadsen III, Syracuse

TE

1. Brock Bowers, Georgia
2. Ja'Tavion Sanders, Texas
3. Erick All, Iowa
4. Jaheim Bell, Florida State
5. Benjamin Yurosek, Stanford
6. Brevyn Spann-Ford, Minnesota
7. Theo Johnson, Penn State
8. McCallan Castles, Tennessee
9. Bryson Nesbit, UNC
10. Michael Trigg, Ole Miss

Chapter 11

2023 Team Previews

AFC EAST/WEST

Andrew Seifter

BUFFALO BILLS FANTASY PREVIEW

KEY LOSSES: Tremaine Edmunds (LB), Devin Singletary (RB), Isaiah McKenzie (WR), Jamison Crowder (WR)

KEY ADDITIONS: Connor McGovern (G), Damien Harris (RB), Latavius Murray (RB), Deonte Harty (WR)

FANTASY IMPACT: Tremaine Edmunds was a big loss in the middle of the defense, but the Bills still project to have one of the league's best defensive units. Connor McGovern will step in for Rodger Saffold, helping Josh Allen stay upright and productive.

Damien Harris replaces Devin Singletary as an early-down complement to the lighter and shiftier James Cook, who should see his role continue to grow in the passing game. Latavius Murray showed surprising late-career juice in Denver last season but is unlikely to matter in fantasy unless Cook or Harris succumb to injury. Deonte Harty earned a decent payday but is more likely to help the Bills' special teams than to overtake Khalil Shakir as Buffalo's primary slot receiver.

DRAFTED PLAYERS OF FANTASY NOTE: Dalton Kincaid (TE, Utah), Justin Shorter (WR, Florida)

FANTASY IMPACT: Thanks to his red zone prowess in one of the league's best offenses, Dawson Knox has finished as a top-12 tight end in fantasy points per game for two years running – but that streak could be coming to an end with the addition of Dalton Kincaid to the tight end room. The fact that Buffalo expended first-round capital on Kincaid indicates that they view him as an upgrade on Knox, and it's conceivable that Kincaid also bypasses Gabe Davis to emerge as the number two option in the Bills' passing game. Justin Shorter is another contender to eventually overtake Davis. Although his college production was severely lacking, Shorter is big, fast, and strong and was once considered the number 1 receiver recruit in the country.

OFFENSIVE OUTLOOK: This one isn't complicated. The Bills have been a Top 3 scoring offense for three consecutive seasons, and there's every reason to believe they can make it four. Allen and Diggs remain among the very best fantasy options at their respective positions.

While the rest of the depth chart is a bit murky, anyone getting regular snaps in this offense belongs on a fantasy roster. That means it'll be important to closely monitor the team's usage patterns throughout the year at RB (Cook vs. Harris), outside WR (Davis vs. Shorter), slot WR (Shakir vs. Harty) and TE (Kincaid vs. Knox). It's also possible that Kincaid takes away snaps from Shakir in the slot.

DEFENSIVE OUTLOOK: The Bills have been nearly as dominant on defense as they've been on offense, finishing in the Top 4 for fewest points allowed in three of the last four seasons. However, that run of dominance is somewhat threatened by the loss of Edmunds, this year's second-best free-agent linebacker, according to Pro Football Focus. While Buffalo will have to try to replace Edmunds in-house via a training camp competition, the good news is that the rest of the defense returns largely intact. The Bills may be transitioning to a smaller and quicker unit, but the bottom line is that they are still a good bet to be an above-average defense – and one you can utilize in fantasy leagues.

2023 OUTLOOK: On paper, the Bills have been the most complete team in the AFC over the last few years, but that hasn't been enough to get them past the rival Chiefs and Bengals in the playoffs. It's hard to argue that the Bills have gotten markedly better this offseason, but they remain one of the only teams (alongside Philadelphia) that can boast having both a top-5 offense and top-5 defense. They are well-positioned to retain their AFC East crown, and perhaps this is the year they finally return to the Super Bowl.

MIAMI DOLPHINS FANTASY PREVIEW

KEY LOSSES: Mike Gesicki (TE), Elandon Roberts (LB)

KEY ADDITIONS: Jalen Ramsey (CB), David Long Jr. (LB), Mike White (QB)

FANTASY IMPACT: The highlight of the Dolphins' offseason has to be the acquisition of Jalen Ramsey, who will pair with Xavien Howard to give Miami one of the most-accomplished cornerback duos in the league. But from a fantasy perspective, it's perhaps more significant that the Dolphins allowed Mike Gesicki to depart and did not replace him with a comparable pass-catching option at tight end. Few teams funnel more targets to their top two wideouts than Miami does, and it stands to reason that Tyreek Hill and Jaylen Waddle could get even more looks with Gesicki gone. One player the Dolphins *did* add is Mike White, who showed promise in spot duty for the Jets and will provide a needed insurance policy for Tua Tagovailoa.

DRAFTED PLAYERS OF FANTASY NOTE: Devon Achane (RB, Texas A&M)

FANTASY IMPACT: The Dolphins were short on 2023 draft picks, but Devon Achane is one selection who will make some noise. Miami's third-round pick is undersized and not built for every-down duty, but he possesses blazing speed, an essential quality for a running back in Mike McDaniel's innovative scheme. The Dolphins opted to run it back by re-signing Raheem Mostert and Jeff Wilson following their successful stints with the team last season, but both backs have lengthy injury histories. Achane may start out as a change-of-pace and/or gadget back, but he should have a path to double-digit touches in this fantasy-friendly offense at some point in 2023.

OFFENSIVE OUTLOOK: While the 2022 Dolphins were not quite on the level of the Chiefs or Bills offensively, they might have been if Tua Tagovailoa had remained healthy. Either way, the team's narrow target tree and McDaniel's ability to get the most out of his players make this one of the league's most fantasy-friendly offenses. Whether you believe in Tua or not, he's proven that he can put up QB1 numbers in this offense, while Hill and Waddle are the rare set of teammates that have a shot to both finish as top-12 fantasy receivers. You don't need to concern yourself with any other pass-catchers in Miami, but any running back getting consistent touches in this offense will be valuable, so Mostert, Wilson, and Achane all have a decent chance to be fantasy relevant.

DEFENSIVE OUTLOOK: The Dolphins were not a very good defense in 2022, but perhaps the addition of Jalen Ramsey can change that. David Long Jr. is set to replace Elandon Roberts at inside linebacker, and rookie second-round corner Cam Smith will add to Miami's loaded secondary. This defense may not be elite in 2023, but it's unlikely to finish again as a bottom-10 unit.

2023 OUTLOOK: The Dolphins will have to contend with the division favorite Bills, perennially tough Patriots, and Aaron Rodgers-led Jets in the AFC East, which is no easy task. But they look the part of a playoff team if Tua can stay healthy and the defense can improve. The Mike McDaniel era is really still just getting started in Miami.

NEW ENGLAND PATRIOTS FANTASY PREVIEW

KEY LOSSES: Damien Harris (RB), Jakobi Meyers (WR), Nelson Agholor (WR), Jonnu Smith (TE)

KEY ADDITIONS: JuJu Smith-Schuster (WR), Mike Gesicki (TE), James Robinson (RB), Riley Reiff (RT)

FANTASY IMPACT: The Patriots experienced their fair share of turnover at the skill positions over the offseason, but the most impactful move may be to the coaching staff, where Bill O'Brien will take over from de facto offensive coordinator (and seasoned *defensive* coach) Matt Patricia. O'Brien will seek to instill some life into New England's middling offensive attack, and his first order of business will be getting Mac Jones back on track after the Patriots' signal-caller regressed badly in his second season. The Patriots shouldn't lose much by replacing Jakobi Meyers and Jonnu Smith with JuJu Smith-Schuster and Mike Gesicki, but they may not gain much. James Robinson would seem to be the logical choice to step in for Damien Harris as the second back behind Rhamondre Stevenson, but at least one Patriots beat reporter has predicted that the team will instead rely on sophomores Pierre Strong and Kevin Harris – and that Robinson won't even make the final roster.

DRAFTED PLAYERS OF FANTASY NOTE: Kayshon Boutte (WR, LSU)

FANTASY IMPACT: The Patriots spent their first seven picks in the 2023 NFL draft on defense, offensive line, or Special Teams, which gives some sense of where Bill Belichick's priorities continue to lie. Still, Boutte is an intriguing talent for the sixth round. Once regarded as one of the top WR prospects in the country, Boutte got off to a strong start as a freshman at LSU in 2020, but an ankle injury ruined his 2021 campaign. He then took a sizable step backward under Brian Kelly last year, and that, plus mediocre combine numbers, caused his draft stock to plummet. There are questions about how Boutte responds to coaching, but if Belichick can get him to buy in, he could eventually emerge as a fantasy factor.

OFFENSIVE OUTLOOK: The Patriots finished 16th in scoring offense last season, which is honestly higher than expected under Patricia. While O'Brien should be a coaching upgrade, it's still hard to expect any dramatic improvement from this unit.

For fantasy purposes, the only truly exciting player is Stevenson, who finished as the RB11 last year and could place even higher now that Harris is no longer around. Mac Jones was barely a QB2 last season and will need to make major strides before he's even a consideration in single-QB formats. Meyers was a reliable WR3 in this offense, and that may be close to a best-case scenario for Smith-Schuster, who hasn't been a true difference-maker since 2018. Gesicki struggled to see consistent targets in Miami, and that should remain the case in New England, where he'll have to compete with Hunter Henry, DeVante Parker, Kendrick Bourne, and others for any touches that don't go to Stevenson or Smith-Schuster.

DEFENSIVE OUTLOOK: The 2022 Patriots defense wasn't quite as dominant as the 2021 edition from a point prevention standpoint, but it was even better for fantasy, finishing as the number one DST last year. Overall, New England has finished as a top-two DST in back-to-back seasons and a top-four DST in four of the last five years. The only major loss to the defense is cornerback Devin McCourty, who retired, but the Patriots replaced him with first-round pick Christian Gonzalez while adding Day Two picks Keion White (Edge) and Marte Mapu (LB) as further reinforcements.

2023 OUTLOOK: The Patriots have remained competitive in the post-Tom Brady era thanks to a dominant defense and a strong offensive line, and Belichick looks set to continue leaning into those attributes in 2023. While there isn't a ton here to get excited about for fantasy football – and the odds of a deep playoff run seem remote – it should surprise no one if New England is once again in the hunt for a wildcard berth when the dust settles.

NEW YORK JETS FANTASY PREVIEW

KEY LOSSES: Elijah Moore (WR), Sheldon Rankins (DT), Nate Herbig (G), Mike White (QB)

KEY ADDITIONS: Aaron Rodgers (QB), Allen Lazard (WR), Mecole Hardman (WR), Randall Cobb (WR), Chuck Clark (S), Quinton Jefferson (DT)

FANTASY IMPACT: The Jets made the single biggest splash of the offseason by acquiring Aaron Rodgers from the Packers for a package of draft picks. Now 39 years old, Rodgers produced more like a QB2 than a QB1 during his final year in Green Bay, but he could be poised for a big bounceback in New York. Garrett Wilson is far and away the best pass-catcher Rodgers has had to work with since Davante Adams. To smooth Rodgers' transition, the Jets also brought in former Green Bay offensive coordinator Nathaniel Hackett, former Packers receivers Allen Lazard and Randall Cobb, and Mecole Hardman, who could serve as a Marquez Valdes-Scantling-esque big play threat.

DRAFTED PLAYERS OF FANTASY NOTE: Israel Abanikanda (RB)

FANTASY IMPACT: Abanikanda generated plenty of buzz in dynasty circles prior to the NFL draft, and it's easy to understand why. He rushed for 1,431 yards and 21 touchdowns during his final season at the University of Pittsburgh and also displayed impressive workout metrics, earning the highest athleticism score of any running back in the 2023 draft class, according to PlayerProfiler.com. Unfortunately, he was not selected until Day Three of the draft and landed in a crowded running back room that already features Breece Hall, Zonovan Knight and Michael Carter. Abanikanda will be worth rostering in redraft leagues if he can overtake Knight and Carter for the number two job, but he's unlikely to make a big fantasy impact unless Hall has a setback in his recovery from knee surgery.

OFFENSIVE OUTLOOK: The Jets cycled through four quarterbacks last season on the way to finishing as the 29th-ranked scoring offense. They are sure to improve under Rodgers, the question is only how much. If the Jets' offense realizes its potential, Rodgers, Wilson and Hall could all finish as top-12 fantasy options at their respective positions, while Lazard and/or Hardman could develop WR3 value. Beyond that, the depth chart is messy, but players like Corey Davis, Tyler Conklin, C.J. Uzomah, Abanikanda, Knight and Carter all have a conceivable path to fantasy utility if Rodgers truly discovers the fountain of youth.

DEFENSIVE OUTLOOK: Robert Saleh is a defensive-minded coach, and his Jets finished fourth in the NFL in scoring defense last season, although they were only a borderline top-12 fantasy defense. Regardless, it was a huge improvement from 2021. The team did lose Sheldon Rankins and Nathan Sheperd along the interior defensive line but signed Quinton Jefferson to help fill the gap. They also upgraded the secondary by trading for Chuck Clark. While it is tough to count on a repeat performance from last year, the Jets should again be an above-average defensive unit.

2023 OUTLOOK: The Jets have finished in the basement of the AFC East for three straight seasons, but they've gradually improved since bottoming out in 2020. Now, with Rodgers in the fold, this team has the playoffs clearly in sight. That is no easy accomplishment in such a tough division, but the Jets have enough firepower on both sides of the ball to get it done if their new-look offense can quickly come together.

KANSAS CITY CHIEFS FANTASY PREVIEW

KEY LOSSES: Orlando Brown (LT), Andrew Wylie (RT), JuJu Smith-Schuster (WR), Mecole Hardman (WR), Frank Clark (Edge), Juan Thornhill (S)

KEY ADDITIONS: Jawaan Taylor (RT), Donovan Smith (LT), Charles Omenihu (Edge), Drue Tranquill (LB), Mike Edwards (S)

FANTASY IMPACT: The Chiefs let Smith-Schuster and Hardman walk in free agency and did little to replace them other than drafting SMU wideout Rashee Rice in the second round (more on him in a bit). That means Kansas City could be set to rely even more heavily on Patrick Mahomes and a now 33-year-old Travis Kelce, not to say the two superstars aren't up to the task. The Chiefs will also be replacing both of their starting offensive tackles from last year, adding a bit of uncertainty around Mahomes' pass protection.

DRAFTED PLAYERS OF FANTASY NOTE: Rashee Rice (WR, SMU)

FANTASY IMPACT: Rice rates highly in terms of burst and catch radius and is coming off a massive senior season at SMU in which he hauled in 96 receptions for 1,355 yards and 10 scores. While he is a somewhat divisive prospect in dynasty circles, there is no doubting the opportunity he'll have in Kansas City, where his competition at wideout is the enigmatic and/or unproven trio of Kadarius Toney, Marques Valdes-Scantling and Skyy Moore. While Hardman and Moore were both disappointing fantasy options during their rookie seasons in Kansas City, you can't completely disregard any player with a path to a heavy target share from Patrick Mahomes. Expectations should be kept in check, but Rice is a reasonable stash in redraft while we wait to see how the Chiefs' depth chart shakes out.

OFFENSIVE OUTLOOK: The Chiefs have led the NFL in yards per game in three of Mahomes' five seasons as the team's starting quarterback, and they haven't finished lower than sixth (2019). The fact they led the league last year – their first without Tyreek Hill – proved that Mahomes can be just fine with a rotating cast of wide receivers. He and Kelce should once again be elite fantasy options, but beyond that, this situation is once again looking tricky to navigate.

The Chiefs re-signed Jerick McKinnon, who quietly finished as the RB21 last year, reuniting him with Isiah Pacheco, who was the RB35. Those two may end up a bit closer in fantasy value this year, rendering both as borderline RB2/3s. Despite playing in the league's most prolific offense, no Chiefs wide receiver finished as a top-24 fantasy option last year, with only Smith-Schuster finishing inside the top-50 at the position. While Valdes-Scantling should remain a situational deep threat, the most pressing fantasy question is whether one of Toney, Moore or Rice can garner a large enough target share to attain weekly WR2 value.

DEFENSIVE OUTLOOK: The Chiefs were a sneaky good defense in 2022, finishing as a top-10 unit in terms of yards allowed, points allowed and fantasy points generated. As far as their offseason moves, newly-signed edge Charles Omenihu should be a solid replacement for Frank Clark, second-year strong safety Bryan Cook looks more than ready to step in for Juan Thornill, and linebacker Drue Tranquill could provide a significant boost to both the pass coverage *and* pass rush. The AFC West will provide some tough matchups, but Kansas City once again looks the part of an above-average fantasy DST.

2023 OUTLOOK: The Chiefs are the defending Super Bowl champs, and Travis Kelce isn't about to let you forget about it. They're also the betting favorite to win it all this year. While Andy Reid's team can be frustrating at times for fantasy purposes, they remain an absolute juggernaut heading into 2023.

LOS ANGELES CHARGERS FANTASY PREVIEW

KEY LOSSES: Drue Tranquill (LB), Troy Reeder (LB), Matt Feiler (LG), DeAndre Carter (WR)

KEY ADDITIONS: Eric Kendricks (LB)

FANTASY IMPACT: The Chargers have had a relatively quiet offseason outside of the NFL draft. To date, their only free agent signing is former Vikings linebacker Eric Kendricks, who was widely considered one of the best coverage linebackers in the NFL before enduring a down year in 2022. The Chargers also retained two key members of last year's squad, offensive tackle Trey Pipkins and defensive end Morgan Fox. The most fantasy-relevant storyline over the offseason involved Austin Ekeler, who received permission to seek a trade after contract negotiations with the team broke down. However, no trade offer has materialized yet, and Ekeler just agreed to a reworked contract with additional incentives for the final year of his deal.

DRAFTED PLAYERS OF FANTASY NOTE: Quentin Johnston (WR, TCU), Derius Davis (WR, TCU)

FANTASY IMPACT: The Chargers' brass must have been awfully impressed by the Horned Frogs' passing attack because LA spent a first-round pick on Johnston, a fourth-round pick on Davis, and even selected TCU quarterback Max Duggan with a seventh-round selection. Of the three, Johnston is far and away the most likely to make some noise in fantasy leagues. The 6'3" wideout is very athletic for a player of his size and profiles as a long-term successor to Mike Williams. In the short term, Johnston should quickly overtake Josh Palmer in three-wide sets, giving him some immediate boom-or-bust WR3 appeal in what should be one of the league's best offenses. Davis is very fast but also very small. He's much more likely to make a living as a kick returner than as a wide receiver.

OFFENSIVE OUTLOOK: The Chargers were an above-average offense in 2022, but given all their talent, you get the feeling they left some points on the table. Injuries were certainly part of the problem. Justin Herbert played through a rib cartilage fracture that he suffered early in the season, while receivers Keenan Allen and Mike Williams each missed a big chunk of the season with their own ailments. However, GM Tom Telesco and Head Coach Brandon Staley evidently agreed that the offense underachieved, opting to replace offensive coordinator Joe Lombardi with Kellen Moore over the offseason.

With an innovative play-caller like Moore now on board, we can anticipate the Chargers rebounding to the top-five offense they were back in 2021. Herbert finished as the QB2 that year and should be closer to that player than the QB11 he was last season. Ekeler was the number one running back in fantasy and could easily do it again this year. Allen may be 31 years old, but he was the WR10 in fantasy points per game last year and remains a high-end WR2 at worst. Williams was the WR22 in points per game last year and has a good shot at returning WR2 value himself, although rookie Quentin Johnston could eventually become a thorn in his side. Tight end Gerald Everett could also lose touches to Johnston, but he's still a decent bet to repeat last year's TE15 finish.

DEFENSIVE OUTLOOK: The Chargers' defense is a unit that tends to get overrated in fantasy circles. Although Staley was trained as a defensive coach, Los Angeles has not finished as a top-20 DST in either of his two years coaching the team. The Chargers' defense has not undergone a dramatic enough overhaul to believe that will suddenly change in 2023.

2023 OUTLOOK: In 2022, the Chargers reached the playoffs for the first time since 2018, only to suffer a heartbreaking defeat to the Jaguars in the Wild Card round. At least one playoff win will be expected this time around, and this team has the talent to do it, provided Kellen Moore can help the offense reach its full potential.

DENVER BRONCOS FANTASY PREVIEW

KEY LOSSES: Dre'Mont Jones (DE), Calvin Anderson (LT), Graham Glasgow (G), Latavius Murray (RB), Chase Edmonds (RB)

KEY ADDITIONS: Mike McGlinchey (RT), Ben Powers (G), Zach Allen (DE), Samaje Perine (RB)

FANTASY IMPACT: While the Broncos were very active in free agency, their biggest offseason acquisition was head coach Sean Payton, who they acquired for two early-round draft picks. Payton's top task is to revive a moribund offense that was long on talent but short on production in 2022. Denver spent big-time cash on upgrading its run-blocking, an early indication that Payton wants to rely on the running game to open things up for Russell Wilson in the passing game, Wilson's recipe for success in Seattle. The question is whether Javonte Williams will be recovered from his devastating knee injury in time for Week 1, and if not, whether the Broncos need to add another veteran running back to work in tandem with Samaje Perine. It's also fair to wonder whether there will be enough targets to go around to support Denver's loaded pass-catching corps featuring Jerry Jeudy, Courtland Sutton, Tim Patrick and Greg Dulcich.

DRAFTED PLAYERS OF FANTASY NOTE: Marvin Mims (WR, Oklahoma)

FANTASY IMPACT: The Broncos expended second-round draft capital on Mims, a clear indication that they envision him eventually playing a major role in their passing attack. But the key word is "eventually." Mims possesses excellent straight-line speed and burst, and he is coming off a 1,000-yard campaign in his final season at Oklahoma. But the Broncos already have three solid options at wide receiver in Jeudy, Sutton and Patrick, who is reportedly fully recovered from the ACL tear that wiped out his 2022 season. While Mims could quickly gain fantasy relevance if one of Denver's other receivers goes down, he'll likely enter the season as a "watch list" player who is much more appealing in dynasty leagues than redraft.

OFFENSIVE OUTLOOK: In a year where many offenses across the league underperformed, the 2022 Broncos were the worst of the worst. Watching them was a weekly trip to the dentist's office. But that all could change in a hurry now that one of the best offensive minds of the 21st century is calling the shots. The Broncos are mostly running it back at the skills positions, banking on Payton's game-planning and a revamped offensive line to spur much better results from Russell Wilson and Co. The Broncos may need a healthy Javonte Williams to fully reach their offensive potential, but it's fair to expect substantial improvement from this unit no matter who is lining up at running back.

DEFENSIVE OUTLOOK: The Broncos were an above-average defense last year in terms of point prevention, which is a decent accomplishment, given how little help they got from the offense. But Denver ranked near the bottom of the league in sacks and was one of only four teams not to score a defensive touchdown, which made them a below-average defense for fantasy purposes. Zach Allen should be able to fill in capably for the departed Dre'Mont Jones, and longer offensive drives should make things easier on the defense this year. Ultimately, though, it is tough to confidently recommend a defense that must face the Chiefs and Chargers twice.

2023 OUTLOOK: Optimism about the 2022 Broncos turned out to be horribly misguided, but a lot of that came down to poor coaching. Denver now has one of the most highly-decorated coaches of the last two decades, so it is just a matter of whether Sean Payton can work his magic with a second franchise. The bet here is that he can. The Broncos play in arguably the toughest division in football, but if the Payton/Wilson tandem clicks, this team can make the playoffs.

LAS VEGAS RAIDERS FANTASY PREVIEW

KEY LOSSES: Derek Carr (QB), Darren Waller (TE), Foster Moreau (TE), Mack Hollins (WR), Rock Ya-Sin (CB)

KEY ADDITIONS: Jimmy Garoppolo (QB), Jakobi Meyers (WR), Austin Hooper (TE), Marcus Epps (S), Robert Spillane (LB)

FANTASY IMPACT: While the Derek Carr era had perhaps run its course in Las Vegas, handing the reins over to Jimmy Garoppolo seems like a lateral move, at best. That said, Raiders head coach Josh McDaniels knows exactly what he's getting in Jimmy G, who should be a solid QB2 in superflex leagues (and a potential streamer in single-QB formats). Meyers is a shrewd addition as a much more reliable second weapon in the passing game than Darren Waller, but he topped out as a high-end WR3 in New England, which may be close to his ceiling in Vegas. Hooper was signed to replace Waller and Foster Moreau, but he'll have to hold off rookie Michael Mayer to have any shot at fantasy relevance.

DRAFTED PLAYERS OF FANTASY NOTE: Michael Mayer (TE, Notre Dame), Tre Tucker (WR, Cincinnati), Aiden O'Connell (QB, Purdue)

FANTASY IMPACT: Mayer doesn't wow you athletically, but he's a big, physical tight end who was very productive at Notre Dame. The odds are against Mayer being a fantasy TE1 as a rookie, particularly with Hooper and O.J.

Howard around, but he's a stable dynasty asset who stands a good chance of becoming the Raiders' long-term answer at the position. Tre Tucker was a surprising pick in the third round, going ahead of his more dynamic and productive Bearcat teammate, Tyler Scott. Tucker has the straight-line speed to keep defenses honest, but he profiles as the kind of situational deep threat who doesn't help much in fantasy. O'Connell isn't much of a threat to Garoppolo, especially in Year One, but he is NFL-ready and should be a solid backup.

OFFENSIVE OUTLOOK: The Raiders were a slightly above-average offense last season, and they appear destined to finish in the middle of the pack again in 2023 – assuming they have all their top playmakers available.

Running back Josh Jacobs has yet to sign his franchise tag tender as he and the Raiders continue to negotiate a long-term contract extension that must be agreed to by July 15. While it's not inconceivable that Jacobs could hold out into the season, the more likely outcome is that he agrees to a new deal or plays out the year on the franchise tag. Jacobs is coming off an unbelievable season, trailing only Austin Ekeler and Christian McCaffrey in fantasy points among RBs. He may not reach those heights again but is a surefire RB1 nonetheless.

The shift from Carr to Garoppolo shouldn't dramatically impact Davante Adams, who remains a top-five fantasy option at wide receiver. Hunter Renfrow is coming off a disappointing, injury-plagued season and is unlikely to be a factor in most fantasy leagues unless Adams or Meyers suffer an injury.

DEFENSIVE OUTLOOK: The Raiders are often a below-average defense, and last season was no exception. The fact they need to play six games against the Chiefs, Chargers and Sean Payton-led Broncos certainly doesn't help matters. While Vegas did invest in some intriguing defensive talent during the NFL draft, this is not a DST that you'll want to turn to in fantasy leagues.

2023 OUTLOOK: The Raiders are coming off of a 6-11 season in one of the NFL's toughest divisions, and it is hard to see this squad taking a massive step forward in 2023. There is too much talent on the offense for the bottom to fall out completely, but barring dramatic improvement on the defensive side, the playoffs seem like a longshot.

AFC NORTH/SOUTH

Nate Hamilton

Cincinnati Bengals Fantasy Preview

KEY LOSSES: Hayden Hurst (TE)

KEY ADDITIONS: Irv Smith Jr. (TE)

FANTASY IMPACT:

The Cincinnati Bengals kept most of their key players, and why not? They have made it to the AFC Championship game in two consecutive seasons, including Super Bowl LVI. Hayden Hurst earned 52 catches on 68 targets which were top-15 among tight ends in 2022. He only found the end zone twice and generated just 414 receiving yards. To say Hurst is a "key loss" may be an overstatement, but it's key given the Bengals' lack of tight-end depth.

The Bengals signed former Vikings tight end and 2019 second-round pick Irv Smith Jr. He's expected to be the lead target at the position and fill Hayden Hurst's previous role. Irv Smith Jr. may not be a fantasy football asset as the Bengals and Joe Burrow's focus will mainly be the stacked wide receiver group. Smith is also an injury risk, as he's missed plenty of football since his sophomore season.

DRAFTED PLAYERS OF FANTASY NOTE: Charlie Jones (WR), Chase Brown (RB), Andrei Iosivas (WR)

FANTASY IMPACT:

Although the Bengals have arguably the best wide receiver group in the NFL, that didn't stop them from adding to it in the 2023 draft. They drafted Purdue wideout Charlie Jones in the fourth round and Princeton WR Andrei Iosivas in the sixth. Both are highly unlikely to make an impact this season, but either has a chance to step up and take over the Tyler Boyd role, as he's expected to be an unrestricted free agent after this season.

The Bengals also made a move at the running back position and drafted Chase Brown from Illinois. I wouldn't expect the fifth-round pick to drive Joe Mixon out of town, but Chase Brown will be in an ideal situation if Mixon misses time with an injury or can't stay out of trouble off the field. Brown is expected to be listed as the RB2 on the Bengals' depth chart.

OFFENSIVE OUTLOOK:

Not much has changed for the 2023 Bengals' offensive. They are expected to have the majority of the key weapons they had last year. Irv Smith Jr. is replacing Hayden Hurst at tight end and is expected to see 50+ targets. Surprisingly, it's looking like Joe Mixon is staying in Cincinnati for now. After all the drama surrounding him, the Bengals showed they are still moving forward with Mixon, as the running back position was not a priority in the Bengals' draft.

DEFENSIVE OUTLOOK

The Bengals' defense struggled to get to the quarterback last season. They wisely utilized their first-round pick (28th overall) on Clemson defensive end Myles Murphy. Expect the Bengals coaching staff to move him all around the defensive line this season. They should see a bump in pressure against the quarterback.

Cincinnati continued selecting defensive players in rounds two and three. They went with Michigan cornerback DJ Turner with the 60th overall pick. Next came Alabama safety Jordan Battle with the 95th overall pick in the third round. Both players have an opportunity to make an impact in 2023. However, it's likely to come later in the season.

2023 OUTLOOK:

This Bengals team is and has been plenty scary with Joe Burrow and his top three wideouts leading the way. Too often, even when all pieces are clicking on all cylinders, organizations will make a bunch of changes. The Bengals' front office has spoken and after a few key defensive moves in the draft, they feel confident with what they have heading into the 2023-24 NFL season. As far as fantasy football goes, you can trust the usual suspects.

Baltimore Ravens Fantasy Preview

KEY LOSSES: Demarcus Robinson (WR), Kenyan Drake (RB)

KEY ADDITIONS: Odell Beckham Jr. (WR)

FANTASY IMPACT:

Odell Beckham Jr. hasn't seen the football field since the 2021 season. In that season, he totaled just 537 receiving yards in 14 games. OBJ hasn't reached 1,000 yards since his 2019 season with the Cleveland Browns. He will turn 31 in November, and although his name still carries some weight, his talents are questionable at best heading into this season.

Rashod Bateman is expected to take on a larger role in his third season, and the Ravens invested their first-round pick on a wideout who is also expected to see plenty of targets in his rookie season. Tight end Mark Andrews remains Jackson's top target despite an improved wide receiver group. Nelson Agholor was also signed by the team, which complicates target shares. As excited as you may be to see Odell Beckham Jr. with Lamar Jackson, tempering expectations come fantasy drafts may be wise.

DRAFTED PLAYERS OF FANTASY NOTE: Zay Flowers (WR)

FANTASY IMPACT:

We are seeing more and more each year how quickly first-round wide receivers impact their respective teams. The Ravens drafted Boston College wideout Zay Flowers with the 22nd overall pick. Teams don't often draft a wide receiver that high to have them sit and develop. Flowers was outstanding after the catch last year (averaged 42.9 yards) and will look to continue that production in the NFL. The Ravens certainly believe he can lead this wide receiver group sooner rather than later. I'd personally draft Zay Flowers over OBJ in fantasy drafts.

OFFENSIVE OUTLOOK:

Last season, no Ravens wide receiver stood out as "the guy." This is likely why the Ravens felt the need to address the position this offseason. They may be an improved group of targets for Lamar Jackson, but I'm still hesitant to trust this offense is going to pivot from what works for them. I still see Jackson throwing to Mark Andrews more than anyone. Rashod Bateman has shown flashes, but we haven't seen enough to feel confident he'll make that leap in year three. Zay Flowers is super talented and a first-round draft pick, but he is a rookie, and it often takes some time to adjust to the NFL. Odell Beckham Jr.'s best years are likely behind him.

Kenyan Drake led the backfield in touches last season. He's no longer on the team, which should finally staple J.K. Dobbins as the lead back this season. Gus Edwards is still on the roster, impacting Dobbins's full potential. All that said, let's be honest, Lamar Jackson is the biggest threat to Ravens running backs. Jackson has rushed over 100 times in each of his five NFL seasons. This offense has the potential to put up many points this season, but if you're looking to spend up for some Ravens on your fantasy teams, Mark Andrews and Lamar Jackson are the only ones worth the draft capital.

DEFENSIVE OUTLOOK

Defense has always been a strong focus for John Harbaugh and the Baltimore Ravens. This year is no different. Although they spent their first-round pick on an offensive piece, the Ravens used their next three picks on defensive weapons. They are becoming younger and faster on the defensive side of the ball. Many platforms had the Ravens among the top 10 defenses in 2022, and it appears they have placed themselves in a position to remain among the NFL's best in 2023.

2023 OUTLOOK:

Now that the drama between the Ravens and Lamar Jackson is over, both sides can finally focus on the task at hand. The Ravens have made Jackson the highest-paid quarterback and have improved his weapons this offseason. This team will be exciting to watch, purely from an NFL standpoint. However, the fantasy side of things has me a bit worried. Outside of Lamar Jackson and Mark Andrews, taking anyone else too early in drafts could leave you feeling some regret. Be cautious with the Ravens wideouts, and try not to lean on J.K. Dobbins as your RB1.

Pittsburgh Steelers Fantasy Preview

KEY LOSSES: N/A

KEY ADDITIONS: Allen Robinson (WR)

FANTASY IMPACT:

The Steelers acquired Allen Robinson from the Los Angeles Rams in April. I don't believe the move makes the team better or is a reason to get excited about Robinson's new landing spot. I'm trying my best to find the positives in this offense for the 2023 season, but it's… difficult. Pittsburgh has added other depth pieces, but Robinson appears to be the "highlight" of the offseason, and that's not saying much. Allen Robinson hasn't had a productive season since 2020. Fantasy impact-wise, Allen doesn't move the needle for me.

DRAFTED PLAYERS OF FANTASY NOTE: Darnell Washington (TE)

FANTASY IMPACT:

The Steelers already have a good tight end in Pat Freiermuth, who finished the 2022 season as the TE8 in fantasy. So, this move to add another viable tight end to the roster was a bit surprising. It's very possible Darnell Washington will mostly be used to block, however, given his size at 6'7", 264 lbs, he presents a major mismatch scenario for red zone targets. I don't expect Washington to play a major role in year one, but his presence could hinder whatever fantasy value the Steelers pass catchers had if he is to catch a handful of touchdowns this year.

OFFENSIVE OUTLOOK:

This offense isn't scaring anyone. The Steelers do have talented wide receivers, but it's tough to imagine they can produce enough for fantasy (given their quarterbacks) to want them on your roster. The Kenny Pickett and Mitch Trubisky combo failed to produce a top-35 fantasy wide receiver last season. Among pass catchers, Pat Freiermuth can still be a late-round option tight end, although the addition of Darnell Washington could make that decision a bit tougher.

Najee Harris was a top-5 running back in carries last season. Given the lack of confidence I have in this offense, I'd expect a similar workload for the third year back this season. He is likely the only Steelers offensive player I'd be happy with on my fantasy team.

DEFENSIVE OUTLOOK

The Steelers defense will be the main event for Pittsburgh in 2023, and they will have to be given their offensive woes. Their defensive leaders T.J. Watt, Cameron Heyward, and Minkah Fitzpatrick will be joined by veteran corner Patrick Peterson. The Steelers spent their 32nd overall pick on Joey Porter Jr. from Penn State. He will likely start the season behind Peterson but has a fairly easy road to playing time should he prove his worth. If you play in any IDP leagues, the Steelers' defensive assets are far more exciting than their offensive pieces.

2023 OUTLOOK:

The Pittsburgh Steelers is my least-favorite team in the AFC North for fantasy football assets. They failed to make any true changes to their team that is likely to result in a boost in fantasy production. Their best wide receiver in 2022 was George Pickens, who finished as the WR36, and the combination of Kenny Pickett and Mitch Trubisky at quarterback was underwhelming, to say the least. They appear to be in a rebuilding phase which doesn't bode well from a fantasy football perspective. I'd stay away from the Steelers altogether unless you can get Najee Harris at a discount.

Cleveland Browns Fantasy Preview

KEY LOSSES: Kareem Hunt (RB)

KEY ADDITIONS: Elijah Moore (WR), Marquise Goodwin

FANTASY IMPACT:

The Browns appear to have moved on from their two-headed monster approach at running back for the 2023 season. With Kareem Hunt out of the picture, Nick Chubb is expected to handle the bulk of the workload in Cleveland's backfield. Although, Chubb was already in that role, given the fact that he had the third-most rushes with 302. It's possible we see a dip in his volume (not necessarily efficiency) if Deshaun Watson can return to his prime form this year.

Elijah Moore can be a useful weapon behind Amari Cooper for Watson this season. Donovan Peoples-Jones was quite productive for the Browns in 2022 and will continue to be part of the Browns' passing attack this year. The Cleveland Browns front office is making it clear that they intend on throwing the ball a lot more with Watson under center, given their offseason moves.

DRAFTED PLAYERS OF FANTASY NOTE: Cedric Tillman (WR)

FANTASY IMPACT:

Speaking of offseason moves, the Browns spent their first pick of the 2023 NFL draft (3ʳᵈ round – pick 74) on Tennessee wide receiver Cedric Tillman. He could be in a position to be the team's WR3 behind Amari Cooper and DPJ. Peoples-Jones is serving the last year of his rookie contract and could potentially see a decline in targets should Tillman and/or Moore out-produce him this season. Cedrick Tillman has promise, but he's more of a dynasty target than a redraft one this year.

OFFENSIVE OUTLOOK:

As I mentioned, it looks like the Browns are loading up on pass catchers for Deshaun Watson. After they signed him to a four-year $156M contract, you better believe they are going to do whatever it takes to make it work. The Browns' wide receivers are talented enough to help Deshaun Watson get to where he needs to be in this offense. Watson and his wideouts all have potential upside and will likely be value picks in fantasy drafts. I'm interested in most of them at the right price.

Of course, we have a stud running back in Nick Chubb. He's been right around the top-10 RBs in each of the last four seasons despite sharing the load with Kareem Hunt and the many uncertainties at the quarterback position over the years. Chubb continues to be worth a high draft pick as your RB1 on fantasy teams.

DEFENSIVE OUTLOOK

The Cleveland Browns' defense is certainly nothing to laugh at with Myles Garrett leading the charge. The Browns added three-time Pro Bowl pass rusher, Za'Darius Smith who had 10 sacks for the Vikings in 2022. Given that key addition and some defensive moves in the NFL draft, the Browns have upgraded their defense this offseason. Smith is expected to take over Jadeveon Clowney's role this season.

2023 OUTLOOK:

It's easy to pick on the Cleveland Browns, but honestly, they are a balanced team heading into the 2023 season. They have the pieces in place at defense to upset opposing quarterbacks and are putting together an offense with plenty of weapons for Deshaun Watson to choose from. What I like most about this team from a fantasy perspective is that you won't have to break the bank to acquire any of the wide receivers and you should also be able to get Deshaun Watson at a discount. All of these have the upside worthy of their average draft position.

Jacksonville Jaguars Fantasy Preview

KEY LOSSES: James Robinson (RB)

KEY ADDITIONS: Calvin Ridley (WR), D'Ernest Johnson (RB)

FANTASY IMPACT:

The Jaguars traded running back James Robinson to the New York Jets in the middle of last season. Travis Etienne is in the driver's seat of Jacksonville's backfield. Don't underestimate the signing of former Browns' running back D'Ernest Johnson. Johnson filled in nicely for an injured Kareem Hunt in 2021. He averaged 5.3 yards per carry on 100 attempts. Johnson also showed he can be an asset as a receiver out of the backfield. He has an opportunity to be the RB2 on the team, but a certain Jaguars third-round draft pick may have something to say about it.

It's been nearly two years since Calvin Ridley stepped foot on an NFL field. He played just five games in 2021 before stepping away to address his mental health. Unfortunately for Ridley, he would be suspended for the entirety of the 2022 season for betting on NFL games in 2021. At his peak, Calvin Ridley showed he could be a WR1. In 2020, he totaled 90 catches for 1,374 yards and nine touchdowns for the Falcons. He'll get the chance to be Trevor Lawrence's top target in 2023, but he's got a lot to prove before that can happen.

DRAFTED PLAYERS OF FANTASY NOTE: Brenton Strange (TE), Tank Bigsby (RB)

FANTASY IMPACT:

Tight End Evan Engram had an outstanding season for the Jaguars last year. He caught 73 of his 98 targets for 766 yards and four touchdowns. He finished as fantasy football's TE5 (PPR). It appears Engram is holding out to work out a long-term deal with the team. The Jaguars answered by drafting Penn State tight end Brenton Strange with their 61st overall pick. Jacksonville doesn't have much depth at the position, so the rookie could be in for a decent workload in 2023.

The Jaguars drafted Auburn running back Tank Bigsby with their third-round selection. He is a high enough draft pick to give the young back an opportunity to put his stamp in this backfield behind Etienne. Bigsby must impress the coaching staff enough to surpass JaMycal Hasty and the newly acquired D'Ernest Johnson. Given his draft cost, Bigsby may be worth a late-round flyer and/or handcuff for Travis Etienne Jr. managers.

OFFENSIVE OUTLOOK:

There are a few question marks heading into the 2023 season for the Jacksonville Jaguars. How will Calvin Ridley bounce back from an extended absence from the game? Will Evan Engram and the Jaguars work out a contract? Regardless of uncertainties, Trevor Lawrence is becoming the leader that Jacksonville drafted him to be. He was the QB7 in 2022 with over 4,000 passing yards and a 25/8 touchdown to interception ratio. Lawrence has proven to be an asset as a runner when needed, finishing as a top-10 QB in rush yards and top-5 with five rushing touchdowns. The benefit of Jaguars' fantasy assets heading into this season is that you can get most of them as low-risk, high-reward picks in your fantasy drafts.

DEFENSIVE OUTLOOK

The Jacksonville Jaguars didn't address many defensive needs early this year's draft. A little surprising, considering the Jags D gave up the fifth-most passing yards in 2022. However, they did show improvement toward the end of last season, so maybe the coaching staff feels confident in the direction they are moving defensively. Although the Jaguars gave up a ton through the air, they appear to be a "bend, but not break" type of unit. They allowed the 12th fewest points against last year. This defense doesn't excite me enough to consider them in fantasy football.

2023 OUTLOOK:

The Jaguars have been in the development stages for years. They finally look like a legitimate contender with Trevor Lawrence leading the way. They have the right pieces in place to be a productive offense in 2023. There will be plenty of options in Jacksonville to give you upside for your fantasy football squads. Lawrence was top-10 in passing yards last year and has some new weapons to target in 2023. I suggest being a bit cautious with wild-card Calvin Ridley as some fantasy managers may push his ADP to a place that can become too risky as we get closer to the season. When it comes to Evan Engram, follow the money. If he does indeed sign with the team, his contract will guide you on what to expect from him from a volume standpoint. As for the other offensive pieces, I have a feeling there will be one or two fantasy football waiver-wire heroes on this team.

Tennessee Titans Fantasy Preview

KEY LOSSES: Robert Woods (WR), Austin Hooper (TE)

KEY ADDITIONS: N/A

FANTASY IMPACT:

The only reason that Robert Woods is considered a key loss is that he led the Titans' wideouts in receptions and receiving yards. It's not saying much, as Woods totaled just 53 receptions on 91 targets, 527 receiving yards, and two touchdowns on the year.

This team didn't make any significant moves in free agency that should have anyone excited from a fantasy football standpoint.

DRAFTED PLAYERS OF FANTASY NOTE: Will Levis (QB), Tyjae Spears (RB), Josh Whyle (TE)

FANTASY IMPACT:

Will Levis is likely to be a season away from seeing significant playing time in the NFL. That is, of course, unless Ryan Tannehill underperforms or gets injured. Even if something like that were to happen, Malik Willis (Titans' 2022 third-round pick) is still on the roster and should back up Tannehill in 2023.

Surprisingly, the Titans didn't do much to improve their wide receiver group considering Derrick Henry is not a lock to return to Tennessee for the 2023 season. That means they are still comfortable with running the ball a ton which would bring immediate value to rookie running back Tyjae Spears. If Henry and the Titans can't come to some kind of agreement, the 81st-overall pick will likely see plenty of opportunity alongside Hassan Haskins.

Cincinnati tight end Josh Whyle was drafted by the Titans in the 5th round. There's still a path to some decent volume for the rookie. The Titans heavily utilized tight ends Austin Hooper and Chigoziem Okonkwo in 2022. Hooper is now on the Las Vegas Raiders and leaves behind 60 vacated targets. Whyle didn't dominate as a receiving option in college, but his 6-foot-6-inch, 248 lbs frame presents as a big red zone target option for Tannehill should he continue favoring the tight end position.

OFFENSIVE OUTLOOK:

This offense has run through Derrick Henry since 2018. If Derrick Henry doesn't stick around, this Titans organization is going to regret not beefing up their pass catchers a lot more. Nick Westbrook-Ikhine had just 25 receptions in 2022 but led the Titans wideouts with a massive three touchdown receptions. Two of which came in Week 10 against the Broncos. Given the Titans' current quarterback position and their underwhelming options at wide receiver, this passing game is going to be something to avoid. One pass catcher that may be worth drafting in fantasy is tight end Chigoziem Okonkwo. He had six more receiving yards and one more touchdown than Austin Hooper last year despite having 14 fewer targets. Okonkwo became more involved halfway through the season, and he's in line for a lot more volume in 2023, especially with Austin Hooper gone.

DEFENSIVE OUTLOOK

The Titans' defense is built to stop the run. In fact, they were the best against the run in 2022. The real problem with Tennessee's defense is through the air. They ranked dead last in passing yards against last year. They tied for allowing the second-most touchdown passes and were middle of the pack in points against. Despite their defensive struggles, the Titans did not use a single 2023 draft pick on defense. They did address defense in free agency and made a handful of defensive coaching hires in the offseason as well.

2023 OUTLOOK:

This team is going to be extremely difficult to trust this year. They are clearly rebuilding and looking to a future with Will Levis. If Derrick Henry departs, then rookie Tyjae Spears immediately skyrockets in value. Even then, it would be difficult to trust him to take over a one-dimensional offense in his first NFL season. Given the Titans' offseason moves, it would be surprising to see Henry walk this season. He is still under contract for this year, but we've seen the last year of contracts turn into a trade or release many times before. Derrick Henry and Chigoziem Okonkwo are the only Titans assets I'm interested in for fantasy football this season.

Houston Texans Fantasy Preview

KEY LOSSES: Brandin Cooks (WR), Chris Moore (WR),

KEY ADDITIONS: Devin Singletary (RB), Noah Brown (WR), Dalton Shultz (TE)

FANTASY IMPACT:

The Texans moved on from consistent producer Brandin Cooks and their 2022 WR2 Chris Moore. This offense is ready to evolve with Nico Collins, John Metchie, and former Dallas Cowboys wideout Noah Brown. C.J. Stroud will most likely be the starting quarterback in Week 1. That also makes another certain draft pick an interesting option for fantasy, but more about that later.

The Texans signed former Buffalo Bills running back Devin Singletary. He's a complimentary piece to Dameon Pierce but has more talent than any Texans backup RB from 2022. This could pose a potential decrease in volume for Pierce in 2023 but should lead to more efficiency in their backfield.

Another Dallas Cowboys player joins the Texans this season. Tight end Dalton Shultz was a top-10 tight end in 2022. He's a viable pass catcher who will be a great weapon and possible safety blanket for C.J. Stroud in Stroud's first NFL season.

DRAFTED PLAYERS OF FANTASY NOTE: C.J. Stroud (QB), Nathaniel "Tank" Dell (WR)

FANTASY IMPACT:

We could see these two rookies connect early and often in 2023. As the number two overall pick in the draft, C.J. Stroud is expected to lead this team from the jump. A risky fantasy football pick in year-one, but a risk worth taking as we've seen rookie QBs step in with immediate success before.

Nathaniel Dell led the NCAA with 1,398 receiving yards and 17 touchdowns last year. What makes Tank Dell an instant consideration for fantasy football teams this season is the fact he was someone C.J. Stroud asked the Texans to draft. The Texans honored their #1 pick's wishes and drafted Dell with their 69th-overall pick. Tank Dell is a smaller receiver, but he's going to get volume given his draft pick and Stroud vying for him in the draft.

OFFENSIVE OUTLOOK:

This offense makes me uncomfortable because there are too many new pieces to trust just how things will shake out. It's not necessarily a bad thing as the weapons that have been added are very talented and capable of producing for the NFL and fantasy. Nico Collins saw a significant uptick in volume from Week 10 last season. He's expected to be the top target, but I think I'd rather draft the upside of Tank Dell.

I expect Dameon Pierce and Devin Singletary to balance each other, allowing Pierce to have fresh legs more often and produce more efficiently. Pierce averaged 4.3 yards per carry on 220 attempts last season. Dalton Shultz becomes the tight end to target in Houston. He presents someone you can draft at a value in 2023.

DEFENSIVE OUTLOOK

Coach DeMeco Ryans, naturally a defensive mind, has been making some beneficial moves to the Texans' defense this offseason. They drafted Alabama pass rusher Will Anderson Jr. with the 3rd overall pick. They added to their defensive line with TCU DE Dylan Horton in the fourth round and followed that pick with Alabama linebacker Henry To'oto'o. The Texans made some key defensive moves outside of the draft as well. They signed free agent linebackers Neville Hewitt and Jermain Carter. Most recently, and likely the biggest splash, was the signing of Pro Bowl cornerback Shaquill Griffin. Griffin offers leadership and still has something left in the tank to make an impact on the field. This defense is looking much improved, and they are just starting under head coach Demeco Ryans.

2023 OUTLOOK:

The Texans are turning the page to a new era in Houston. They are getting younger and faster and have plenty of high expectations heading into the 2023 season. There is a lot of buzz and excitement surrounding the offensive assets on this team. This is expected when a team land one of the top quarterbacks in the draft. There is cause to approach drafting Texans in fantasy drafts this offseason. There could be some growing pains at least this season with so many changes happening all at once. I'm not saying to avoid drafting Texans because I'm a believer in the upside. Just weigh the possible risk and take a look at your supporting fantasy pieces before pulling the trigger.

Indianapolis Colts Fantasy Preview

KEY LOSSES: Matt Ryan (QB), Paris Campbell (WR)

KEY ADDITIONS: Gardner Minshew (QB), Isaiah McKenzie (WR)

FANTASY IMPACT:

Matt Ryan was a shell of his old self during his time with the Colts. It's easiest to put the blame on him, but the offensive line did little to protect Ryan. He was facing immediate pressure as soon as he was looking to his first read on many plays. I digress. It's clear Indianapolis had to move on, and they did. They signed free agent quarterback Gardner Minshew just two days after letting Ryan go. Minshew is a short-term solution if he plays at all this season as the Colts utilized their first-overall pick on a quarterback.

Wide receiver Paris Campbell was the Colts' WR2 last season. He caught 63 of his 91 targets for 623 yards and three touchdowns. Something newly acquired wideout Isaiah McKenzie can handle. McKenzie wasn't far off from Campbell's production last year as the third, sometimes the fourth option in the Bills' passing attack. McKenzie will fit in nicely with this wide receiver group in 2023.

DRAFTED PLAYERS OF FANTASY NOTE: Anthony Richardson (QB), Josh Downs (WR)

FANTASY IMPACT:

With the first pick of the 2023 NFL Draft, the Indianapolis Colts select... Anthony Richardson, Quarterback, Florida. The Colts are ready to move on from mediocracy with their new weapon at the quarterback position. However, it's unclear whether Richardson will be the starter in Week 1. Gardner Minshew is a quarterback capable enough at the NFL level to give the rookie some time to develop should he need it. Whenever Anthony Richardson is ready to go, he gives opposing defenses a lot to think of as a diverse quarterback who can also produce on the ground.

The Colts have enough wide receivers to not force their third-round pick onto the field too early. Josh Downs was a great pick for the Colts and is someone who can make an immediate impact if needed. There's plenty of offseason left for Downs to do enough to move up the depth chart. For now, he's not someone I'd consider drafting in fantasy unless you can get him late.

OFFENSIVE OUTLOOK:

If Gardner Minshew starts the season under center for the Colts, it's not enough to scare me off their key pass catchers. Michael Pittman Jr. was one of my favorite wide receivers heading into last season. Unfortunately for him, the combination of the offensive line and Matt Ryan did him in from a fantasy perspective. I'm doubling down on Pittman this season, especially at his fallen price. To me, it's a toss-up between Alec Pierce, Isaiah McKenzie, and Josh Downs as to who will step up and become the WR2 in this offense. I'd lean toward McKenzie at least to begin the season.

Jonathan Taylor has fallen too much to not take him at his ADP, regardless of where it is come draft time. This team should be performing much better than they did last season and one of the key pieces will be Jonathan Taylor. He's among the top players on my bounce-back list.

DEFENSIVE OUTLOOK

The Colts have seen some significant changes to their defense this offseason. Linebacker, Bobby Okereke moved his talents to the New York Giants and the Colts traded star cornerback Stephon Gilmore to the Cowboys. The Colts' front office wasted little time addressing their defensive needs in the draft. They took Kansas State cornerback Julius Brents with the 44th overall pick. They went on to draft a defensive tackle (Adetomiwa Adebawore, Northwestern) in the fourth round and two more defensive picks in the fifth round (South Carolina CB Darius Rush and California safety Daniel Scott). Although they are making the appropriate moves to address weaknesses, the Colts defensive unit has lost key leaders heading into this season and they will look to the young draft picks to step up early.

2023 OUTLOOK:

Like the Texans, this team has had plenty of changes this offseason. The changes are encouraging enough for me to trust this team's key fantasy assets again. As I mentioned, both Michael Pittman and Jonathan Taylor are likely to be a discount in this season's fantasy football drafts and both are well worth the picks at whatever their ADP will be on draft day. I'd prefer the quarterback position to be figured out already, but Gardner Minshew is a solid option to start the season and has enough to dish out fantasy production to his receivers. My biggest hesitation is this offensive line. If they can't step up and improve from last season, I'll be eating this page of the Fantasy Football Black Book.

NFC EAST/WEST

Chris Meaney

Dallas Cowboys Fantasy Preview

KEY LOSSES: Ezekiel Elliott (RB), Dalton Schultz (TE)

KEY ADDITIONS: Brandin Cooks (WR), Stephon Gilmore (CB), Ronald Jones (RB)

FANTASY IMPACT:

The Dalton Schultz loss is significant to Dak Prescott as the tight end totaled 13 touchdowns over the past two seasons. However, the Cowboys desperately needed someone opposite of CeeDee Lamb since moving on from Amari Cooper and they got that with Cooks. He joins his fifth team since 2016 and he brings six 1,000-yard seasons to Dallas. Six of those campaigns have come over his last eight years. He hasn't scored more than six touchdowns since 2017, but he could top that with the move from Houston to Dallas.

The biggest change on this team is at the running back position as they released Ezekiel Elliott after seven seasons. Zeke remains a free agent and the keys to the offense officially belong to Tony Pollard.

DRAFTED PLAYERS OF FANTASY NOTE: Luke Schoonmaker, TE (Michigan), Deuce Vaughn, RB (Kansas State), Jalen Brooks, WR (South Carolina)

FANTASY IMPACT:

A feel-good moment for Dallas' assistant director of college scouting Chris Vaughn as he made the call to select his son Deuce on draft day. The sixth-round selection means the Cowboys feel pretty good about Pollard as their lead back heading into the season. Vaughn will compete with Ronald Jones and Malik Davis for touches, and he should come out ahead of both. Despite his 5-foot-5, 179-pound frame, Vaughn led all FBS backs with 1,936 total yards last year and he racked up 24 touchdowns in his last two seasons. He had 42 and 49 catches in his last two campaigns with Kansas State and he saw 124 targets over that span. He was a true bell cow back in college as he finished with 234 carries, 1,404 yards and 18 touchdowns in 2021. He followed that up with 293 carries, 1,558 yards and nine touchdowns in 2022. The burst and lateral quickness is there, but he'll unlikely be an option for us fantasy players due to his size. Brooks will open up camp behind Michael Gallup and Jalen Tolbert, but both were disappointing in 2022.

OFFENSIVE OUTLOOK:

Dallas finished in the middle of the pack in Total DVOA (15) and Pass DVOA (13) last season, according to Football Outsiders. They were a top 10 rushing team, but I believe they'll miss Zeke more than some may think, especially as a pass blocker and near the goal line. Nonetheless, Pollard has been the better back over the past couple of seasons and he's finally free of Elliott. Pollard had his season cut short last year due to a broken fibula and it remains to be seen if he can handle a full workload, or if he can be productive near the goal line. Dallas doesn't seem to be worried about those questions. He's a low-end RB1 with upside to finish as a top five running back at the position.

Lamb has top five upside at his position as well, but the same can't be said for Prescott. The Cowboys' QB threw a career high 15 interceptions last season and he only played 12 games. Dak and the offense could become more run heavy with Brian Schottenheimer in as OC and Kellen Moore now with the Chargers. Dak is a better target in superflex leagues.

DEFENSIVE OUTLOOK:

As I mentioned last year in the Black Book, Dan Quinn is a big reason this defense has been one of the best units in football since his arrival. Dallas ranked second in Total DVOA, third in Pass DVOA and fifth in Rush DVOA. Only the 49ers allowed fewer points per game than Dallas in the NFC (20.1). Gilmore and Trevon Diggs make for a solid duo at cornerback, but the heart and soul of the defense is Michah Parsons.

2023 TEAM OUTLOOK:

There's no question the Cowboys are contenders in the NFC. They'll compete with the Eagles in the NFC East and if we're following trends, they may win it as there hasn't been a repeat winner in the division since 2004. They are +185 to win the NFC East and they check in with a 9.5 win total which only trails the Eagles and 49ers in the NFC. The conference is extremely weak, so the fact you can get 16-1 for them to win the Super Bowl is appealing.

New York Giants Fantasy Preview

KEY LOSSES: Richie James (WR), Kenny Golladay (WR), Julian Love (S), Nick Gates (C), Jon Deliciano (LG)

KEY ADDITIONS: Darren Waller (TE), Parris Campbell (WR), Jamison Crowder (WR), Bobby Okereke (LB), A'Shawn Robinson (IDL), Rakeem Nunez-Roches (IDL)

OFFSEASON FANTASY IMPACT:

The Giants made a few moves on defense, but their biggest splash on offense came when they traded for tight end Darren Waller. The former Raider had back-to-back seasons with 90+ catches and 1,100+ yards in 2019 and 2020, but his last two years have been very disappointing. Waller has only played 20 games in the last two seasons due to multiple injuries and he only has five touchdowns to show for it. Although I like the fit and he could certainly lead New York in targets, he's on the wrong side of 30.

Campbell's first full season in the NFL came at the right time as he received a new contract from the Giants. Despite playing 17 games, he only finished with 623 yards and three scores. Campbell has 32 games, 97 catches, 983 yards and five touchdowns in four seasons. He's been held under eight games in three of his four years. He'll compete with Isaiah Hodgins, Darius Slayton, Wan'Dale Robinson, Jalin Hyatt and Sterling Shepard for targets at WR.

DRAFTED PLAYERS OF FANTASY NOTE: Jalin Hyatt, WR (Tennessee), Eric Gray, RB (Oklahoma)

FANTASY IMPACT:

Good value on Hyatt as some had him mocked to go in the early second round. Hyatt brings a ton of speed to a Giants squad that lacked explosiveness in their game last season. Hyatt's seven grabs of 50+ yards ranked first in FBS. Hyatt could play a similar role as Gabe Davis did for Brian Daboll in Buffalo. That means he'll likely be very boom or bust for the first couple of seasons.

OFFENSIVE OUTLOOK:

In his first year as a head coach, Daboll brought this offense from the worst in the NFL to 10th in Total DVOA. They finished 10th in Pass DVOA and seventh in Rush DVOA. In Daboll we trust as he was able to get Daniel Jones paid. Jones may have only tossed 15 touchdowns, but he set career highs in completion percentage (67.9%), passing yards (3,205), rushing yards (708) and rushing touchdowns (7). Best of all, he only threw five interceptions after racking up 29 in his first three seasons. He's a low end QB1 that nobody seems to want, but this offense should be better in year two with Daboll and some of the weapons that were added.

Don't fool yourself in thinking the offense doesn't run through Saquon Barkley. The Giants' back put all the injury prone talk to rest last season. He played 16 games and finished with a career high 295 carries and 1,312 rushing yards. He caught 50+ balls for the third time in his five years and his 10 rushing touchdowns were the most he's had since his rookie season.

DEFENSIVE OUTLOOK:

The Giants improved on offense, but they still had plenty of issues on defense last season. Only Chicago, Las Vegas and Atlanta ranked worse in Total DVOA. They finished 22nd in Pass DVOA and dead last in Rush DVOA. The additions of Nunez-Roches and Robinson will help the run defense.

2023 TEAM OUTLOOK:

The Giants squeaked into the playoffs last season with nine wins and they even won a playoff game on the road. It was their first playoff win in over 10 years. They ranked 22nd in average scoring margin (-1.6). Five of their wins were decided by seven or fewer points and three of their losses were by one score or less. The Giants are long shots to win the division (+600) and their win total is 8.5 in most spots. I'd lean to over 7.5, but it's a stay away for me at 8.5.

Philadelphia Eagles Fantasy Preview

KEY LOSSES: Miles Sanders (RB), Javone Hargrave (DE), Isaac Seumalo (LG), Andre Dillard (LT), Kyzir White (LB), T.J. Edwards (LB), Chauncey Gardner-Johnson Jr., (S), Marcus Epps (S), Gardner Minshew (QB), Zach Pascal (WR)

KEY ADDITIONS: D'Andre Swift (RB), Rashaad Penny (RB), Dan Arnold (TE), Marcus Mariota (QB), Olamide Zaccheaus (WR), Terrell Edmunds (S)

OFFSEASON FANTASY IMPACT:

The Eagles lost some key pieces on defense, but they were able to bring back Jason Kelce, Fletcher Cox, Brandon Graham and James Bradberry. It seemed like Darius Slay was on his way to Baltimore before signing a two-year contract extension with Philadelphia.

After a zero-touchdown season from Sanders in 2021, Miles bounced back in a big way as he set career highs in carries (259), yards (1,269) and touchdowns (11). Sanders only had nine in his first three seasons in the NFL. The Eagles chose to let him walk to Carolina and now they have a running back room that consists of D'Andre Swift, Rashaad Penny, Kenneth Gainwell and Boston Scott. All four of those backs make up less than $6 million dollars and 2% of their cap. Swift and Penny are fantasy darlings in the community but both have issues staying healthy. This has a committee written all over it but the o-line is strong, so if one can emerge it could be a difference maker for the Eagles and your fantasy team. Penny could be their short yardage and goal line back. Swift's ceiling is high and the Philly native is explosive as a pass catcher.

DRAFTED PLAYERS OF FANTASY NOTE: Jalen Carter, DT (Georgia), Nolan Smith, LB (Georgia), Kelee Ringo, CB (Georgia)

FANTASY IMPACT:

A year after drafting Georgia defenders Jordan Davis and Nakobe Dean, the Eagles took three more Bulldogs in this year's NFL Draft. GM Howie Roseman continues to build through the trenches, and he's had a lot of success doing so.

OFFENSIVE OUTLOOK:

The Eagles were dominant on both sides of the ball last season. According to Football Outsiders, they were first in Rush DVOA, ninth in Pass DVOA and sixth in Total DVOA. They'll be hard pressed to repeat what they did last season, as they have a new OC, tougher schedule and team's will be more prepared for this offense. However, they have one of the best WR duos in the league in A.J. Brown and DeVonta Smith. The Eagles led the NFC in points per game (28.1), which was good for third overall. Brown is a WR1, Smith is WR2 and Dallas Goedert has upside to be a top five tight end.

As for Jalen Hurts, the breakout many expected last season happened. In his second full season as a starter in the NFL, he finished with a career best 3,701 passing yards, 22 passing touchdowns, a 66.5 completion percentage, and 13 rushing touchdowns. He was first in fantasy points per game and was on his way to a potential MVP if he hadn't suffered a shoulder injury towards the end of the season. Hurts has 1,500 rushing yards and 23 rushing touchdowns in the last two seasons. He finished last year with a 16-2 record, and he's won 21 of his last 25 games. It's only part of why Philly handed him $255 million in the offseason.

DEFENSIVE OUTLOOK:

The Eagles finished first in Pass DVOA and sixth in Total DVOA in 2022. They lost some pieces on this side of the ball, but they'll have one of the best cornerback duos in the league once again. However, they're weak in the middle of the field and that's where teams will attack them. They were 21st in Rush DVOA, but they still have a strong run defense. Teams just failed to have success throwing against them, so some of the rushing numbers are skewed. However, the schedule is much tougher in 2023, so the secondary will be tested more than they were last season.

2023 TEAM OUTLOOK:

Not listed above is the loss of OC Shane Steichen and DC Jonathan Gannon. It can be tough to lose one coordinator, let alone two. Brian Johnson takes over at OC and Sean Desai at DC. Eagles' fans will tell you the loss of Steichen is much bigger than Gannon's departure. The Eagles win total is juiced at 10.5 and they're +110 favorites to win the division. They also have the shortest odds in the NFC to win the Super Bowl (+850). They have the toughest schedule in the NFL this season, based on their opponent's winning percentage from last season.

Washington Commanders Fantasy Preview

KEY LOSSES: Carson Wentz (QB), Taylor Heinicke (QB), J.D. McKissic (RB), Wes Schewitzer (C), Cole Holcomb (LB)

KEY ADDITIONS: Eric Bieniemy (OC), Andrew Wylie (RT), Jacoby Brissett (QB), Cody Barton (LB), Nick Gates (C)

OFFSEASON FANTASY IMPACT:

The Commanders will open up the season with Sam Howell as their starting quarterback after parting ways with Carson Wentz after just one season. Howell is Washington's 13th different starting quarterback since Kirk Cousins left in 2017. He should open up as the team's starter in Week 1 but don't be surprised if you see Brissett at some point. The biggest addition to the Commanders is Eric Bieniemy at OC. He's served as the offensive coordinator for the Chiefs over the last five seasons. He'll bring plenty of creativity to the Washington offense which they've lacked.

DRAFTED PLAYERS OF FANTASY NOTE: Chris Rodriguez Jr., RB (Kentucky)

FANTASY IMPACT:

The Commanders only drafted one skilled player on offense and it was Rodriguez Jr. with pick 193 in the sixth round. He's nothing more than a short yardage back, but he'll be behind Brian Robinson Jr. on the depth chart. He'll also be behind Antonio Gibson and he won't cut into his work through the air. Gibson is the big winner in the offseason as the team parted ways with McKissic.

OFFENSIVE OUTLOOK:

The Wentz experience in Washington went exactly how you thought it may have. He was benched halfway through the season and later cut in the offseason. Washington ranked 28th in Total DVOA and 26th in both Pass and Rush

145

DVOA. Howell isn't the answer, but it'll be interesting to see how this offense looks with Bieniemy. Terry McLaurin desperately needs a QB to get him the ball. He's going a bit too early for my liking, but I will have shares of Joahan Dotson once again. Dotson only caught 35 passes over his 12 games, but he scored seven touchdowns.

DEFENSIVE OUTLOOK:

The Commanders had a top 10 defense last season and they finished eighth in Rush DVOA (13th in Pass DVOA). Defense hasn't really been the issue with Washington over the years. They took cornerback Emmanuel Forbes with their first pick last season, which should help their pass defense. Their defense kept them in a lot of games, and they were a nightmare for opposing running backs as they allowed the fourth-fewest fantasy points per game to RBs.

2023 TEAM OUTLOOK:

The Commanders are 13-1 to win the NFC East and 80-1 in some spots to win the Super Bowl. Their win total is 6.5 and it's a number I could see them surpassing but the division is very tough and there are plenty of questions about their QB. Their defense will keep them in games again in 2023 but they may have a bottom 10 offense yet again.

Arizona Cardinals Fantasy Preview

KEY LOSSES: J.J. Watt, (DE), Chosen Anderson (WR), Byron Murphy (CB), Zach Allen (IDL), DeAndre Hopkins (WR)

KEY ADDITIONS: Jonathan Gannon (HC), Kyzir White (LB), Zach Pascal (WR), Jeff Driskel (QB)

OFFSEASON FANTASY IMPACT:

The Cardinals hired Monti Ossenfort to be their new GM and he hired Jonathan Gannon to be their new head coach. Gannon did some good things with the Eagles over the past two seasons as their defensive coordinator. Unfortunately, the Cardinals don't have close to the same talent on the field that Gannon had in Philadelphia. It'll be interesting to see how Kyler Murray and the offense looks without Kliff Kingsbury and with Drew Petzing as the OC. This will be his first season as an offensive coordinator.

DRAFTED PLAYERS OF FANTASY NOTE: Paris Johnson Jr., OT (Ohio State), Michael Wilson, WR (Stanford), Clayton Tune, QB (Houston)

FANTASY IMPACT:

Michael Wilson is the only fantasy-relevant player the Cardinals drafted, and he may not bring much to the table in his first season in the NFL. Wilson has only played 14 games over the last three years due to multiple injuries (foot & collarbone). DeAndre Hopkins has officially been released, leaving Marquise Brown and Rondale Moore as the top two receiving options in Arizona. Wilson has more appeal in keeper and dynasty formats.

OFFENSIVE OUTLOOK:

Petzing will have his hands full in the first few weeks of the season as Murray could miss the first 4-6 weeks and potentially even longer as he recovers from a torn ACL. Look for Colt McCoy and Jeff Driskel to fill the void until he returns. He makes for a risky pick and someone to only really consider in redraft formats. If DeAndre Hopkins gets traded, it'll open up a path for Wilson, but the offense will take a big hit.

DEFENSIVE OUTLOOK:

The Cardinals will have one of the worst defenses in football this season. Last year they ranked 24th in Total DVOA, 21st in Pass DVOA and 22nd in Rush DVOA, according to Football Outsiders. Arizona allowed the 10th most fantasy points to quarterbacks, the thid-most to running backs and the most to tight ends.

2023 TEAM OUTLOOK:

It's going to be a long season for first-year head coach Gannon and the Cardinals. Arizona has a league-low 5.5 win total and I have a lean to the under. We could see Hopkins and Budda Baker get traded at any moment, which will only make them worse. Don't be surprised if the Cardinals have another top five pick in next year's draft. This will be a team to stack against in NFL DFS.

San Francisco 49ers Fantasy Preview

KEY LOSSES: Jimmy Garoppolo (QB), Mike McGlinchey (RT), Robbie Gould (K), Jimmie Ward (S), Samson Ebukam (EDGE), Emmanuel Moseley (CB), Azeez Al-Shaair (LB), Daniel Brunskill (RG), Hassan Ridgeway (IDL), Tyler Kroft (TE), Charles Omenihu (EDGE)

KEY ADDITIONS: Javon Hargrave (IDL), Clelin Ferrell (EDGE), Sam Darnold (QB), Brandon Allen (QB), Jon Feliciano (LG), Isaiah Oliver (CB), Zane Gonzalez (K), Chris Conley (WR)

OFFSEASON FANTASY IMPACT:

The 49ers were inside the top 10 in sacks last season, and they added Hargrave, who had a career-high 11 for the Eagles last season. Despite losing a few players on the defensive side of the ball, this team will yet again have one of the top-ranked defense of the year. Jimmy Garoppolo's departure opens up the door for Trey Lance to compete with Brock Purdy for the starting gig. Sam Darnold is also on the squad, and it's possible we see him at one point. Lance and Purdy are coming off a season in which they suffered season-ending injuries. It sounds like Purdy will have a chance to be the Week 1 starter.

DRAFTED PLAYERS OF FANTASY NOTE: Cameron Latu, TE (Alabama), Jake Moody, K (Michigan), Brayden Willis, TE (Oklahoma), Ronnie Bell, WR (Michigan)

FANTASY IMPACT:

The Niners selected not one but two tight ends, and you guessed it, they'll play behind George Kittle. Latu has a higher ceiling than Willis, and he'll provide a breather for Kittle. We could also see more two tight ends sets from San Francisco's offense. The 49ers didn't pick until the third round, and they selected kicker Jake Moody with their second pick in the third (99th). He should beat out Zane Gonzalez, who SF traded for.

OFFENSIVE OUTLOOK:

The strength of this team is defense and there's really no debating that. However, they do have some very skilled offensive players, including Deebo Samuel Brandon Aiyuk, George Kittle and Chris McCaffrey. CMC's game took off when he was traded to SF. The former Panther racked up 13 touchdowns in 14 games with the Niners. GM John Lynch said Purdy has earned the right to start for the 49ers, and he's progressing really well. Purdy finished 6-0 in the regular season and won two playoff games. He had a rock solid 13:4 TD:INT and finished with a 67.1 completion percentage. He tossed at least two touchdowns in all six games, but he only threw more than 250 yards once in those six regular season games and never more than 284 (332 in the playoffs).

DEFENSIVE OUTLOOK:

The 49ers had the NFL's best defense last season, according to Football Outsiders. They were fifth in Pass DVOA and second in Rush DVOA. They surrendered the fewest fantasy points to running backs and the sixth-fewest to quarterbacks. Steve Willks takes over as San Francisco's DC after they lost DeMeco Ryans to Houston. Like Robert Salah, Ryans received a head coaching job thanks to his work on the defensive side of the ball. The 49ers allowed a league-best 16.3 points per game.

2023 TEAM OUTLOOK:

The 49ers are NFC West favorites at -149. They have an 11.5 win total, and they're 10-1 to win the Super Bowl. The path to the SB from the NFC is much easier than the AFC. The only question I have about this team is the QB play.

As mentioned, Purdy was great in a small sample size. Let's see if he can do it again. I'm willing to bank on Kyle Shanahan playing to Purdy's strengths.

Seattle Seahawks Fantasy Preview

KEY LOSSES: Rashaad Penny (RB), Travis Homer (RB), Quinton Jefferson (IDL), Jonathan Abram (S), Marquise Goodwin (WR), Ryan Neal (S), Cody Barton (LB)

KEY ADDITIONS: Bobby Wagner (LB), Devin Bush (LB), Jarran Reed (IDL), Dre'Mont Jones (IDL), Evan Brown (C), Julian Love (S)

OFFSEASON FANTASY IMPACT:

Eight-time Prow Bowl linebacker Bobby Wagner is back in Seattle after one season with the Rams. He finished 2022 with a career-high six sacks. He brings a ton of leadership to this defense. As you can see, the Seahawks added defensive players through free agency.

DRAFTED PLAYERS OF FANTASY NOTE: Jaxon Smith-Njigba, WR (Ohio State), Zach Charbonnet, RB (UCLA), Kenny McIntosh, RB (Georgia), Devon Witherspoon (CB)

Seattle drafted the best wide receiver and cornerback in the draft. They also took Carbonnett and McIntosh, who will compete with each other for touches behind Kenneth Walker III. Charbonnett should win the job, but if he struggles as a pass blocker, he'll ride the pine. JSN's will open up the season as the team's number three wideout. However, he's worthy of being the first WR taken off the board, and his future looks bright.

FANTASY IMPACT:

The selection of Charbonnet at pick 51 was a touch surprising, considering Seattle drafted Kenneth Walker III with pick 41 last year. His 152.7 scrimmage yards per game last season ranked third in FBS. I love the player, Seattle isn't the best fit, and it cuts into Walker's production as well. Look for him to step up as the third down running back with Travis Homer and Rashaad Penny no longer around.

OFFENSIVE OUTLOOK:

Geno Smith led the NFL in completion percentage last season, and he finished as the fifth-best QB in fantasy (ninth in points per game). Smith has three solid options at WR and two very promising running backs, to go along with an improved defense. Smith, DK Metcalf, JSN, Tyler Lockett and Noah Fant make for a cheap stack to target in best ball formats. Lockett is undervalued again in drafts this season, but it's worth noting that the Seahawks have three good wideouts now, not two. Metcalf only scored six touchdowns, but he finished with a career-high in targets (141) and catches (141).

DEFENSIVE OUTLOOK:

The Seahawks ranked in the bottom 10 in Total DVOA defense last season and 25th in Rush DVOA. However, they are much improved on this side of the ball after landing the top corner in the draft to go along with the return of Wagner. He'll help the run defense get back to where they used to be. Seattle allowed the fourth-fewest fantasy points to RBs.

2023 TEAM OUTLOOK:

I'm feeling the Seahawks quite a bit this season. If I would have told you that they would have a top 10 pick the following year after trading away Russell Wilson, that would make sense. However, their top 10 pick was Denver's first, and Seattle made the playoffs in their first year without Wilson. I believe the Seahawks will make the playoffs again and compete with the 49ers for the division. Give me over 8.5 wins on the season and a sprinkle on them at +275 to win the NFL West.

Los Angeles Rams Fantasy Preview

KEY LOSSES: Jalen Ramsey (CB), Allen Robinson (WR), Baker Mayfield (QB), Bobby Wagner (LB), Matt Gay (K), A'Shawn Robinson (IDL), John Wolford (QB), Greg Gaines (IDL), Nick Scott (S)

KEY ADDITIONS: Hunter Long (TE), Brett Rypien (QB)

OFFSEASON FANTASY IMPACT:

The Rams lost two solid players in Jalen Ramsey and A'Shawn Robinson. Allen Robinson was a major disappointment in Los Angeles as he only played 10 games (33 grabs and 3 td). It seems like years and years ago since A-Rob was fantasy relevant at wide receiver.

DRAFTED PLAYERS OF FANTASY NOTE: Steve Avila, G (TCU), Stetson Bennett, QB (Georgia), Davis Allen, TE (Clemson), Puka Nacua, WR (BYU), Zach Evans RB (Ole Miss)

FANTASY IMPACT:

The Rams spent their first pick on the offensive line for the second straight season. That's great news for Matthew Stafford, who suffered two concussions in 2022, and his season was cut short due to a spinal cord contusion. Bennett will back up Stafford, Allen will play behind Tyler Higbee and Evans will play behind Cam Akers, who was fantastic down the stretch last year. Akers truthers (me) shouldn't worry too much about Sean McVay's selection of Evans. The Rams have selected a running back every year with McVay as head coach and Evans was taken in the seventh round. The most exciting player from a fantasy perspective that the Rams drafted is Pauka Nacua. The Rams didn't get much production from Van Jefferson, Ben Skowronek or Tutu Atwell when Cooper Kupp went down. They also moved on from A-Rob, so Nacua has a chance for targets right away. Cam Akers finished the season with three straight 100-yard games

OFFENSIVE OUTLOOK:

If Matthew Stafford or Cooper Kupp go down again, it'll be all over for the Rams. The Rams finished with a 5-12 record one year after winning the Super Bowl. Their 340 points scored was the second-worst mark in football.

DEFENSIVE OUTLOOK:

The Rams had one of the best defensive units in the league two seasons ago, but last year they ranked 24th in Pass DVOA. I don't know if we'll see much of an improvement with the loss of Jalen Ramsey to Miami. Seattle had a great offseason via free agency and the draft.

2023 TEAM OUTLOOK:

Talk about a Super Bowl hangover for the Rams, as almost everything went wrong for them in 2022. Stafford and Kupp will have to remain healthy all season in order to stay competitive. The Rams feel like they're rebuilding, but there's still a lot of star power on the squad. LA opens up at +750 to win the NFC West; their win total is 6.5.

NFC North/South

Chris McConnell

Detroit Lions Fantasy Preview

Key losses: Jamaal Williams (RB), D'Andre Swift (RB)

Jamaal Williams is no longer with the team, instead signing with the Saints in free agency. I bet you thought that meant D'Andre Swift was finally going to be set free, huh? Well, that was true…and then even more true after draft night when Swift was traded to the Eagles. The backfield will be okay, though (more on that in a minute), but it's not every year you see a team let go of both their highly productive RBs, especially when one of them led the league with 17 rushing TDs.

Key additions: David Montgomery (RB), C.J. Gardner-Johnson (CB)

Montgomery replaces the departed Jamaal Williams, signing a 3-year, $18M deal. Monty is coming off a career low in rushing yards and rushing TDs, so there seems to be some room for positive regression here. if he can overcome a talented newcomer (again, more on that in a minute). CJG sign a 1-year, $8M deal with Detroit, which seems like a steal of a deal for a consensus Top 10 free agent this past March. Gardner-Johnson reunites with former Saints DBs coach Aaron Glenn, Detroit's defensive coordinator, and should give the Lions secondary quite the boost as he looks to build off a solid 2022 season and earn a massive payday as a free agent in 2024.

Drafted Players of Fantasy Note: Jahmyr Gibbs (RB), Hendon Hooker (QB)

If you read my write-up on the Falcons, you could probably tell I thought the pick of RB Bijan Robinson with the 8th overall pick was the dumbest pick of the entire first round…that is, until Detroit decided to take the second-best RB in the draft with the 12th overall pick (if you haven't noticed, taking RBs in the 1st round is beyond stupid). Having said that, I've been a Georgia Tech fan all my life, and Jahmyr Gibbs is no slouch. He's an incredible talent and should thrive in the NFL. In PPR, he's going to have a ton of value. It was a puzzling pick on its own in the 1st round, but then D'Andre Swift was traded to the Eagles, and suddenly things brightened up a bit for Gibbs. He's a do-it-all RB but will operate the role that Swift vacates as the primary receiving back and big, chunk-play option in the backfield. He has a legitimate chance to be a fantasy RB1 in year 1. Hendon Hooker was drafted in the 3rd round and seems like he could be their franchise QB of the future, or at least that's their plan. Hooker enters the league at 25 years old, so his age apex isn't exactly the most appealing thing about him. But he's a talented thrower of the football who could actually see some starts this season. He's best looked at as a dynasty stash for the time being, albeit with a very high upside.

Fantasy Impact:

Jared Goff is no Pat Mahomes, but he's proven to be a rock-solid QB2 in fantasy, and that honestly shouldn't change in 2023. Amon-Ra St. Brown returns as the newly-minted alpha on offense, and when it finally looked like we'd see a lot of Jameson Williams…he gets suspended six games for gambling. Regardless, he'll be a huge addition in his second season to this Lions offense, and while ASB is gobbling up targets in the short & intermediate range, Jameson will eventually be tasked as the lid-lifter with a ton of chunk plays with explosion to boot. Will David Montgomery be better than Jamaal Williams? Probably not, but Jahmyr Gibbs should be better than both Swift AND J-Will, so the Lions won't lose much, if anything, in the RB room. There is no TE worth your time or a roster spot on the Lions roster, but that won't keep them from sporting a fantasy-friendly offense this season.

Offensive outlook:

What if I told you the Lions were a top 3-ranked offense in 2022? Well, believe it. Will there probably be a little bit of a regression there? Sure, but it's not like this offense will fall off the hinges completely. They should easily be a top 10 unit in 2023 and play in a division that doesn't have a bunch of fearsome defenses. Yeah, they'll be just fine.

Defensive outlook:

So why were the Lions only 9-8 with a top 3 ranked offense last year? Well, things like that tend to happen when you're sporting the worst defense in the NFL (so yeah, taking a RB in the 1st round makes sense, right?) But this is why they went out and signed CBs C.J. Gardner-Johnson and Cam Sutton in free agency, then went and drafted LB Jack Campbell from Iowa and CB Brian Branch from Alabama. All of these are big-time additions for a defense that is gasping for air heading into 2023, and if they want to capitalize on the expectations they're now faced with, they will need all the help they can get.

2023 Outlook:

The Lions surprised everyone last year and now enter 2023 as the favorites to win the NFC North, with no more Aaron Rodgers to contend with in Green Bay. Their offensive weaponry and defensive improvements are impressive, but is the latter enough to put them over the top? We should get a good sense of what and who the Lions are this season early on the year. The division is up for grabs, so they have every reason to be optimistic.

Minnesota Vikings Fantasy Preview

Key losses: Patrick Peterson (CB), Dalvin Tomlinson (DT), Adam Thielen (WR)

Patrick Peterson heads to the Steelers as he enters the final years of his career. He was more than solid for Minnesota last year, but it was time for them to pull the ripcord sooner rather than later. The bigger loss will likely be top-end run-stopper Dalvin Tomlinson, who heads to the Browns to beef up that defensive front further. In a division with some incredible runners, they'll need to plug this hole soon to ensure there's not a large drop-off in production. Adam Thielen was a fan favorite for all his years with the team, but he's now a shell of his former self, and the Vikings upgraded the WR room this offseason.

Key additions: Byron Murphy (CB)

Byron Murphy was one of the best corners available in free agency this year, and while he's not an elite player at age 25, he's still a solid addition for a team that needed to fill the void by losing Patrick Peterson so there's no reason to think much will change in regard to production from the CB unit.

Drafted Players of Fantasy Note: Jordan Addison (WR), DeWayne McBride (RB)

Many people had Jordan as the top WR in this year's class, and perhaps they were right. Regardless, he's a huge talent at the position, and Justin Jefferson needs help on the other. Addison will be the WR2 from the moment he steps foot on the field and could also wind up with some solid WR2 numbers in fantasy if he transitions quickly. He'll likely be a first-round pick in all rookie drafts and should immediately have a good chunk of production ready for your team in 2023. McBride is more of a "stash-and-see" player, as he won't see any playing time this year if Dalvin Cook stays with the team. However, if Dalvin departs in any way, McBride should be the favorite to backup then-starter Alex Mattison and in doing so, he'd likely see a healthy amount of snaps this season and would only be one injury away from a massive opportunity. Anything can happen with RBs as we've seen, so McBride is well worth a late 2nd-early 3rd round selection in your rookie drafts.

Fantasy Impact:

Well, we know what to expect from a few players. Justin Jefferson has been a top 6 fantasy WR every season he's been in the league so far, ending 2022 as the WR1 overall. He'll be the first WR off the board in almost all drafts this year, and another top-flight season is in the chamber, barring injury. Kirk Cousins should give us another solid QB2 fantasy season, while Dalvin Cook should also continue to do his normal routine, though that could change if he's cut or traded. The Vikings offense is in for another highly fantasy-friendly season, and I haven't even mentioned T.J. Hockenson yet.

Offensive outlook:

The Vikings were a top 7 offense last year, which should surprise no one. They are even more loaded this season than they were this time last year, so it's conceivable that they will only get better in 2023. Dalvin Cook's future is still in limbo, but either way, they should be fine at the RB position. There's barely a weak spot on this roster, as

T.J. Hockenson is also manning the TE position and will continue to provide high TE1 numbers. So, let's just put it simply: Draft Vikings players.

Defensive outlook:

So, this is where things get interesting. The Vikings offense is among the best in the league. But the defense? Well, they were ranked second-worst in the NFL overall, and this is the team's Achilles heel. Even if your offense isn't built to score WITH them, you will definitely be able to score ON them. They drafted 2 CBs and a DT in April, so some help should be coming, but it doesn't seem like they've made the required moves this offseason to improve this unit very much. Expect Minnesota to struggle mightily on defense yet again.

2023 Outlook:

As you probably guessed, this team's bread and butter is the offense. And that part of it will be fine. But as always, the Vikings success will hinge solely on two things: Their defense and the play of QB Kirk Cousins. Kirk has been pretty steady in his tenure there, so we know what to expect from him: He'll show flashes of brilliance, and then all of a sudden, he'll wet the bed randomly. In order to make a Super Bowl run, however, these two aspects of the team will have to simply be more consistent because otherwise, it'll be the same ole story: Decent-to-great regular season and underwhelming in the playoffs…if they can even make it there in 2023.

Chicago Bears Fantasy Preview

Key losses: David Montgomery (RB), Riley Reiff (OL)

David Montgomery departed for the Lions in free agency, leaving Khalil Herbert as the team's RB1 heading into 2023…we think (we'll get to that shortly). Perhaps the last thing the Bears needed was to let Riley Reiff walk in free agency, but they did. Now the offensive line arguably heads into 2023 with even more questions than answers, and that's probably not a good thing for Justin Fields' uniform cleanliness.

Key additions: D.J. Moore (WR), D'Onta Foreman (RB)

Speaking of Justin Fields, he was desperate for more help at WR last season, and Chase Claypool just wasn't cutting it. Instead, the team traded for the Panthers' D.J. Moore. Heading into his age 25 season, Moore has never been a fantasy (or real life) alpha WR (being the best WR on the Panthers roster doesn't mean you're an alpha), but the good news was he finally eclipsed four receiving TDs in a season for the first time in his career, though the trade-off was that his yards and reception totals took a dip. Listen, DJM has never had solid QB play in his career, and while on the surface, the move to Chicago seems like a good thing, it could just as easily be a terrible thing if Justin Fields doesn't take a step forward as a passer this season (just because you're arguably a top 5 fantasy QB doesn't mean you will elevate a WR to the next level either). Proceed with caution in fantasy. Foreman also comes over from Carolina, to the dismay of all the Khalil Herbert fans. His arrival likely means a pretty frustrating RBBC in Chicago, made only more frustrating by the rookie they just drafted…so let's get to him, shall we?

Drafted Players of Fantasy Note: Roschon Johnson (RB)

Roschon was taken in the 4th round, but only because his backfield-mate at Texas was Bijan Robinson. Johnson has serious do-it-all talent, and the Bears got themselves a good one here. The issue for Johnson is he doesn't have a pathway to immediate playing time behind Khalil Herbert & D'Onta Foreman. However, if he shows well this summer and in training camp, he has a real chance to ultimately be the RB1 on this team, though he's more likely to have to wait a bit before getting that chance. Regardless, this looks to be a headache-inducing RBBC this season, so if you're a zero RB guy (please stop), don't make any of these guys your RB1. RJ has the all-around game to be a fantasy asset if he gets his opportunity to go to work.

Fantasy Impact:

Justin Fields. That's the blurb.

Okay, so maybe there's more than Fields here, but we probably shouldn't be expecting Cole Kmet and D.J. Moore to break the fantasy bank this season. There are even questions on whether Fields will repeat or surpass what he did last season, but that shouldn't keep you from drafting him as a top-flight fantasy QB. He has the wheels you want and knows how to use them. Justin's issue will be health and the offensive line because if he's constantly running from pressure and getting sacked like last season, there's no way he will hold up all season long.

Offensive outlook:
Chicago had a bottom 5 total offense last season, and that's with how good Justin Fields was on the ground. Have they really improved enough for us to think this team will take a stab at a top 10-15 offense? Unlikely, and I wouldn't bet on it. Odds are, this team will still struggle mightily on the offensive side of the ball but should be better than they were last year, for what that's worth. The key to the whole offensive machine will be, like usual, the offensive line...and even with top 10 pick Darnell Wright drafted out of Tennessee to play OT, it just hasn't improved enough.

Defensive outlook:
The Bears were outdone on offense by how bad their defense was. This unit was bottom 4 in the NFL, but they drafted some serious talent on this side of the ball, and prior to that, Chicago inked LB Tremaine Edmunds to a contract. So at worst, they shouldn't be a bottom 5 defense in 2023. Any improvement for this unit will be a welcomed development for the fans and for the offense. Chicago can't have another bottom 5 offense and defense in 2023, or else head coach Matt Eberflus will likely be out the door.

2023 Outlook:
The Bears sported the No. 1 overall draft pick this season before trading it to Carolina. The entire organization doesn't want this to happen in 2023. However, just how much did this team improve overall? We won't know for several more months, but odds are they will still be fighting to get out of the NFC North basement, even with their owner in a new division (Aaron Rodgers).

Green Bay Packers Fantasy Preview

Key losses: Aaron Rodgers (QB), Allen Lazard (WR), Robert Tonyan (TE)
Thank the almighty that this saga is over. For months we knew WHERE Rodgers would play, and for months we waited for it to become official, and it has. He's a Jet. This means that Jordan Love (where this entire saga seemingly began three years ago) is now set to be the franchise QB in Green Bay. Time will only tell if he can fill Rodgers's shoes the way that Rodgers filled Favre's upon his departure, but Love has all the tools necessary to make it happen and an exciting young offense around him with good coaching. He won't have any excuses and will need to prove he can get the job done. Allen Lazard reunites with Rodgers in NYJ (as does Randall Cobb), and Robert Tonyan heads to the division rival Bears. Neither of them seems to hold any fantasy relevance in 2023.

Key additions: No key additions

Drafted Players of Fantasy Note: Jayden Reed (WR), Luke Musgrave (TE), Tyler Kraft (TE)
Robert Tonyan is replaced by two rookie tight ends in Musgrave and Kraft, drafted in the 2nd & 3rd rounds, respectively. That draft capital tells us that they will both play a lot of snaps, and one should reveal himself to us as the go-to target for Jordan Love this season. Jayden Reed is a 5'11" 187lb speedster out of Michigan State taken in round 2. He has solid hands and is a competitive player on the outside. Watson and Doubs are still largely unknowns and need to show us more than just one season of productivity, so there should be every chance for a player like Jayden to slither his way into significant snaps in his rookie season.

Fantasy Impact:
Look, this is all about Jordan Love at the end of the day. He has the keys to the kingdom now and everything around him to succeed. He's got incredible physical traits and can make all the throws on the field, but that doesn't

automatically mean you're a 10-year franchise QB. But regardless, he actually has a really good chance to be on the fantasy QB1 radar this year with his tools and mobility. I'm a believer, and as someone with a ton of dynasty shares of Love, I will rise and fall with him. Aaron Jones & A.J. Dillon will be Aaron Jones & A.J. Dillon, so there are no worries about the RB room, but the Doubs, Watson, and Reed and the two rookie TEs will go as Jordan Love goes. If Love is great, they will be too. If Love is a disaster...well, you can probably guess.

Offensive outlook:
The Packers sported the 17th-ranked offense last season in the NFL, and that was WITH Aaron Rodgers. So naturally, they should get worse, right? Not exactly. As I mentioned before, Jordan Love has incredible QB attributes and will need to put it all together in order for this offense to improve from last year. With all of the primary weapons returning to Green Bay, this team is one to keep an eye on this season, as they have no expectations but a very high ceiling.

Defensive outlook:
Call them consistent. The 17th-ranked offense coupled with the 17th-ranked defense. Green Bay drafted LB Lukas Van Ness with the 13th overall pick in April, and there are big expectations for him to be a jolt to this defense that has lately been the epitome of average. Unfortunately, they may need more than just one first-round linebacker if they want to find themselves in the top 10 of the NFL in defense in 2023. This unit still has a ways to go if they want to fully stop guys like Justin Fields, Amon-Ra St. Brown, and Justin Jefferson in their own division. Just as they are likely to live and die by Jordan Love this season, they could just as easily do the same with their defensive unit.

2023 Outlook:
As they begin their post-Rodgers world, the good news for the Packers is that the NFC North isn't exactly the epitome of strength. Sure, the Lions will probably open the season as the favorites to win the NFC North crown, but this division is another that is truly up for grabs, and the Packers, even with Jordan Love as their new starting QB, should be well within the mix to take the division in 2023.

Atlanta Falcons Fantasy Preview

Key losses: Every defensive rookie they could have drafted instead of a RB at 8th overall
We have a lot to discuss on this topic. Since there were no significant losses from last year's team, let's move on to "key additions," and we'll revisit this shortly.

Key additions: Jessie Bates III (S)
Jesse Bates moved from Cincinnati on a 4-year, $64M contract. He has played excellent football in his five seasons in the league so far, and he's just what the Falcons need in the secondary. Bates was named a Second-team All-Pro in 2020 and has amassed 14 interceptions and 479 tackles in his career. He will immediately enhance a Falcons pass defense that permitted the eighth-most passing yards (231.9) last season.

Drafted Players of Fantasy Note: Bijan Robinson (RB)
In real life, this pick was questionable, as running backs are often devalued. However, in fantasy football, it's going to be a dream. Bijan Robinson could end the season as the best RB in football and maintain that title for the next 5+ seasons. He's as elite an RB prospect as you can find and is arguably the best RB prospect since Adrian Peterson & Saquon Barkley. From day one, Bijan is a top-tier fantasy RB1. However, according to Warren Sharp, the Falcons' scheme last year led their RBs to rank highly in numerous categories.

They also had THREE RBs rank in the top-20 in efficiency out of 69 qualifying RBs. Rookie Tyler Allgeier broke Atlanta's rookie rushing record last year, and he ranked #2 in the NFL in EPA/att among all RBs with 100+ carries. His 3.6 yards after contact per carry ranked #5. Among all rookie RBs since 2000 with at least 175 attempts, he ranked #9 in success rate. While Bijan is a great pick in fantasy, it was arguably a misguided pick in reality.

Fantasy Impact:
Solid offensive line? Check.
Fantasy RB1? Check.
Fantasy WR1? Check.
Fantasy TE1? Check.
Fantasy QB1? ...well, let's just say "TBD." Desmond Ridder has a great skill set and arguably an even better mindset. Mentally, he embodies a true franchise QB, saying all the right things, and doing everything you want him to do. Now it's time to see it all come together. Since he was a 3rd-round QB selection and not a 1st-round selection, he doesn't get the benefit of 2-3 years to prove it. 2023 is the year, and he's going to have to demonstrate he can execute with all the resources around him to succeed. The offensive line, which ended the season as a top 10 unit, will aid him in this. Entering Week 15, Atlanta's offensive line had allowed just 78 pressures all season, the second-lowest total in the league. They helped block for the most run-heavy team in the league, rushing a league-leading 52.5% of the time. With another season of run-heavy football on the way and immense talent in every position, Ridder is arguably better prepared than any 1st or 2nd-year QB in the NFL. There are no excuses.

Offensive outlook:
This team is going to run, and run a lot, especially after drafting an RB in the top 10. This team was highly competitive last season, largely due to their offensive play. That should only improve in 2023 with a healthy Pitts, a better QB under center, Drake London in his second season, and two highly talented RBs in the stable, supported by a top 10 offensive line from 2022. The offense should not pose an issue for these guys, enabling them to compete in an NFC South division that is truly up for grabs.

Defensive outlook:
Last season, the Falcons ranked 27th on defense, a ranking that seems typical for Atlanta. They struggled to rush the passer and to halt opponents. Despite being competitive in nearly every contest, they squandered several games due to their defensive inadequacies. The signing of Jessie Bates as Safety in free agency should offer some improvement. They also signed 37-year-old Calais Campbell, who, in his prime, would have been a stellar addition. The challenge is, at his age, he is unlikely to generate sacks for the team and is more of a locker room leader at this stage of his career. Zach Harrison, drafted out of Ohio State, is expected to be the edge rusher tackling opponents' quarterbacks. However, with only 3.5 sacks at Ohio State in 2022, it remains to be seen if he can step up in the NFL. There's little to suggest this unit will significantly improve from last season, and they could easily perform as poorly, if not worse, than in 2022.

2023 Outlook:
The success of the Falcons' season will likely hinge on the performance of the defense. This suggests we might see more squandered leads and another "good but not quite good enough" season. Desmond Ridder will also play a substantial role in the team's success, but with the offense poised for him, he would have to be a complete disaster to prevent them from being in the playoff hunt throughout the season in such a lackluster division.

New Orleans Saints Fantasy Preview

Key losses: None
Ordinarily, former 1st round pick Marcus Davenport would count as a significant loss, but after five years in the NFL, he hasn't established himself as a key contributor to a defense. So, we move on.

Key additions: Derek Carr (QB), Jamaal Williams (RB)
The Saints are set to pay Derek Carr $150 million over four years. Although this reunites Carr with Dennis Allen, it seems to be an excessive price for a quarterback who hasn't yet proven himself as one of the league's top-tier talents. Jamaal Williams had an outstanding 2022 season, leading the league with 17 rushing touchdowns and

accumulating just over 1,000 yards. He is expected to replace Mark Ingram and eventually form a duo with Alvin Kamara.

Drafted Players of Fantasy Note: Kendre Miller (RB)

In my opinion, Kendre Miller was one of the top five running backs in this class, and the Saints have secured a valuable addition. Their running back group is now fully stocked. Miller is more of a dynasty stash than a redraft darling. Barring an injury or suspension for Alvin Kamara, Miller likely won't have many opportunities in 2023. However, if he gets his chance, I expect him to seize it fully.

Fantasy Impact:

The Saints' offense is poised to improve from its 19th ranking last season. Despite being overrated, Derek Carr should bring vitality to the offense, something Taysom Hill and Andy Dalton failed to provide. With a fully recovered Michael Thomas and a second-year wide receiver Chris Olave, this offense could be lethal if Carr performs well. Alvin Kamara's potential suspension at the start of the season might reduce his draft value somewhat, providing an opportunity for fantasy owners to snag him later in the draft. The addition of Jamaal Williams could also impact Kamara's ADP, despite the fact his days as a top-tier RB1 are likely over. Carr should be capable of supporting a top-tier WR1, either Thomas or Olave, while the other remains a high-end WR2. Both should do well this season. Juwan Johnson might become a solid TE1, especially now that Adam Trautman isn't around to take snaps. The Saints' offense promises to be fantasy-friendly in 2023.

Offensive outlook:

The Saints' offense should flourish. While it won't rival the Bengals, Eagles, or Chiefs, it should comfortably rank among the better "tier 2" offenses in the league and improve upon its overall 19th ranking from last season. There's a lot to like about this team.

Defensive outlook:

The Saints, who had the 6th best defense last year, used their first two draft picks to secure Clemson DT Bryan Bresee and Notre Dame edge rusher Isaiah Foskey. These rookies are expected to play as many snaps as they can handle. In a division ripe for the taking, this unit should have a successful season going up against quarterbacks Baker Mayfield, Bryce Young, and Desmond Ridder.

2023 Outlook:

The NFC South is up for grabs, and the Saints are the clear favorites for the division title. Atlanta and Carolina will be competitive and also aim for the crown, while Tampa could be a dark horse if Mayfield performs well. However, as long as the Saints maintain their defensive prowess and enhance their offense, they shouldn't face many obstacles. They are undoubtedly the most complete team in the division, and given the weaker NFC overall, they could even be contenders for a Super Bowl run.

Carolina Panthers Fantasy Preview

Key losses: D.J. Moore (WR), D'Onta Foreman (RB)

The decision to part ways with Moore was a shock to some. DJM had been a pretty steady, solid presence for Carolina since he was drafted in 2018. He never evolved into an elite talent at his position and probably won't in Chicago either. However, this is about the Panthers, and their trade was about acquiring the No. 1 overall pick in this year's draft to select Bryce Young as the new face of their franchise. Bryce is set up for success as Terrace Marshall, Adam Thielen, D.J. Chark, and Laviska Shenault currently headline the WR room, along with the promising young rookie Jonathan Mingo.

Key additions: Frank Reich (HC), Miles Sanders (RB), Adam Thielen (WR), Hayden Hurst (TE), Vonn Bell (S)

You can argue that Frank Reich never got a fair shot to lead Indy in the right way. After three failed veteran QBs had stints in Indy, one might wonder if Reich would ever get the chance to draft his guy... well, here it is. He was armed with the No. 1 overall pick in the draft, so let's finally see what Reich can do with a team when his QB is in place. Miles Sanders never seemed to become the player we all thought he would be in Philly. Instead, he was just a decent talent at the RB position behind a perennially good offensive line with great QB play. Now in Carolina, things will likely be tougher, and expectations should be kept low. Adam Thielen joins the fold at WR but is a shell of his former self and likely won't be a significant fantasy contributor moving forward. Hayden Hurst won't be a fantasy superstar either, but he will be a great safety blanket for Bryce Young. Vonn Bell is a fantastic signing, plucked away from Cincinnati. This will easily be the most impactful addition for the team this year on defense.

Drafted Players of Fantasy Note: Bryce Young (QB), Jonathan Mingo (WR)

The Panthers allegedly told Bryce months in advance that they were going to draft him. Well, they kept their word, as they traded up to No. 1 overall to select the most seasoned and refined QB prospect in this class. Young should step in instantly and demonstrate flashes of his football IQ and raw talent. There will be adjustments he'll have to make and peaks & valleys he'll have to navigate as a rookie, but with a solid WR room and the addition of rookie WR Jonathan Mingo, Bryce is in a position to succeed immediately. Mingo is a big, strong receiver in the mold of a true alpha. He has 4.4 speed and great athleticism. Mingo should be a day 1 impact player but may not be an immediate fantasy star. Either way, both are 1st round picks in 1QB leagues, with Mingo being an early 2nd round pick in SuperFlex.

Fantasy Impact:

We likely won't see any tier 1 fantasy players on the Panthers this year. Miles Sanders is a good player but firmly on the shaky RB2 radar. The WR room has some solid real-life talent, but it would take an out-of-the-box season for any of them to be a WR1 in fantasy. Hayden Hurst could be on the low end of the TE1 radar this year as Bryce's safety blanket, but he's probably not a player you want as your starting TE in fantasy. As for Bryce himself, he should have a solid rookie season. In fantasy, he should be a more than serviceable QB2 and, in my opinion, will be a top-20 QB for most, if not all, of the fantasy season.

Offensive outlook:

The Panthers ranked 29th in total offense last season, a ranking that surprised no one, especially after trading away Christian McCaffrey. This year, however, things are looking bright in Charlotte, and the offense seems head and shoulders better on paper. With his QB finally and firmly in place, Frank Reich should be able to showcase his abilities as an offensive-minded head coach in what should be a very underwhelming division.

Defensive outlook:

The Panthers didn't expect to have the 22nd-ranked defense in 2022, but they added much-needed pieces in the draft, including more pass rush help off the edge across from Brian Burns. This, along with an excellent free agent signing of safety Vonn Bell from the Bengals, should improve the Panthers' defensive fortunes at least a little bit in 2023.

2023 Outlook:

The defense should see some improvement. The offense is likely to undergo a near-complete 180-degree turn, and the team will be much better coached than they have been in the past few seasons. This team has all the elements of a squad that is unquestionably going to be very competitive week in and week out, and a division crown isn't out of the question, as the NFC South is as much of a toss-up as it's been in a decade.

Tampa Bay Buccaneers Fantasy Preview

Key Losses: Leonard Fournette (RB), Tom Brady (QB)

Farewell, partner! Tom Brady retired – again – for good this time, right? It seems so, and even if he were to return, it wouldn't likely be for Tampa. Regardless, his departure leaves a void at the quarterback position, and I don't count Baker Mayfield as the ultimate solution. With Fournette gone, the Bucs will lean on Rachaad White, who spent his rookie season sharing duties with the veteran. Now, it's the Rachaad show, and he has every chance to emerge as the primary back.

Key Additions: Baker Mayfield (QB), Chase Edmonds (RB)
But are these genuinely key additions? Chase Edmonds is like the running back version of Baker Mayfield. He had his chance in Arizona to secure the role of the franchise back, but he underwhelmed, leaving his fantasy backers disappointed. His brief stint in Miami was equally uninspiring, and he hasn't shown any reason to suggest he could challenge Rachaad White's workload. Baker showed a bit of a resurgence with the Rams late last season, which probably prompted Tampa to gamble on him. But as we've seen, Baker tends to underperform, settling comfortably into a mediocre backup QB role.

Drafted Players of Fantasy Note: None
Tampa hardly addressed the offense in this draft until the fifth round, when they picked rookie TE Payne Durham, who likely won't see much action in his first season. Given their other positions, this strategy seems sensible.

Fantasy Impact:
With Tom Brady, Gronkowski, and Fournette gone, can we still find excitement in Mike Evans, Chris Godwin, Rachaad White, and Cade Otton? Rachaad White should provide fantasy owners with a solid season. The offense won't be terrible, but it will certainly differ from the last several years and probably won't reach the level of Jameis Winston's era. Baker is the current QB, but it's uncertain how long he'll maintain the starting job. Odds are, Kyle Trask will make a few starts this season before Tampa inevitably shifts their focus to the 2024 draft with prospects like Caleb Williams, Drake Maye, and Michael Penix. Mike Evans and Chris Godwin should still provide decent WR2 production. Cade Otton, who has a lot of talent, might find himself on the TE1 radar this year as a potential late-round steal. But in fantasy terms, Rachaad is the player to target, unless there's a late free-agent acquisition like Ezekiel Elliott, Kareem Hunt, or a Leonard Fournette comeback. Rachaad should be a solid high-end RB2 or low-end RB1 in 2023.

Offensive Outlook:
As mentioned above, this Tampa offense will differ from what we're used to seeing. Despite ranking in the top 14 in 2022, with Baker as the QB, things might not run as smoothly in 2023. Nevertheless, the team should remain highly competitive.

Defensive Outlook:
Almost all of their draft picks were on the defensive side of the ball, signaling a desire to maintain or improve upon their top 11 defense from 2022. In theory, the defense could improve, which would be beneficial considering the potent offenses of the Falcons and Saints, and a much-improved Panthers offense. This unit will indeed have its work cut out this season.

2023 Outlook:
In this division, anything is possible. While the Saints are the favorites to win the crown, realistically, all four teams have an equal shot. It all comes down to whether Baker Mayfield can channel his Rams performance rather than his Carolina self. If we see the latter, the Bucs may well surprise many in 2023.

Chapter 12

2023 NFL Futures Betting Cheat Sheet

Joe Pisapia

Top 10 NFL Awards Bets

10 Dan Campbell Coach of the Year +1000

9 Bijan Robinson AP Player of the Year +4000

8 Jalen Carter Defensive ROY +600

7 Jalen Hurts MVP +1200

6 Anthony Richardson Offensive ROY +700 AP

5 Joe Burrow MVP +700

4 Micah Parsons DPOY +700

3 Ja'Marr Chase AP POY +1200

2 Bijan Robinson AP Offensive ROY +300

1 Patrick Mahomes MVP +700

Top 10 NFL Futures

10 Arizona Cardinals Under 4.5 Wins -114

9 Philadelphia Eagles Over 10.5 Wins -158

8 Atlanta Falcons to Make the Playoffs Yes +128

7 New York Jets to Win AFC East +250

6 Detroit Lions to Win the NFC North +145

5 Patrick Mahomes Most Passing Yards +400

4 Cincinnati Bengals to Win the AFC +500

3 Cincinnati Bengals vs Philadelphia Eagles in SB +2400

2 Philadelphia Eagles to Win the SB +850

1 Philadelphia Eagles to Win the NFC +330

Printed in Great Britain
by Amazon